AIRPOWER AND TECHNOLOGY

AIRPOWER AND TECHNOLOGY

SMART AND UNMANNED WEAPONS

David R. Mets

PRAEGER SECURITY INTERNATIONAL
Westport, Connecticut • London

Library of Congress Cataloging-in-Publication Data

Mets, David R.
Airpower and technology : smart and unmanned weapons / David R. Mets.
p. cm.
Includes bibliographical references and index.
ISBN: 978-0-275-99314-6 (alk. paper)
1. Airplanes, Military—Armament. I. Title.
UG1270.M48 2009
358.4′24—dc22 2008033898

British Library Cataloguing in Publication Data is available.

Library of Congress Catalog Card Number: 2008033898
ISBN: 978-0-275-99314-6

First published in 2009

Praeger Security International, 88 Post Road West, Westport, CT 06881
An imprint of Greenwood Publishing Group, Inc.
www.praeger.com

Printed in the United States of America

The paper used in this book complies with the Permanent Paper Standard issued by the National Information Standards Organization (Z39.48–1984).

10 9 8 7 6 5 4 3 2 1

Contents

Preface

I have been studying the story of American aviation for about 70 years now. It began in 1935 when my uncle took me for a ride in an airplane at the Groton airport in Connecticut. The military dimension started with a visit to the *USS Lexington*, docked on the west side of Manhattan during the fleet visit of 1937. She was all decked out for Navy Day and was literally glistening everywhere with the holiday colors displayed above and the biplanes on her flight deck with the brilliant yellow wings. I subsequently made a special study of military leadership that culminated in writing a biography of General Carl A. Spaatz and with a 14-year stint of teaching airpower history at the USAF's School of Advanced Air and Space Studies. Much of that work was a matter of analysis—examining the parts of the story in detail. Now, it appears to be the time to attempt the synthesis in one volume that may be useful in a small way to busy military leaders and citizens seeking a summary treatment of the third dimension of warfare: air, space, and cyberspace.

American airpower started its growth in the wake of the industrialization and urbanization of the United States—the transition from an agrarian country with continental interests to a global power with worldwide concerns. For us, war in the third dimension has had both a naval and a land-based aspect, and few syntheses have attempted to treat both of them. That in part was a contributor to the many controversies surrounding its development. Also, much of the writing has been done by people with backgrounds in either one or the other dimension of the subject, and sometimes by folks with no practical experience in either. It is hoped that the study will help the various partisans better appreciate the viewpoints of other services and of the general public.

The scope of the work that follows is limited to the twentieth century and the beginning of the next one, and it deals with foreign airpower in only peripheral ways. It is focused on military air, space, and cyberspace and gives little attention to commercial aviation or civilian space efforts. Being a synthesis, the book is dependent upon secondary sources where appropriate, although some primary source material helps build the foundation.

My goal is to produce a readable work for the interested citizen that will yield insights to the problems and choices facing America in developing and employing air, space, and cyberspace power to support her national interests. I hope to deliver some understanding of the theories, doctrines, organization, and technologies of land-based and sea-based air and space power. I will include passages on the technologies and techniques of precision-guided weapons, unmanned aerial vehicles, information warfare, and space that will assist in making judgments connected with those dimensions of the subject. In general, the development of the story will be along chronological lines.

I wish to acknowledge a few of the many people who helped me along the way. The first was the uncle, Eino Ojala, who took me on that initial flight. My regret is that he did not live long enough to witness my earning of wings nor to see this book—he was a veteran of World War I and a great American. Dr. Irving B. Holley, Jr., of Duke University is the greatest living airpower historian. He has been a mentor of mine for 40 years now, and I have profited greatly from his interest and expertise. The biographer of Admiral Chester Nimitz, Professor E. B. Potter, was a teacher of naval history at Annapolis when I attended, and he whetted my interest in the subject. My many colleagues from the history departments at the Air Force Academy and West Point, as well as at the School of Advanced Air and Space Studies, were as fine a group of teachers as one could hope for and greatly helped me along the way. My fellow aircrewmen in the 341st Strategic Bomb Wing, the 463rd Tactical Airlift Wing, and the 388th Tactical Fighter Wing educated me in the ways of the fighting Air Force, and even saved my life on some occasions. Finally, I thank my partners from the staff of the old *Air University Review* for adding to my education in airpower theory and doctrine plus introducing me to the world of editing and journal production, and thus further whetting my appetite for reading, writing, and publishing.

For many years, I was privileged to work in the same building that houses both the greatest airpower library on the planet and the marvelous archives of the USAF: the Air University Library and the Air Force Historical Research Agency, both of Maxwell AFB, Alabama. That same structure also houses the School of Advanced Air and Space Studies. I enjoyed participating in the learning of 13 generations of its students—in my opinion, the very finest field grade officers in the service. Their brilliant and inquisitive minds are a joy to behold. Among the other archives I have used for this book are the Manuscripts Division of the Library of Congress, the National Archives, the archives at the Naval War College, the collections of the American Military Institute at Carlisle Barracks, the archives at the U.S. Military Academy at West Point, the Nimitz Library in Annapolis, and the Air Force Academy Library. Air University gave me the opportunity to repeatedly tour the holdings of the Air Force Museum at Wright-Patterson AFB, the Air Force Armament Museum at Eglin AFB, the National Museum of Naval Aviation at Pensacola, and the Aviation and Space Museum of the Smithsonian Institution in Washington, DC. All those libraries, archives, and museums are truly American national treasures. Air University also gave me the chance to visit the Imperial War Museum and the RAF Museum in the United Kingdom, a memorable experience. Without those establishments and people, this book would not have such quality as it does; any faults in the tome are entirely my own responsibility.

1

Introduction

Can there be any valid reason for busy citizen-leaders to overload their reading lists with works about air and space history, theory, and doctrine? After all, in the popular vernacular when we say, "That's purely theoretical," we mean that it is not real. Almost every doctrine manual ever written asserts that nothing in it excuses the leader from the necessity of applying good judgment to the case at hand. This is the same as saying that leaders get paid to decide when to violate doctrine. Michael Howard, one of the leading military historians, has asserted that doctrine is always wrong.[1]

Yet without some vision of what the future is likely to bring, we enter new conflicts unarmed with any ideas and highly vulnerable to confusion and paralysis. Thus, Howard said, it is necessary that we try to develop military theory and then doctrine to have some idea of what we should be doing in preparing plans, acquiring weapons, training people, and building our organizations—notwithstanding their imperfections. He argued that our job is to make our doctrine less wrong than our enemy's and our organization flexible enough to react more quickly to the lessons of combat than can the adversary.[2] It almost follows that the leader must also be well read in the history of politics and war if they are to gain the perspective to judge which theories are sound and which are not.

What is it all about? The purpose of this work is to help the aspirant American leader toward building their own personal theory of war and air and space power, including an understanding of what doctrine is and what its utility and limitations are. We will explore the evolution of American air and space history and technology and relate them to evolving theory and doctrine in summary terms. We will conclude with a brief look at information warfare and with some speculations about the future. We do this with the thought that no matter how thorough the technologies and techniques of gathering and interpreting information, they will likely never be able to get the last scrap of knowledge desired. This condition will make it necessary for citizen-leader and military officer alike to make choices that in the last analyses are partially dependent upon assumptions—guesses. What we are trying to do here is to reduce the number of unknown factors and increase the number and accuracy of the known ones so as to improve the odds that that final guess will be a correct choice—or at least more correct than those of America's enemies.

What exactly is theory? The meaning I assign herein to the word *theory* is that it is a body of ideas about the organization of military forces for war and their employment in war. As I use it, *doctrine* is also a body of ideas about the organization and employment of forces. The difference is that doctrine has the formal approval of the highest authorities of an organization; theory does not. Theory is more tentative than doctrine. One of the earliest air theorists, Giulio Douhet, declared that that air superiority is essential; the same idea is in Air Force Doctrine Document 1 (AFDD-1). The difference is that AFDD-1 has the signature of the Chief of Staff of the Air Force—Douhet's book is not so endorsed. But the current doctrine document also contains the words, "The doctrine in this document is authoritative but not directive. Therefore, commanders need to consider not only the contents of this AFDD, but also the particular situation when accomplishing their missions."[3] In other words, commanders get paid to decide when to violate doctrine. Were doctrine to become directive, then it would also have become dogma instead of doctrine.

What are some of the practical uses of doctrine? It is one of the inputs in determining what the research program shall be for the Air Force and Navy research laboratories—whether the money should be put into self-protecting weapons for the shooters or dedicated defense suppression aircraft, for example. It is one of the factors considered in training programs—whether to increase the number of loadmasters or missile technicians being trained. Combined with political objectives, intelligence, weather, and force availability, doctrine is often one of the factors going into the building of strategies, along with theory in cases where the commander decides that doctrine does not apply. We know doctrine can never be as precise as a blueprint but we hope that it will be near enough to reality that our strategies will be approximately correct—or at least more correct than that of our adversaries.

Where does doctrine originate? In part, doctrine emerges from the historical experience. We know from Stonewall Jackson's attack on Joseph Hooker's right flank at Chancellorsville (and many other cases) that surprise is usually desirable. Unhappily, in the formative years of air theory and doctrine its historical data base was pretty thin. Similarly, the theory and doctrine for space warfare does not yet have much of an historical database. Cyberspace has hardly existed for 40 years. What happens when there is insufficient experience to determine the probabilities? We then fall back on deductive reasoning—speculation. Thus, the initial theories of airpower during the interwar period arose from the limited experience with air fighting in World War I and the vast imaginations of airmen everywhere.[4] Our ideas on space warfare right now are based on a little experience from the 1991 Gulf War onward, and a large amount of deductive reasoning heavily based on assumptions. Let us now turn to a look at the ways in which experience and imagination helped us solve some problems and complicated others.

ORGANIZING THEMES

Since biblical times at the latest, Western culture has placed a premium on the worth of the individual. One dimension of this has always been the effort to preserve life in war by developing the ability to deliver projectiles with maximum accuracy from a maximum distance—precision and standoff. David was able to sling his stone at Goliath accurately from a standoff distance that kept him out of the giant's reach. Nowhere is this phenomenon more pronounced than it is in the United States. Among our European ancestors, the people were numerous but the arable land was scarce (in relative terms). In Colonial America, the land was abundant and generally free for the taking but the labor supply was short. Land was cheap but wages were high (again, in relative terms). This was one of the reasons why American farms were generally mechanized earlier than those of the rest of the world. In the military realm, this basis is why America has often been described as ever ready to substitute bucks for bodies—to develop precision and standoff. It is among the reasons for the great appeal of air and space power to many Americans, notwithstanding its expense. They deem that it can achieve the security of our safety and our prosperity with a minimum loss of life, and perhaps more humanely and even with less expense in some cases. Those dreams have been a long time reaching fruition, and we still have a way to go—but the dream is still among us.

An Air and Space Theory and Doctrine Time Line

1903	Wright Brothers flight
1911	First use of aircraft in war
1915–17	German bombing of Great Britain
1918	Founding of the Royal Air Force

1921	Publication of Douhet's *Command of the Air*
1921	Commissioning of *USS Langley*, CV-1
1921	Sinking of the *Oestfriesland*
1925	Publication of Mitchell's *Winged Defense*
1926	Mitchell court-martial
1927	Launching of *USS Lexington*, CV-2
1929	End of Trenchard's Command of RAF
1933	Death of Admiral Moffett in airship crash
1935	Foundation of US GHQ Air Force
1935	First flight of B-17
1939	*Luftwaffe* in invasion of Poland
1940	Strategic bombing of Great Britain
1941	Writing of AWPD-1 air plan
1941	Pearl Harbor
1942	Battles of Coral Sea and Midway
1942	First flight of German V-2
1943	*Schweinfurt*/Publication of FM-100-20
1945	Hiroshima
1947	Foundation of USAF
1948	Berlin blockade
1949	Soviet nuclear explosion
1957	*Sputnik*
1959	First nuclear carrier, *USS Enterprise*, CVAN-65
1959	Brodie's *Strategy in the Missile Age*
1961	Onset of flexible response
1969	Astronauts go to Moon and back
1975	Fall of Saigon
1988	Warden's *The Air Campaign*
1991	Gulf War/End of Cold War
1997	Publication of AFDD-1
1999	Kosovo Campaign
2003	Second Gulf War

The Evolution of Air and Space Thinking and Technology

The Reconnaissance and Spotting Age: Airpower in the Great War

The initial uses of airpower were merely extensions of old army and navy functions: reconnaissance and artillery spotting. Very soon, the ground commanders demanded that the aerial spies be denied, and so the air superiority mission was born. Ground attack was coming into use as the war ended, and strategic bombing was tried by both the Allies and Germany.

Pursuit and Command of the Air: First Fighter Age

In the American case, the flyers came away with a conviction that air superiority was a firm prerequisite for everything else. But unlike Giulio Douhet in Europe, they generally felt that it was best achieved by fighters in an air battle rather than by sudden attacks on the airdromes and aircraft factories of the enemy. Mitchell and his cohorts advocated a preponderance of pursuit but also demanded tactical support aircraft and units as well as bombers. The ancestor unit of the Air Corps Tactical School was established right after the Great War and from the outset, it was near the vortex of airpower thinking. Mitchell's 1925 book and his court-martial that same year, among other things, guaranteed that there would be a good deal of public attention to the evolution of airpower theory, technology, and organization.

Naval Aviation before Pearl Harbor

The disappointment with the outcomes of World War I led to the virtual starvation of the US Army, and to a lesser extent its air arm, until the mid-1930s. Things were not quite so bad with the Navy because it still enjoyed its role as the first line of defense, and apparently could not get us involved in another European war. Also, it was quickly apparent that aviation would be highly useful to battleship sailors and their gunnery as well as in a direct attack role for command of the sea.

The Era of the Industrial Web: Rise of the Strategic Bomber

There were antecedents for the idea of the Industrial Web in Mitchell's War College lectures of 1921 and 1922. Gradually, from 1926 through about 1935 the Air Corps Tactical School and some of the other Air Corps leaders developed it. By the end of the interwar period, the idea that the nodal points of an enemy economy could be hit by unescorted daylight bombers and that would cause their capitulation was the dominant (though not the exclusive) thought in the American air force. At the time, RAF thinking was similar and the notions resonated among many political leaders. However, the experience of World War II exposed the defects in the dominant theory: first, the defenses in large part because of the unanticipated development of radar proved too potent for the unescorted bomber; second, the finding and hitting of the target was more difficult than had been thought; and finally, the targets and passive countermeasures proved much more resilient than had been predicted. But all of that was masked by the sudden appearance of atomic weapons at Hiroshima and Nagasaki.

The Coming of the Balance of Terror: Heyday of the SAC Bombers

The period of the American monopoly of nuclear power was much shorter than anyone had dreamed. Even before the Soviets exploded their first atomic device, the Berlin Airlift faintly suggested that perhaps nuclear weapons would not be the complete solution for economic security. But the Korean War soon soured most Americans on any thought of future conventional conflict, and the United States' superiority in delivery systems enabled a reliance on nuclear massive retaliation at much lower expense than would have been the case with ample conventional forces. Many have cited the Cuban Missile Crisis as the turning point that caused the Soviet leaders to vow that they would never again would be cowed by U.S. nuclear superiority, and they moved to quickly close the gap in strength by the development of ICBMs—or so America thought.

Nuclear Parity and Flexible Response: Return of the Fighters

As the nuclear strength of the USSR grew, many in the United States and Europe began to doubt the robustness of the extended deterrence of our nuclear umbrella. Even before the end of the Eisenhower administration, Generals Lauris Norstad and Maxwell Taylor were speaking and writing that the conventional forces of NATO needed strengthening. They argued that it was necessary to give the president other options than choosing between world nuclear annihilation and capitulation. Also, the Europeans doubted the validity of the United States' guarantee if the president had to sacrifice American cities to attempt to save, say, Paris. All this stimulated some restoration of tactical airpower thinking, equipment, and training even before the Vietnam War broke out. The limits of nuclear air power having already been demonstrated, the Vietnam War cast doubt on the efficacy of conventional airpower. Though many would argue that the war was lost for reasons having nothing to do with airpower, the outlook was about as dark as at any time since *Schweinfurt*. But it had not been a free ride for the Communist world, notwithstanding that it was hard to see its strain in the West.

The End of the Cold War and the Diffusion of the Threat: Command and Control (C^2) and Precision-guided Munitions (PGM)

The end of the Cold War was about as surprising as was its beginning. The great battle on the northern European plains had never occurred, but apparently the internal stresses the struggle had imposed on the Warsaw Pact, along with communism's inherent contradictions, caused an erosion not very visible in the West. Presidents Truman and Johnson had tread very gingerly in Korea and Vietnam because of their high concern to avoid a war with the USSR. But that threat was gone in 1990 when a former Soviet patron, Saddam Hussein, created an intolerable situation in Southwest Asia. President Bush was able to react much more vigorously, and this time airpower was enabled to operate in a much less constrained manner. Its advocates argued that it was therefore able to bring all its power to bear with splendid results. This made possible a quick victory with only four days of ground battle. Though airpower was much more constrained in the 1999 Kosovo Campaign, its advocates argued that it again demonstrated that the potency of conventional airpower, armed with precision weapons and controlled by a superior command and control system assisted by space, could achieve quick results at minimal cost—sometimes without any ground fighting but always with last-resort nuclear power brooding in the background. At the time of this writing, the Second Gulf War seemed to indicate that the technological and information trends had continued through the early part of the twenty-first century.

2

Airpower Thinking and Technology before Hiroshima

THE RECONNAISSANCE AND SPOTTING AGE: AIRPOWER IN THE GREAT WAR

Guns were fired from aircraft at College Park, Maryland, as early as 1911; bombs were dropped before the First World War. But in a highly traditional way, the new technology was at first used as cavalry had been in days of old. Aircraft were used to gather information for the ground commanders to help them build the enemy order of battle to avoid surprise and to improve the accuracy of artillery fire. Both these things contributed to the deadlock on the Western Front during the First World War, and both led to a strong desire on the part of the ground commanders to demand that those advantages be denied to the enemy leaders. Thus, the idea of air superiority in the first instance did not arise from the airmen but rather from the soldiers.[1] Although airmen are fond of pointing out that aerial reconnaissance identified a gap in the German Armies wheeling around Paris in 1914 at the first Battle of the Marne and thus defeated the von Schlieffen Plan,[2] a case cannot be made that airpower was a decisive factor in that war.

Albeit not decisive, the record of air fighting in World War I soon was very much a current and crucial topic of debate and study everywhere. The limited engine power available and the demand for air superiority fighting led to increasing specialization of aircraft units.[3] The first to emerge were the fighter units, but the other modern roles and missions were conceived shortly after and specialized aircraft were developed for some of them, like armored ground attack airplanes and long-range strategic bombers.[4] In the years that followed, operations designed to further the missions of the Army, Marines, and Navy by battlefield support and the like came to be called "tactical." Those intended to directly affect the enemy decision-making or capability for war were soon described as "strategic." Samples of the latter would be attacks on cities or on munitions industries. Attacks on oil fields would therefore be "strategic," and those against finished petroleum en route to the battlefield would be "tactical" interdiction.

Even during World War I, air superiority was seen as an enabler of all the other air missions. Although it was already dangerous to fly too low over the battlefield, the focus after the war was very much on air fighting. Technology and tactics were changing so rapidly that the balance swung to and fro with amazing frequency. There were so many different accelerations involved in maneuvering in the third dimension that for a long time, it was next to impossible to hit an enemy in a swirling fight. It was obvious from the beginning that the way to factor out all of the accelerations would to be to get behind an enemy on the same course and speed. However, that maneuver was inhibited by the fact that it required an airplane that was faster than and more maneuverable than the enemy, and it practically mandated that the pursuit (as fighters were known until after World War II) be a one-seat craft. With the limited power of those days, the additional weight of a gunner would be prohibitive. The guns and ammunition were still so unreliable that they could not be mounted on the wings outside the propeller arc but had to be mounted where the pilot could reach them and reload or clear jams. An effective synchronizer that would fire the weapons between the turning propeller blades was not invented until the middle of the war, and that made the air fight all the more deadly. The technological balance was fairly even through the war, and in the end the Allies managed to command the air mostly through numbers and offensive tactics.[5]

Even before the end of 1914, the British Royal Naval Air Service under the guidance of Winston Churchill had undertaken some offensive counter-air missions against the German Zeppelin sheds. The results were mixed. The idea of bombing cities for purposes of undermining will or the capability to continue the war had existed before the war. The Germans happened to be better equipped for it at the outset because of their airship programs, but there were production and political restraints that kept them from undertaking such raids on England until 1915.[6]

One of the political constraints in the first couple of years of the war was Kaiser Wilhelm's reluctance to attack enemy civilians or, especially, to risk the British royal family. However, his power to control such things eroded as the war went on and, among other things, the blockade of Germany became more effective. The Zeppelin raids of 1915 and 1916 did cause some panic in Great Britain, for sure, but they were quite expensive. Some were shot down and there were many accidents. However, by 1917 the Germans had developed long-range bombing airplanes that took over the mission, and that caused some diversion of resources on the Allied side. The British created an Independent Bombing Force by 1918, the aim of which was the deliberate bombing of Germany for two purposes. One was a counterforce attack to reduce the capability of the enemy bombers to attack London. The other was retaliatory to put enough pain on the enemy that the will to do so would be diminished—or at least, the productivity of the German workers would be reduced. Meanwhile, the Royal Air Force was created in the spring of 1918. In the end, the results of the strategic bombing campaigns on both sides were far from decisive.[7]

Most of the other missions of airpower appeared in primitive form during World War I as well. Aerial resupply was tried during the siege of Kut in 1915.[8] Close air support from low altitudes was tried on all sides, and was discovered early to be a highly dangerous mission, albeit sometimes very effective.[9]

At the Armistice in November, 1918, Europe was on the point of economic collapse, Woodrow Wilson and the League of Nations were promising that there would be no more wars, and America was following her usual pattern in drawing down to minimal military forces. In that environment, rivalry among services was certain to be intense, and all were striving to build a better theoretical case for a larger share of what remained of the military budget.[10]

PURSUIT AND COMMAND OF THE AIR: THE FIRST FIGHTER AGE

The great Italian air theorist, Giulio Douhet, published his *Command of the Air* a few months after the war ended (1921). His message was clear: There had been a revolution. Land war and sea war had been reduced to conducting a short defense only long enough to permit the air force offensive to bring about victory in a few days. For the most part, only bombers would be required and they would first achieve air superiority by destroying the enemy air forces at their airdromes and in their factories. If that did not persuade the enemy leadership that the war was futile, then the air forces would go on to make a direct attack on the adversary population to cause it to rise up against its own leadership. In so doing, they would force a capitulation in a few days time. Inherent in all of that were several assumptions. One was that the enemy would, in all likelihood, be an advanced industrial society. Another was that civilian morale is inherently fragile—much more fragile than soldier morale. A third assumption was that the bomber would always get through, or at least if escort were needed, a bomber airframe laden with guns would suffice. Finally, there was the assumption that airpower is inherently offensive, and the surface forces would remain stronger in the defense than the offense for the foreseeable future.[11]

Brigadier Billy Mitchell came back from the war aboard the *SS Aquitania* early in 1919. He was full of ideas about the future of airpower, and he was not bashful about sharing them with a fellow passenger, Jerome Hunsaker of the United States Navy. Within weeks, those ideas had been fully passed on to the General Board of the Navy.[12] At that point, Mitchell shared many of the assumptions and ideas of Douhet but was not as great a fan of the bomber or strategic attack.[13] He was for a more balanced force, and the elite units would be the pursuit squadrons that would achieve command of the air, at least in part through the air battle.[14] His main points in the early 1920s were that the United States needed a separate air force that would be equal to the Army and Navy. He further asserted that all three should be under a department of defense. He fully agreed with Douhet's idea that command of the air was the first mission, that airpower was inherently offensive, that any adversary would likely be a fully developed industrial power, and that future war was highly likely, if not inevitable. Mitchell did not recognize Douhet as the source of any of these ideas, but some of the Air Service people around him had indeed enjoyed extensive consultations with Count Gianni Caproni, a close associate of the Italian theorist.[15] Also, Mitchell himself did meet with Douhet during his travels of 1922.[16]

Both Douhet and Mitchell early argued that the airplane was revolutionary and demanded both doctrinal and organizational changes. In the case of the United States, the air organization that emerged in the early 1920s remained organic to the Army. The Army Chief of Staff and his General Staff were the ultimate military decision makers. This concept did not at all resemble what Mitchell and some members of Congress had in mind. Like Douhet, he wanted an autonomous air force equal to the other services and all under a department of defense. In the 1920s, the Air Service included three specialized groups: the First Pursuit Group, the Second Bombardment Group, and the Third Attack Group. For all the accusations that the Air Service and Air Corps were so obsessed with strategic bombing that they ignored the requirement for ground support, it is noteworthy that the Third Attack Group remained a part of the organization throughout the interwar period.[17] Only one other air force in the world maintained a like organization through the period, and that was the Italian. But there was more to American airpower than the Army's Air Service. Unlike the rest of the world, long-range, land-based bombing in Japan was under the province of the navy, not the army nor air force as in the United States and Great Britain.[18] But the US Navy was quick to realize that at the very least, airpower could extend its standoff by observation to permit precision fire of its big guns before the enemy battle line could come over the horizon.

NAVAL AVIATION, 1911–1941

Aviation came to the United States Navy on the tail end of a long string of major technological changes and in the wake of one great doctrinal change. The technical improvements included steam propulsion, conversion from coal to oil for fuel, rifled breech-loading guns, iron ships, steel ships, hardened armor, electrification, torpedoes, destroyers, turbine steam engines, beyond visual-range fire control, submarines, and improved mine warfare methods. The doctrinal change occurred in the 1880–1900 period and converted the organizing concept of the United States Navy, which had been one of a coastal defense, commerce-protecting force for an agrarian nation preoccupied with internal development.[19] The new Navy was designed to achieve command of the sea through the use of battleships engaged in great sea battles with other navies in the name of an industrial-urban power with vital interests in overseas markets and sources of raw materials.[20] By most measures, the US Navy was the third-ranking in the world at the dawn of aviation shortly before World War I (behind the British and German).

The passages in the chapters that follow cover the origins of naval aviation, the initial combat experience in World War I,[21] the era in which it served as an auxiliary to the battle line and in which Billy Mitchell was a principal adversary, its transformation into the main striking arm of naval power, the interregnum between World War II and Korea in which it fought for its existence against the nuclear Air Force (or so it was perceived), the heyday of naval aviation during Korea and after as the agent in command of the sea and charged also with power projection ashore, and finally the recent post-Cold War period as it searched for another mission after the disappearance of the Soviet threat—the "From the Sea" era.

The Origins

The Navy was fully aware of the US Army's activities in aviation before World War I. There were naval observers present at the Army's tests of the first aircraft ordered from the Wright Brothers. It could hardly be otherwise, as the fire control methodology had lagged the technical development of ordnance and ammunition in the naval context. It had standoff but not precision. One of the measures to take full advantage of those improvements was to physically raise the location of the gunnery spotters aboard ship so as to extend their visual horizon, but the guns could potentially fire beyond that visual range nonetheless. If for no other reason, the mariners had a built-in interest in aviation from the start. Aircraft could elevate the gunnery observers to whatever height required above the masthead. Almost as soon as it was tried from aircraft, the aircraft as a spotter dramatically improved the precision of gunnery fire.[22]

The first landings and takeoffs were made from ships in 1911, and naval flight training got started that same year under the tutelage of Glenn Curtiss at Hammondsport, New York. Even at that early date, visionaries anticipated an offensive role for naval aircraft. One of the experiments done at Curtiss' school was in bomb-dropping, and he laid out an outline of a battleship as a target. But the vast preponderance of thought at that stage looked toward aviation as an auxiliary of the battleship to improve the latter's effectiveness in its offensive role.

Notwithstanding the early shipboard landings and takeoffs, a serious problem was how one might operate aircraft at sea without interfering with the gun power of the combatant ships. There had been the thought that the fire control observers might be elevated in balloons and kites, and some got thrilling rides in experiments along those lines. From early days, it was clear from the launching methods of both Samuel Langley and the Wright Brothers that aircraft might be catapulted, but the recovery was a continuing problem—as was the plane and apparatus for launching, for space aboard the combatants was at a premium.

Before and during World War I, the United States led the world in flying boat technology. The planes used at Vera Cruz had been flying boats. But counting on shore-based planes, or even those nearby operating from seaplane tenders, being overhead when needed was a shaky proposition. The thought of dedicated aircraft carriers with landing decks was conceived immediately, but opening up a whole new line of specialized ships with the personnel to operate and maintain them was a daunting proposition. There was no easy solution in view when America went to war in 1917.[23]

Naval Aviation in World War I

As noted, neither Army nor Navy aviation was in any way decisive in the First World War. But the activity of both probably was much more extensive than appreciated by today's citizens. The great sea battle did not materialize for Alfred Thayer Mahan's navy,* and the principal use of naval aviation was in the submarine war and as an element of land-based airpower at the northern end of the Western Front.

One of the notions coming out of that conflict was that no American-designed and built airplane ever made it to the war. This was indeed true of the Army (although some American-built, British-designed DH-4s made it over just before the end) but it omits the fact that Curtiss flying boats did make a substantial contribution. They did so in the submarine war. They had precious little offensive capability against the U-boats but their very presence forced the enemy vessels to submerge; in itself, that was a substantial advantage. Because of the limitations of U-boat speed and endurance underwater, keeping them submerged for long periods had the effect of reducing the number of submarines that could be a threat to the sea lanes at any given time. However, any lessons that might have emerged from that were overshadowed by the preoccupation with the Battle of Jutland, and how aviation potentially might make another clash like that much more decisive.[24]

---

* Mahan graduated from the US Naval Academy before the Civil War and wrote the great doctrinal work, *The Influence of Seapower on History*, late in the century, which made him famous.

When the German Navy steamed into Scapa Flow after the war for its surrender to the Allies, there were Americans present to witness the spectacle. Two of the most prominent impressions they came away with were that all the British capital ships (battleships and battle cruisers) were already equipped with their own aircraft for reconnaissance and spotting, and the Royal Navy already had three aircraft carriers at sea. A third impression was the scuttling of what had been the world's second strongest navy, the German battle fleet.

As we have seen, at war's end Captain Jerome Hunsaker had been in Europe on Navy technical business and it was his lot to come home aboard the *SS Aquitania* with General Billy Mitchell as company. He received a full dose of the Mitchell treatment. Hunsaker soon made known to the General Board of the Navy that notwithstanding the scuttling of the German fleet, there was a new threat on the horizon: Mitchell with his ideas of a separate air force and a unified department of defense.[25]

Naval Aviation as an Auxiliary to the Battle Line

If the Army's Billy Mitchell had not existed, then the Navy would have had to invent him.[26] In the end, he served as a great stimulus to naval aviation. In large part a response to the threat posed by Mitchell's ideas, the Navy created the Bureau of Aeronautics in the summer of 1921, before the famous bombing tests. Its first chief was a former battleship captain, Rear Admiral William Moffett, who was able to use the threat of Mitchell to pry funding and other considerations out of admirals not so inclined.[27] But there were some who were so inclined—many more than today's citizens might assume: Admirals William Sims, Joseph Reeves, William F. Fullam, W. V. Pratt, and later people like Ernest King and William Halsey.[28] But there was little thought even among the most air-minded of them that the aviation forces ought to be separated from the Navy. The trend was rather strongly in the direction of making aviation an organic part of the sea service. That model almost automatically led to opposing any thought of a third service for an air force.[29]

General Mitchell launched a campaign for the separate air force soon after his homecoming, and as a part of it, he proposed bombing tests that would (in his vision) prove that the day of the *Dreadnought* was done. After considerable agitation, and with assistance from some friends in Congress, the tests were scheduled using the captured German battleship *Ostfriesland* as a target. Mitchell put together the First Provisional Air Brigade for the tests—using all of the personnel of the Air Service Tactical School, whose sessions were suspended. Both the Army airmen and the sailors attempted to stack the deck but the battleship went down in the full view of the media and countless dignitaries. It really did not mean much, as the conditions were highly artificial (like those at Pearl Harbor) in that the ships were not moving, undefended, close to Langley Field, and Mitchell's Martin bombers needed navigational assistance even for that short distance to a location known to the attackers beforehand.[30] All that mattered little to the media, and it was widely seen as the dawn of a new day in naval warfare.

Meanwhile, the Navy was moving as fast as it could to develop its organic aviation so that it could advertise itself as the wave of the future. Moffett was hardly in office when he went off to Pensacola to go through an air observers' course that he set up to give some of the old sea dogs wings (and hopefully credibility in the aviation community), theoretically including all the elements of flight training that the fledgling pilots were undergoing except the solo.[31] It would be some time yet before the pilots entering the ground floor of aviation would have enough seniority to qualify for command of major ships or shore stations.[32]

The General Board of the Navy had recommended a forced draft aviation program in the summer of 1919, and that was implemented insofar as funding and arms control negotiations would permit. The latter constraint grew out of the Washington Conference of 1921–1922 held in the wake of the bombing tests. Largely on U.S. initiative, the emerging treaties provided for[33]

- A complete freeze on the building of battleships for ten years.
- The sizing of the American, British, Japanese, French, and Italian fleets in the ratio of 5:5:3:1.75:1.75.
- The same ratios to be applied to aircraft carriers with the United States and Great Britain, capped at a total tonnage of 135,000 tons.
- All vessels above 10,000 tons with guns larger than 8 inches to be defined as "capital ships."
- Individual carriers limited to 27,000 tons, except that the British, Americans, and Japanese would be permitted to complete two of their battle cruiser hulls already in process above that up to 33,000 tons.
- Each power would be permitted one experimental aircraft carrier that would not be counted against the 135,000-ton cap.
- No new fortifications would be built in the Pacific between Hawaii and Singapore.

During the years immediately after the Washington Conference, the naval aviators were usually careful not to suggest that airplanes were anything but auxiliary to the battle line. They had already done work to take them to sea aboard battleships, launching them from platforms atop turrets for recovery ashore (and in wartime for ditching at sea) and, as noted, had some marvelous results in improvements in gunnery accuracy at longer ranges than ever before.

The responsiveness of flying boats was still a question, and the recovery of catapult aircraft still required stopping a ship at sea—a highly dangerous practice in the presence of enemy submarines or ships. The collier *Jupiter*, a newer vessel, was selected for conversion to a carrier. It was a little over 10,000 tons, had a modern propulsion plant, and it had huge spaces (originally intended for coal stocks) that could be converted into a workable hangar deck for aircraft storage and maintenance. The aviation enthusiasts seemed to be biding their time before claiming an offensive mission for the airplane until some real results were available from the *Langley* (CV-1) experiments at sea.[34]

The *Langley* truly was a test bed in the hands of Admiral Joseph Reeves, a naval observer, sometimes said not to fully understand the details of the aviators' work but certainly more knowledgeable about the larger implications of naval aviation than practically anyone else in the Fleet. He pushed the aviators to the limit, and enabled U.S. carriers to pack many more airplanes aboard and to get more sorties out of each one than could any other navy. In the annual Fleet Exercises, he developed imaginative ideas leading to the development of independent fast-carrier task forces and to power projection ashore—all this before the Roaring Twenties were gone and before the great ships *Lexington* (CV-2) and *Saratoga* (CV-3) were at sea. As the theory was developing, aviation was still mainly to be used for reconnaissance and spotting, though there were ideas here and there that it might also be used to attack enemy battleships (Japanese capital ships were generally faster than ours) to slow them down so that our line could catch up with them for the final kill.[35] However, from early on surface sailor and aviator alike well understood that air superiority over the sea battle was essential.[36] They also shared with their land-based air brethren the assumption that airpower is inherently offensive. In the naval case, that was all the more so because the defensive value of the carriers themselves was weak and lay mostly in their superior speed, allowing them to flee other ships—but not enemy aircraft.[37]

There was little hope that such air superiority could be achieved with catapulted airplanes or with flying boats—neither could be numerous enough nor agile enough to have any effect on the air battle in the presence of enemy aircraft carriers. This led to important support for the development of carriers on the part of the most hardened battleship sailors, and to the notion that air superiority could be most quickly achieved through sinking the enemy aircraft carriers. That latter function then became the primary duty of the air groups aboard the carriers.

The reasons underlying the evolutionary way in which aviation was incorporated into the Fleet are open to debate. "Battleship sailor" has become an euphemism for "hopeless reactionary" well beyond the boundaries of the USAF, but I am not altogether sure that it is justified.[38] Moffett himself was a first-class battleship captain; Admiral Chester Nimitz, the leader in the Pacific War, commanded a cruiser; the victor at Midway, Raymond Spruance, was not an aviator but rather a cruiser sailor. Arguably, just as Arnold confessed at the end of the day that the Air Corps had received real airpower just about as soon as it was technically feasible, the naval aircraft of the 1920s and early 1930s perhaps were just not robust enough to get battleships. The bombs Mitchell used to sink the *Ostfriesland* had been 2,000 pounders.[39] Until the SBD Dauntless went aboard carriers in 1940, the largest bomb that could be carried any distance by carrier-based aircraft was but a 500 pounder—not likely to penetrate the horizontal armor aboard battleships, although it might well tear up the superstructure and slow them down. The point is that if Pearl Harbor had come in 1931 or even 1936, it certainly would have been quite a different story.[40]

Meanwhile, the intellectual dimension of the work was being carried on at the Naval War College at Newport, Rhode Island, and in the pages of the *United States Naval Institute Proceedings*. The student can find any number of war games at the former and articles in the latter to support the assertion that Jutland was being replayed endlessly. But they can also find plenty of evidence that the gamers were increasingly including submarines and aircraft,[41] and there are enough articles on aviation in two decades' worth of *Proceedings* to fill several books. However, it must be admitted that at the public level both aviation and submarines were seen only as auxiliary to the Fleet. Admiral John Towers himself, one of the first naval aviators, attended the War College in 1934 and his thesis was explicit on insisting that aviation was a supporting arm for the battle line.[42] On the very eve of war, the aviators on the faculty at Newport were still carefully avoiding any debate of aircraft versus battleship.

However, immediately after Pearl Harbor the submariners were to come out of the closet with a full-blown unrestricted submarine warfare offensive. The theory is that they developed these ideas by playing the red team commanders in the war games at Newport while publicly denying that any American skipper would use German methods against commercial sea transportation. That this campaign was not immediately more effective is due largely to major technological deficiencies in U.S. torpedo design. Presumably, the aviators and some surface sailors had also given some thought to alternative uses of naval air power even before Pearl Harbor nailed down the lesson for them once and for all. They themselves had practiced Sunday morning carrier air attacks on Pearl Harbor as early as 1932,[43] and Billy Mitchell had predicted such attacks on that station in the early 1920s.

The *Lexington* and *Saratoga* were a major acquisition preoccupation during the 1920s, having plenty of schedule and cost overrun troubles. They finally went down the ways in the last weeks of 1927, and by 1929 they were both up and running as major elements of the Fleet. However, even before they became operational sea plane tenders and the like were assigned the role of aircraft carriers during Fleet Exercises, with but one airplane representing a carrier air group. Once the big ships went to sea, red on blue war exercises with real airpower on both sides became possible. Both procedures and technology had been developed on the *Langley*, and they were quickly adapted to the new carriers.[44]

There is much more of an interdependence between ship and aircraft technology than most Americans would suspect, and a great deal of debate as to the optimum design occurred during the interwar period.[45] For example, during a crucial phase of the 1982 Falklands War, the air was calm and the Argentine carrier, the *Veinticinco de Mayo*,[46] just could not get up enough speed to launch its A-4 attack aircraft with any sort of a payload, and they were out of the fight just as surely as if they had been shot down or their carrier sunk. Once the ship is built, one is liable to be stuck with its constraints for a very long time. The *Forrestal* came on line in 1955, and has just recently gone out of service (1993).

The requirements for the *Ranger* were laid down before the results from the sea trials of the *Lexington* and *Saratoga* were received. The Washington Treaty had limited the United States to a total of 135,000 tons, and 66,000 tons were used up by the latter two ships. There was much thought that numbers matter in the air superiority struggle above the great sea battle. It was argued that those numbers were more dependent upon the number of decks engaged in launch and recovery than the size of the individual ships.[47] In consequence, the *Ranger* (CV-4) was designed at about 14,000 tons, less than half that of either CV-2 (*Lexington*) or CV-3 (*Saratoga*). The two greater ships could steam at 33 knots but the CV-4 could only get up to 27 knots, and there was not much that could ever be done to boost that. Six knots may not seem like much to a modern jet flyer but it was twenty percent of the ship's speed, which could make a radical difference in the design of fighter aircraft, especially. The result was that *Ranger* was confined to Atlantic operations through the whole of World War II, even during the dark days of the winter of 1942–1943.[48]

One of the reasons the *Ranger* had to stay in the war against Hitler was that the Japanese surprised us with their fighter design in the Zero. The bomber losses over China after 1937 had led to the demand for a long-range escort fighter, which was developed in the Zero. It had exceptional range and agility but sacrificed speed and robustness to get it. For a time after Pearl Harbor, it got the better of U.S. pilots but once the Americans learned of its weaknesses, revised tactics enabled them to hold their own in the Wildcats and to achieve superiority in the Hellcats and Corsairs.[49] The standard American deck load in 1941 was made up of F4F *Wildcats*, which were no match for the Zero. The design of a higher-speed successor was imperative, and that was the F6F Hellcat—which helped win the war but which was generally too hot in landing aboard a small-deck, slow-speed carrier. (The Wildcats nonetheless remained in production throughout the war for service aboard escort and light carriers not intended to face the highest Japanese threats but where the decks were small.)

There was little anticipation of radar in either the Japanese or the US Navy until late in the 1930s. In any event, the offensive spirit was strong in both services, and deck space was so short that the incentives were great to put as much offensive power as possible on that which was available. Thus, the emphasis was on bombers and torpedo aircraft because of their offensive natures. However, radar technology was earlier in coming to the US Navy, and that service was earlier into the development of a shipboard command and control system in its Combat Information Centers—which turned out to be a substantial advantage later in the war.[50]

There was some movement back toward larger carriers once the budget constraints of the 1920s were loosened a bit after Franklin Roosevelt, a naval enthusiast, took office in 1933. At first it was a work relief effort, and later a response to growing Nazi and Japanese threats—including that implied by the Japanese refusal to renew the naval disarmament arrangements past December 31, 1936. These later ships included the *Hornet*, *Wasp*, *Yorktown*, and *Enterprise*. (Only the *Ranger*, *Saratoga*, and *Enterprise* of the prewar carriers survived the war.) The *Wasp* was not far from the *Ranger* in displacement and spent most of her combat life in the Atlantic, though she came to an early end in September 1942 in the South Pacific, falling to a Japanese submarine. The others were all about 20,000 tons, and the next class, the *Essex*, went up to 27,000 and became the backbone of the carrier task forces that won the Pacific War—one of them being the second carrier *Lexington*, which was a training vessel at Pensacola into the 1990s.[51]

Even before World War I, growing antagonism between Japan and the United States led American naval thinkers to contemplate war against her.[52] The Japanese were imperialistic enough during the First World War to lend credibility as a threat to the U.S. interests in the Far East, and although that subsided for a time after the Washington Conference, the imperialist march resumed in the early 1930s. The American Navy lost a part of its reason for being when the Kaiser's fleet disappeared and war with Great Britain had become unthinkable. The scheme that emerged from all of this was called War Plan Orange, which assumed a one-on-one war between Japan and the United States. It also assumed the Japanese would wait on the far side of the Pacific for the US Navy to progress across that sea, and its strength would be diminished in the process—or so the Japanese thought, to the point where they would have a good chance of defeating it in a Mahanian battle somewhere around the Philippines.[53] That done, they would be free to exploit their command of the seas for the betterment of Japanese industry and capitalism, with the end result that they would be impregnable in the region. However, the American Plan Orange sought to go across the Central Pacific, building a base structure among the captured islands as it went. In that way, the infrastructure would support the Fleet at full strength, the great sea battle would go our way, and the markets of the Far East would be preserved for American enterprise forever more—and democracy developed along the way. The plan was updated many times and it did not enjoy the enthusiasm of the Army, which was to provide the troops (bait) in a forlorn hope in defense of the Philippines, to be rescued by the US Navy but only after an interlude in Japanese prison camps.[54]

How did aviation play into all this? One of the principal ways that an inferior navy (in numbers only: Japanese torpedoes, fighter technology, and night gunnery among other things were not inferior) could use land-based airpower from the many islands was to attrit the superior fleet as it strove to cross the Pacific. Not having many such islands, the United States would have to rely on carrier-based airpower to a greater extent. This put her at a disadvantage because aircraft were much smaller then than they have become. Therefore, the penalty incurred in arresting gear and built-in strength to survive carrier landings was a far greater proportion of the whole than is the case today. There was some substance to the notion that carrier-based airpower was inferior to its land-based counterpart. Thus, there was to be wisdom in Admiral William Halsey's decision to launch Jimmy Doolittle early once the strike force had been discovered by the Japanese trawler, and in a reluctance by carrier admirals to enter the Mediterranean until the juice had been taken out of the Italian and German air forces by other means.[55]

On the eve of World War II, it was already clear that the assumptions underlying War Plan Orange were faulty in some ways. It was not to be a one-on-one war, nor would the Pacific War be the primary effort. The idea that Orange would nonetheless be valid as a plan for the Pacific part of World War II was still strong, and that we would have to develop a base structure across the Central Pacific and have a great battle on the far side was similarly strong. The idea that the carrier in addition to the battleships (or instead of the battleships) might be a capital ship had more adherents than theretofore. There were substantial numbers of both categories of vessels in the plans for new construction and the program for the *Essex*-class carriers was well underway, although the first samples would not be ready for action for close to two years. Doubtlessly, the idea that the battleship was to be supported and the carrier was in a supporting role was still predominant, although Pearl Harbor was to make the issue moot. The Navy and the other services were building up at a rapid pace already for three years, and the production and training programs were beginning to bear important fruit.

One of Orange's assumptions that went wrong at the last minute was that the Japanese Navy would wait on the far side of the Pacific for the US Navy to come to it for the climactic battle. It had been a sound assumption for a long time but Admiral Isoroku Yamamoto, who was reluctant to tackle America for good and sound reasons, thought otherwise. If Japan was to have any chance at all in a war that his countrymen were insisting upon, then it would have to open with a massive attack on the main strength of the U.S. Fleet.[56] That would be intended to yield the time for the Japanese to consolidate their initial gains. It was a dim hope in Yamamoto's mind but it was the only way he could see that might yield enough time for war weariness to set in the United States to the point where she might accept a compromise peace. He was wrong. Meanwhile, as we shall see in the next chapter, the sleeping giant on the other side of the Pacific had not been altogether inactive.

3

The Foundations of American Airpower

THE ERA OF THE INDUSTRIAL WEB: RISE OF THE STRATEGIC BOMBER

Although Mitchell came out of World War I mainly concerned with what we now call tactical airpower, even in the early 1920s the strategic bombing idea was present in his public lectures and speeches, as well as those at an ancestor unit of the Air Corps Tactical School (ACTS).[1] Some of Mitchell's remarks were precursors of the ACTS industrial web theory, that an industrial society resembles a spider web made up of interdependent parts. Nodal points existed in the web. If one or a few of these were destroyed, then the entire web would collapse. Gradually, through the 1920s the prestige of the bomber units consequently increased so that in the 1930s they constituted the main force in the US Army Air Corps.

As noted, the ACTS moved to Maxwell Field in 1931, and thereafter it reached its heyday. Its curriculum always covered the airpower spectrum and included courses dedicated to ground attack and pursuit throughout. However, there can be little doubt that the Air Force (strategic bombing) course was emphasized. Arguments did go on about the capability of fighters to intercept incoming bomber raids (always in the absence of any suspicion that radar would soon appear) and about the practicality (or impracticality) of escort fighters.[2] Perhaps as the result of wishful thinking, the theory that emerged by the mid-1930s was that the bomber could always get through in daylight with acceptable losses.[3] It could do so without escort, and it could find and hit its targets with a high degree of accuracy. It could get its standoff by flying at very high altitudes; it could get its precision by flying in daylight and using advanced bombsight technology. Once those nodal targets were hit, the entire enemy industrial system would tend to collapse, and capitulation would necessarily follow. Whether for moral or public relations reasons, the theory always specified that industrial objectives—not the civilian population—were to be the targets. Douhet, Mitchell, and the ACTS all argued that this would happen so rapidly that the stalemate in the trenches would be much shorter than it had been in the "Great War." Thus, the total human suffering would be less notwithstanding the violence done to cities or industrial targets.[4]

There were skeptics on the ACTS faculty, and there is also some evidence that some of the students did not believe everything they were told.[5] Notwithstanding all the emphasis on strategic bombing, arguably the United States led the world in fighter development until the Spitfires, Hurricanes, and Bf-109s came on the scene in 1937. Also, the first monoplane aircraft in U.S. service reached the line in 1928 as a ground attack weapon, the A-8. The B-10 was the first monoplane bomber and did not go operational until 1932—the same year that the all-metal monoplane fighter, the Boeing P-26, arrived in the units.[6]

The first Flying Fortress B-17 flew in 1935 and arrived in units in 1937. Its first assignment was to the Second Wing of the General Headquarters (GHQ) Air Force at Langley Field. Under the Command of Major General Frank Andrews, the GHQ Air Force was then thought to be a partial response to the technical changes in military forces and the doctrinal developments since the First World War. Some thought of it as a type of halfway house to an independent air force and a strategic bombing doctrine. The Army General Staff did allow that it could fly in independent operations prior to the contact of the ground armies. It was established in 1935 and had three wings of varying composition. One was at Langley Field and it had all the heavy bombers, few though they were. It also had some of its own fighter units. Another was at Barksdale Field, Louisiana, and it was heavy on attack aircraft, although it too had fighter squadrons. The third was at March Field, California, and it had both bomber and fighter groups.[7]

In general, there are three main elements of organizing forces for war: people, ideas, and material. We have seen previously that the ideas relating to both employment and organization were developed to some degree long before Pearl Harbor. Although they were not universally accepted within the American military, they were rather well-developed and discussed. As to material, the American aircraft industry was not behind those of other nations in any across-the-board sense. Our engines were competent; those of radial air-cooled design were the best in the world and proved to be a substantial advantage over the Axis powers. As noted, our four-engine airplanes were second to none, and production of both the B-17 Flying

Fortress and the B-24 Liberator was well underway before we went to war. Both were in the 70,000-pound region of gross weight at takeoff. They had a high altitude capability for the day, and during operations they generally bombed from 20,000 feet or more, relying on height for their standoff. They both were equipped with the Norden bombsight, which was thought to yield surgical precision from that standoff altitude—and which had achieved accurate results over the dry bombing ranges in California. The United States also developed smaller bombers, always with radial engines, that served well in tactical campaigns around the world and were in high demand by our allies. They included the B-25 Mitchell and B-26 Marauder at about 30,000 pounds, and the A-20 Havoc at slightly less. The Mitchell earned fame in the bombing of Tokyo in April 1942, and the A-20 acquired fame in the Battle of the Bismarck Sea, eleven months later.

America was in for some nasty surprises in fighter design, for she had led the world in that category as late as 1935. The Navy went into the war with deck loads of F-4 Wildcats and TBD Devastator torpedo bombers, both of which were hard pressed by the Japanese. However, the Germans and British had pulled ahead in the late 1930s with the Messerschmitt Bf-109, the Spitfire, and the Hurricane. Even the Japanese surprised us with their agile, long-range and well-armed Zero, which was deadly against American Navy and Army aircraft in a turning fight until well into the war. In general, with an important radar assist from the British, the U.S. electronics industry put both our bombers and fighters at an advantage over those of the Axis powers. This yielded a communications and a search advantage over all the members of the Axis, although the lead was greater in the Pacific than over Germany.

Whatever the technological shortfalls, the basic strength in American science and industry enabled us to overcome them in fairly short order. This was soon evident in the Pacific as the F-6 Hellcat and F-4U Corsair came on the line with 2,000-horsepower engines, which made them more competitive with the Japanese and were the airplanes that won air superiority in that theater. Not only was industry able to turn out great numbers, but also as the war went on it had enough surplus capability to continue development of new designs at a faster pace than was possible for both Germany and Japan. Atop that, the oil industry in the United States was producing superior fuels that, combined with better engine technology, enabled America to surpass both Germany and Japan—and to deliver important help to both Great Britain and the USSR. At that time, America was not dependent upon overseas sources of crude oil.

One of the reasons for the technology and production advantages was that the United States had a population that alone exceeded the combined total of Germany and Japan, and when added to that of our allies, the Axis was hopelessly outnumbered. Also, as in Germany but not Japan, literacy was just about universal in the United States. But more than that, since

Colonial times the ratio of population to land area was so much less in the United States than in Europe or the Far East, and that from the beginning meant there had been a greater affinity for labor-saving devices in America than elsewhere. As we noted, the result was that our farms were mechanized much earlier than they were elsewhere and the industrial revolution came to America just a little after Great Britain, and once it got rolling it had surpassed that of every other nation before Pearl Harbor. Thus, it was more than just a cultural conceit when Americans claimed to have more mechanical aptitude than others, and that counted not only in design and production but also in the operation of the equipment in battle.

The huge land areas of the United States helped in many other ways. It provided a large free-trade area that made industrialization and mechanization profitable. It was conducive to the early development of railroads and the associated technologies. It provided practically all the raw materials that were needed up to that time. Plus, when aviation came along in the twentieth century there was a greater advantage in large countries than smaller ones. That stimulated the early development of aviation and airlines (the U.S. airlines got another huge boost during World War II when those of most other countries were out of business). The time savings between San Francisco and New York inevitably were greater than those to be had between, say, Dresden and Hamburg. Thus, in addition to the ideas and technology, American airpower had a leg up in the area of aviation personnel, although other countries had been more determined in pushing that dimension than Americans had been. A case in point was the development of the Air Transport Command of the US Army Air Forces. It was largely done by merely mobilizing the airlines and putting them into uniform, and it was by far the largest and most competent air transport organization anywhere in the world.[8]

The United States had the good fortune to have a couple of years to prepare for war. Hitler marched in September 1939, and Pearl Harbor did not come for more than two years. The United States was an "arsenal of democracy" for those two years, and had shipped some B-17Cs to the British. They were quickly found unsuitable by our future allies, but the Air Corps did not want to believe it. The argument was that properly employed, in sufficient numbers and in daylight, they could succeed. During those two years, the aircraft was changed to include tail guns and power turrets above and below, and the American aircraft factories were run up to full production and beyond.[9] Meanwhile, the RAF had gone to war with a strategic bombing theory not too far removed from that of the Air Corps. It was not at first accompanied by compatible technology in that the British four-engine heavy bombers were not due out of the British factories until 1942. It had been reorganized in 1935 to include a dedicated strategic bombing unit, Bomber Command. For nearly three years, Bomber Command fought on with unimpressive two-engine bombers with practically no escort. It was so badly bloodied that in 1940, it quickly reverted to night bombing to preserve the force. Still, it took some time to realize that the RAF could neither hit targets nor even find them in the darkness.[10]

The ideas developed by Giulio Douhet, Billy Mitchell, and many others had great appeal to many in Congress and the media. The technologies intended to implement those ideas were ingenious and innovative. But it all depended upon a massive and innovative industrial capacity to bring it to fruition.

HOW HAD WORLD WAR I CHANGED THE ROLE OF INDUSTRY IN AMERICA?

In some ways, the First World War experience was essential to American success as the "arsenal of democracy" in the last years before Pearl Harbor. The Great War had demonstrated that the *laissez-faire* economic system did not always work. Many dimensions of our armament program were failures, especially airframe design and production. The mismanagement of the railroads also demonstrated that planning and centralized organization might have their virtues in some circumstances—like total war. Although the war had not been nearly as tough on American working populations as it had been on the Europeans, it nonetheless gave additional impetus to the mechanization of both agriculture and industry to get maximum production with minimal expenditure of labor. There was already a good deal of admiration and envy of the American industrial and agricultural systems in Europe, and the major contribution that the United States made to the Allied victory was economic, and all hands knew it. One dimension of this was that the United Kingdom shot its capital out of the barrels of cannons during the First World War (17 train loads of artillery ammunition per day) and the consequence was that New York took London's place as the financial capital of the world. The American automotive industry got a huge boost from the war, and the electronic and aviation industries got a start, although the latter was decimated after the war because of the disappearance of government orders. Civilian demand sustained the other two during the 1920s. The huge demands of the war emphasized the importance of mass production by semi-skilled and unskilled labor.[11]

THE CHANGING ROLE OF THE FEDERAL GOVERNMENT

It is often written that the First World War brought the government into the economy in a big way, and set precedents that it used later to cope with the Great Depression, big labor, and big business. Many of the bureaucrats and politicians involved in the First World War were the senior folks of the New Deal and World War II. Franklin D. Roosevelt had been Woodrow Wilson's Assistant Secretary of the Navy; George Marshall had been a colonel and a planner on Pershing's staff. Much of the routine they used in the problems of the first war was utilized to fight the problems of the Great Depression and then the second conflict. It did not work in the case of the Great Depression, but who can argue that U.S. productivity was not a major factor in the outcome of the Second World War? Big government was already in place and had two more years to prepare for World War II than the earlier conflict, and that made a huge difference. All of the fighter planes that Carl Spaatz had at Issoudon in 1917 and 1918 were manufactured in France or the United Kingdom (1,000 aircraft). By the end of the African Campaign in 1943, the RAF had more American-manufactured aircraft there than their own. Practically all of those used there by the USAAF and USN were built in the United States (there were a few Spitfires used by the USAAF at the outset of the campaign).[12]

THE CULTURE OF WORLD SCIENCE AFTER WORLD WAR I

For a long time prior to the "Guns of August," there had been a cosmopolitanism in the world of science that was not found among other professions. Nationalism reached a zenith between 1914 and 1945 that got in the way of communication among many centers of scientific inquiry. This came to seriously hurt Germany in that her persecution of the Jews caused many of the most prominent scientists in Germany and other parts of central Europe to migrate to the United States, much to our benefit in aviation and nuclear sciences. Much of that happened in the interwar period, and then again at the end of World War II when the Russians and the United States competed to get as many of the German scientists as possible to migrate to those countries.[13]

THE WORLD ECONOMY AFTER THE ARMISTICE

The center of the world economy had been Europe for centuries, but the war decimated those countries by 1918 so that the United States became a sort of an economic hegemon as a result. The European powers wound up with huge war debts owed to the United States. The United States held most of the money and gold. The only way Europe could have paid would have been through foreign trade or reparations from Germany. The reparations dried up quickly; the Republican Congresses of the 1920s enacted high tariff barriers, which stimulated others to do the same thing. There was a substantial start to globalization in the nineteenth century, what with the coming of steamships, cargo refrigeration, and specialized mass production. Although the petroleum industry was in its infancy, that was also a contributor just as was the British Navy that represented a country dedicated to the propositions of free trade and freedom of the seas. However, after the Great War foreign trade dried up and the Europeans could not pay their war debts that way. In the end, the United States had to swallow all of the debts except the one from Finland, which was the only European country to pay up. The case has often been argued that World War I caused the Great Depression, which in turn caused World War II. The USSR in the late 1920s went on a forced draft industrialization that ultimately resulted in it becoming a heavyweight, and Japan made a huge profit out of World War I that furthered its industrialization and national wealth. The war had been a pleasant experience for the Japanese, who had suffered almost no casualties and made enormous gains, and perhaps they therefore wished to repeat it in 1941. The apparent success of the Communist Revolution in Russia set up a conflict between capitalism and Marxism that lasted for most of the rest of the century.[14]

THE MAGINOT LINE AND MILITARY THINKING IN AMERICA

Notwithstanding economic hard times, the greatest army in the world, the French, dedicated itself to building a giant fortification in the east: the Maginot Line. That was based heavily on the notion emerging from the conflict that the defensive form of war is much stronger than the offensive. In the years that have passed, the term "Maginot Line mentality" has become a euphemism for "stupidity." But it is not completely accurate, and that type of thinking was certainly not limited to France. It potentially was an important economy of force method that would have released resources to build a formidable mobile striking force that could have been used to meet a German invasion in a sort of Schlieffen Plan II.[15] The original German plan was indeed to wheel around the north end of the Maginot Line, and the British-French plan aimed to meet it in Belgium.[16] More or less fortuitously, the German plan was to be compromised and Hitler knew it, which caused him to change the scheme. The new one was for a thrust through the Ardennes straight at the Channel Coast. That would strike right at the hinge of the British-French wheel into Belgium, and resulted in a smashing victory for the Germans. Nobody knows what would have happened had the original plan been followed, but perhaps the *Blitzkrieg* would not have succeeded and the history of the world would be different.[17] In any event, the Maginot idea resonated with isolationists in America.

Certainly, the entire Western world had been appalled at the awful waste of World War I and the Great Depression and was trying to find a way to defend at a minimum cost, especially in infantrymen's lives. For a long time, the British were defensive and had little or no intention of getting back into combat on the Continent. The United States also looked to its Navy as a first line of defense[18] and had no intention at all of getting into a ground war again. A major argument of Mitchell was that the United States could be defended with one air force instead of two navies and at a much lower cost. The original thought behind naming the B-17 the "Flying Fortress" was that fortifications cannot move and thus are necessarily defensive. Thus the B-17, they hoped the isolationist public would believe, was a defensive weapon, and an economical one at that.

DISASTER AND REFORM

A great many writers, especially after the fall of France, came to argue that the Germans succeeded because of their humiliation in the First World War—implying, at least, that disaster is essential to real reform in the face of inherent military conservatism. A corollary to that has often been that civilian intervention in military affairs is necessary to overcome the rigid "military mind." I think that Stephen Rosen makes a good case that disaster is not essential.[19] He uses some fine examples wherein militaries had brought about substantial and beneficial change in the absence of defeat:

a. The USMC came up with an amphibious warfare doctrine, technology, and innovation after World War I, in which we had been victorious.
b. The Navy had been on the winning side in World War I, and yet brought about major change in integrating aviation into the fleet between the wars.
c. The RAF, victorious in World War I and firmly dedicated to the notion that airpower is inherently offensive, brought about major change in building a complete defensive system around radar and Fighter Command.

The German example after World War I is certainly suggestion enough that defeat is conducive to reform. Also, the major changes made by the USSR in the 1920s and 1930s at huge cost in the wake of the sufferings of World War I is additional evidence that it is conducive to change. Only occasionally do large military organizations make major changes in the presence of victory and prosperity.[20]

CIVILIANS AND MILITARY REFORM

I agree with Rosen that the role of civilians has been exaggerated some, especially in the case of the Battle of Britain. Air Marshal Hugh Dowding took a major bureaucratic risk in putting money onto radar development, and started building an integrated command and control system long before Sir Thomas Inskip ever came into office to beef up fighter production.[21]

In a much later case, there is no doubt that Robert McNamara did good things in systematizing the U.S. acquisition and budgeting systems, but some of what he did was not that impressive. His insistence of commonality in the absence of a really good handle on what airpower is about resulted in no gun in the F4-C when it did need one. He also made the F-111 into a side-by-side seating arrangement against Air Force wishes so that it would fit onto carrier elevators—and then the Navy refused to buy the airplane. My Army officer friends would probably not agree, but I still think he pushed us into helicopters for the Army too fast and too deeply, and it is a fortunate thing that they were never tested on the Northern European plain against the USSR. This was of later interest in that Secretary of Defense Donald Rumsfeld had been pushing for "transformation" in all the services, but especially the Army. Daily news reports from Kosovo and the Second Gulf War suggest that he then had more ammunition to bring about substantial reform in the Army, reluctant to give up its heavy formations in favor of lighter, more deployable forces.[22] But more on that later; for now, I agree with Stephen Rosen that sometimes civilian intervention can help but it is not always necessary, and sometimes it can even be hurtful.[23]

As Rosen also pointed out, civilians are almost inevitably deficient in the understanding of the technical and doctrinal dimensions of the military profession.[24] Many of them also seriously underestimate the power of the military (and most other) bureaucracies.[25] I think that they are sometimes given to oversimplification of military problems and are often insufficiently cognizant of the Clausewitzean axioms on fog, friction, and uncertainty.[26] It often does not seem that way because the civilians frequently have better access to the media, not the least due to the frequent built-in bias of the latter against things military and for scandal.

Reformers within the military do have some dilemmas to face when trying to innovate. General Pershing (with President Wilson's blessing) had not been eager to meld American forces in with those of the British and French. Other military leaders have often been accused of failing to understand the political dimensions of coalition warfare ever since. Further, it is often said that too many military planners have been insufficiently educated on the economic dimensions of warfare—which was one of the reasons for the founding of the Industrial College of the Armed Forces in the 1920s (originally the Army Industrial College.)[27] Yet the U.S. military has been unwavering in its obedience to the principle of civilian supremacy since the days of George Washington. There can be little doubt that many of the armed forces' leaders, maybe even a majority, are conservative and are unsympathetic to "amateur" intervention in matters of strategy and military technology. Still, a case could be made that Abraham Lincoln was the best military strategist the Union had, and maybe a similar case could be made for FDR.[28]

It is sometimes argued in decision theory courses that along with economic considerations, cultural factors are important and can even be determinant. Perhaps a good case can be made that military officers often can stand more education and thought on this subject. No one can watch old World War II motion pictures and doubt that Americans in general had a pretty weak understanding of Japanese culture—and consequently underestimated them.[29] Notwithstanding our continuing nationalism and insularity after World War II, our own culture was far closer to that of Germany than it was to that of the USSR. Our reconstruction of the former was successful, but it may have been a special case. With the Soviet threat in the east in the German case, reform was facilitated by their choice of what might have seemed the lesser of two evils—and here again, the German culture was closer to the American than the Russian. Our later experiences in Vietnam and later in Iraq suggest that no easy generalizations are possible.

One of the reasons why military thinkers have often been seen as more pessimistic and conservative than their civilian counterparts is that they will usually proclaim that they are not ready for battle or war, that they need more resources. They will emphasize enemy capability over threat and go for a maximum amount of force. If you can kill the cat, you can kill the kitten. They will tend to want to compensate for uncertainty with more mass. Rather than base their planning on an enemy's uncertain intentions, they strongly tend to base it on their capabilities.[30] But that will be difficult because they will also want to cover all the bases, and in so doing will weaken mass. They will therefore tend to exaggerate the enemy's capability and understate their own to get more financial and political support, and maybe sometimes to prepare in advance an excuse for failure. Perhaps there was some of this in the Second Gulf War, wherein reports suggested that Secretary Donald Rumsfeld insisted on starting the campaign with much less ground force than desired by some of the Army planners. Our intelligence was much more voluminous on Iraq than it was on Germany in World War II but the cultural gap was greater.

TO STIMULATE MILITARY INNOVATION

For all the lamentation about the lack of innovation in the military, how would one go about stimulating change in the services? According to Thomas Hone and Stephen Rosen, one would look a long way into the future and create a protected career track for spacemen and unmanned combat air vehicle (UCAV) people—or whomever you thought you would need. You might instruct the promotion boards to make sure that such space and UCAV people received a quota of promotions in each cycle. If you were like Admiral Moffett, you might want to dilute some of the normal professional requirements for advancement. The religion in the Navy has long been that one must be a naval officer first and an aviator (or other specialist) second. Thus, one must go through tours as a department head in all the departments of large ships (navigator, gunnery officer, engineer, supply, and on and on) to qualify for command at sea. Without having had command of a major combatant, one could not advance into the ranks of the admirals. The trouble with that was that one simply did not have enough time to do all those things and yet be proficient enough as an aviator to survive. Identifying and caring for talented individuals may be more important than getting money for programs. Money does count but time may count for even more—as has been noted endlessly, in wartime when time is short change tends to be incremental.[31]

It has been argued that although the military is far less isolated from the parent society than it was in the days of the "Yellow Legs" on the frontier, it nonetheless remains somewhat apart and perhaps not as alive to political and social change as some of the other professions. One consequence, it is argued, is that military doctrine in the usual case excessively lags change in political, social, and technological affairs. But critics cannot have it both ways; either the military is obsessed with technology or it is insufficiently cognizant of it, but probably not both.[32] There can hardly be any question that some lag is inevitable. The faster and greater the political, social, and technological change, then the longer the lag in doctrine. The coming of the nukes was highly disruptive to politics and military doctrine and it took at least ten years or so for things to stabilize, and we might even ask how this was possible in such a short time.[33]

I suppose that all militaries have some tendency toward conservatism, but the American military is notorious for being less so than its NATO colleagues and the Allies in World War II. One sometimes see it argued that the U.S. military is too unstable to suit the tastes of its allies. No doubt that accounts for some of the nervousness in the Security Council of the United Nations prior to the Second Gulf War and in the aftermath with regard to U.S. policy toward Syria. Insofar as one manifestation of slowness to change is related to interservice rivalry, it is questionable that the United States leads the pack in that. The controversies among the services in Great Britain were every bit as bitter in the 1920s as they were in America at that time or in the late 1940s. In Japan, the want of cooperation between army and navy far exceeded that in either Great Britain or the United States. Inevitably, the parent culture affects these things.[34]

Many of the critiques of the alleged conservative nature of militaries in general, and air forces in particular, have arisen at least in part from the wisdom of hindsight. What is often discounted is that there is a long journey to be made between the discoveries of basic science and the appearance of new weaponry in sufficient numbers to make a difference. Further, it is also unrecognized that the real success of new weapons usually comes in areas that were unimagined by the scientists and developers. Rather, once the device is fielded it very often happens that it is combined with other mature technologies and put to purposes altogether different from those imagined by the originators. All these things take time.[35]

Rosen claims that all innovation has been good, but I have my doubts about that. I do believe that it is possible that innovation can sometimes be premature. I do believe that had the nation completely bought Mitchell's case, it would have been premature because the technology was simply not there until much later. As it was, the appearance of radar came close to making obsolete a huge cost sunk in strategic bombing, and then we would have thought that change premature. Had the Navy switched to carriers as fast as Admiral Sims and Mitchell would have liked, and the had war started in 1931, then we would have regretted it, for the battleships would surely have blasted the carriers out of the water in short order.[36] One simply did not have the planes and the bombing techniques necessary to hit battleships with big enough bombs until the late 1930s. I think I would argue that premature innovation is as bad as tardy change. Although it is not military, the case of the Concorde supersonic airliner may be another case.[37] The costs have been enormous, and both France and Great Britain have better uses for the money. The benefits of subsidizing high rollers so that they can get across the Atlantic in four hours instead of seven did not seem to be commensurate. The technology spin-offs for either the economies or the militaries involved did not seem commensurate, either.

CULTURE AND MILITARY REFORM

Perhaps it is a conceit of the West, and especially of the United States, that our culture is inherently more innovative than those of the Far East or the Islamic worlds. Of course, there is no stereotype that applies universally to any culture. However, it is often written that Western culture is more innovative for a variety of reasons. One reason may be that the Western family is less authoritarian than those in other cultures. The women have a higher status in the West than they do in either most of the Asian cultures, or certainly within Islamic culture. Also, there is considerably less ancestor worship in the West than elsewhere, and that may be related to a more reverential attitude among Asian and Islamic children toward their parents.[38] Religion appears to be a stronger force in Islamic cultures and in many of those in the Far East as well. This is often taken to be a factor inhibiting innovation because it is based on faith rather than on what we call reason.[39]

The Renaissance and Enlightenment were movements away from faith-based reasoning toward humanism that began several centuries ago in the West, but insofar as it has happened at all in the East Asian and Islamic cultures, it started later there. I think that Russian culture resides somewhere between those extremes and is probably closer to the West than not, although I do guess that the Russian family is more authoritarian than those in the West. There are those theories that also hold that the Protestant Reformation, though faith based, was another factor conducive to innovation. In many of the denominations, earning money or charging reasonable interest on loans was not as reprehensible as it was in the Islamic or Asian cultures, and even in Catholic Europe. In turn, this was a factor leading to capitalism and competition, and again to innovation.[40]

It has even been argued that climate has something to do with innovation. In temperate zones, one had to get in the habit of planning ahead for the winter to survive. That led to saving against harder times, and further to legitimizing the banking industry and hard work and competition. But according to Arnold Toynbee and some others, in the tropical areas food was available all year around. That meant that one did not have to save against the hard times of winter, and societies in those regions thus did not get the original impetus enjoyed by the folks in Northern Europe. At the other extreme, in Arctic areas the people expended all their energy in killing one more seal, so that there never was any surplus to devote to science, technology, and other forms of innovation. That theory has taken plenty of heat, it is true. It is not politically correct, to be sure.[41]

If one is needed, a case in point is the Yom Kippur War of 1973. In general, tactical airpower had been a smashing success in World War II, and the USAF came out of Korea with a pretty strong perception that it had saved the Army's bacon at the time of Pusan and elsewhere in Korea. Thus, while the funding and fame was going to the strategic air forces in the 1950s in large part, there was probably some complacency within the tactical air forces as well. Some of the same factors seem to have affected the Israeli Air Force (IAF) prior to 1973, although our American tactical air forces had already assimilated the lessons of Vietnam in that regard. After the 1967 war, the French had abandoned their connection with Israel, and the United States reequipped her with American air technology—and thus the relationship with the USAF became much closer. The IAF is basically a short-range tactical force designed for war against relatively primitive enemies over a short period. All those enemies are of the Islamic culture, albeit that they were often equipped with Russian or Western air technologies. Thus, those enemies had not had much of an organic capability in electronics or surface-to-air missiles (SAM), and that may have been conducive to complacency. Also, the IAF had achieved one of the greatest air victories in history in 1967 even as the United States was losing the war in Vietnam. Thus, one suspects that there was complacency, especially in the IAF, to the effect that the 1967 cakewalk could be easily repeated and that there was nothing much to learn from the USAF. Unhappily, after 1967 the Arabs imported knowledge, technology, materiel, and even Soviet personnel that changed the equation radically. But in that case, more than technology was involved; rather, the Egyptian strategy employed was indeed innovative and combined with the new technologies to provide the IAF with a first-rate surprise. The result was a near-disaster in the opening hours of the 1973 war, and it was only with the greatest of pain that the Israelis survived the initial attack.[42]

Like the pilots of most air forces, those of the IAF are a self-confident lot. Some folks, like Carl Builder, have argued that they are also conservative and generally against missiles and UCAVs because of a fear of technological unemployment. Yet it was the so-called bomber barons from the World

War II generation who presided over the bringing of ICBMs onto the line of the Air Force in the 1950s, and in so doing led the rest of the world. General Bernard Schriever was the technical/managerial leader of all this, and he has pilot wings and flew in combat in the Southwest Pacific in World War II. Also, the man supposed to be the most avid bomber baron, Curtis LeMay, was in charge of the Strategic Air Command (SAC) in the 1950s, and then Vice Chief of Staff even as SAC was going over to missiles and the bombers were beginning their decline as the main pillar of deterrence. There was to be a pretty good argument in favor of covering all the bases with the Triad[43] in the days of the Cold War, where the price of failure was the annihilation of civilization. It seems clear to me that the reason why the UCAV is destined first for the suppression of enemy air defenses (SEAD) mission is that it is usually the most dangerous one we have and the pilots, like other rational animals, are generally free of a death wish. Also, ignorance is not a prerequisite for pilot school, and some aviators are as smart as engineers. The idea gets wide circulation because of its appeal to the rest of humanity, who react to perceived elitism among our pilots.[44]

At the other end of the spectrum, there is the conventional wisdom in our logistical commands that scientists are too enamored with odd ideas to be left in charge of getting practical weapons to the units in numbers and in a timely way. As the story goes, true imagination and practicality are not usually found in the same package. Although procurement is much more expensive than research and development, both cost a lot. One can be sympathetic with the managers' desire for some accountability in the laboratories, yet it is clearly necessary to leave room for exploration without yet having any tangible piece of equipment in view as the outcome. A case in point may be Vannevar Bush's *Modern Arms and Free Men*, published in 1949 and predicting that we would not see intercontinental ballistic missiles in our lifetimes.[45] He was probably our most distinguished scientist at that moment. Yet a little more than a decade later, it seemed that the world was quivering in fear during the Cuban Missile Crisis. On the other side of the equation, Vannevar Bush stoutly resisted the integration of the scientists working on national defense with the government or the military precisely because he thought it would stifle their imagination.[46] It is certainly true that during World War II, people working under his direction did produce some very practical and decisive things, like the proximity fuse.

Alfred Thayer Mahan, the great American naval theorist before World War I, argued that authoritarian governments have an advantage over pluralist societies when it comes to organizing military forces for war. Although the great man would certainly not have advocated that type of government, he did lament that authoritarian outfits had an advantage in that they can be more swift than we are at getting consensus, getting organized, and getting effective ships (or airplanes) on the line in large numbers. Certainly, the British have a reputation of muddling through but Mahan surely did admire those folks; we will return to this subject in our chapter on intelligence. It is difficult to read the story of the interwar period without seeing the RAF as muddling through, but then the *Luftwaffe* had its share of muddlers, for sure.

The Battle of Britain has been offered as a special case study for many different things: the importance of air superiority, a school on strategic bombing, a demonstration of the importance of innovation. Further, the Battle came at a very bad hour in the history of the Western democracies. Thus, in the historiography of airpower we have usually given more than the usual attention to the subject.[47]

4

The Battle of Britain/America Prepares

At the end of World War I, there was hardly any doubt that command of the air would be a prime requirement in any future wars. From the beginning, many people thought it was an enabler more than an end in itself. (Giulio Douhet did assert that possibly the loss of air superiority would be so obviously deadly that the political leaders might decide to throw in the towel without requiring that the air attack move into the exploitation phase.) Why then were the arguments in Great Britain and the United States about airpower in the 1920s so vicious? The debate was more about what it should enable (an attack downtown or support on the battlefield) and how it should be accomplished (an air battle, an attack against air resources on the ground, or some combination of the two). Soldiers and sailors everywhere thought it should be used to enhance the effectiveness of armies and navies; some airmen thought it should enable the attack downtown to bring about the decision without the necessity of a prolonged and bloody surface fighting. Douhet thought it might be achieved with an attack against the enemy airpower on the ground; Billy Mitchell thought it might be achieved by a combination and that the air battle was paramount. Possibly the British, too, thought that a combination would be required.

As military aviation really did not have much of a history, thinking about its role in war required more assumptions than necessary for land or sea warfare. There was a pretty strong assumption among airmen that the offensive was to be preferred. This may have led in the direction of the Douhet version of the achievement of command. There also was an assumption on the part of some that the decisive blows would come from the infantry or the battle fleet, which led to the notion of local air superiority over the scene of the battle and the command of air forces by the older services. There were also strong assumptions that it would remain difficult to find another airplane in the footless halls of space, and that a long-range escort fighter for bombers was impractical because range and agility were contradicting qualities.

Notions about air superiority did change in the two decades before the Battle of Britain. In the United States, we moved by the end of the 1920s from fighter predominance to bomber predominance in the air superiority battle—moving closer to Douhet, although not all the way. Perhaps in the absence of knowledge of radar this was a result of desiring a decisive impact without the agony of the trenches. Perhaps among American airmen it was because it was the only practical (in the long run) independent mission that might yield a separate air force and a separate promotion list. It was probably some combination of the two, with the emphasis varying from individual to individual. I remain convinced that there is a natural preference of initiative and activism in America that is conducive to the bomber approach because it is offensive in nature. Standing by and waiting for the attack to come was not a congenial idea to many Americans. Even a case for isolationism might be possible in that bombers might be able to keep conflict away from American shores, whereas soldiers were less likely to do so.

In Great Britain, the commitment to bombers came earlier and possibly was even stronger than in the United States.[1] The United Kingdom had an enormous technological lead at the end of World War I, but the poor condition of its treasury prevented her from maintaining the lead. However, geography made a huge difference, and the single fattest target in the world was probably London, within easy flying distance of France. Thus, the need for interceptors was quite clear in Great Britain once the German threat began to be perceived. But in the United States, the Morrow (1925) and Baker Boards (1934) were probably correct in deciding there was no similar threat to the Americas for the foreseeable future[2] (the first one came in September 2001, and even then all the attackers took off from U.S. airfields). Also, the air leaders in Great Britain began to get a glimmering that radar might be possible earlier than was the case in the United States. General Hap Arnold, Chief of the US Army Air Corps, was dimly aware that it was a possibility in the summer of 1939, but by then the British were well along in the development. So in Great Britain, from about 1935 onward the bomber predominance was diminished partly at the insistence of civilians and partly at that of Air Marshal Hugh Dowding.[3]

The U.S. airmen really did not begin to get a handle on the new technology until the summer of 1940, when both the technology and the organizational ideas were shared with Arnold's men in England during the Battle of Britain.[4] But by then, we had a huge cost sunk in large bombers, and the momentum was very great. In any case, the United States had developed a whole string of fighters in the 1930s (P-26, P-35, P-36, P-37, P-38, P-39, and P-40). This was done notwithstanding that there was no real threat against the North American homeland. For a time, a case could be made that the United States led the world (or was one of the leaders) in fighter development being the first into monoplanes, all-metal construction, retracting landing gear, closed cockpits, internal wing bracing, controllable pitch propellers, superior fuels, and radial engine development. As we have seen, at the end of the period the Spitfires and Messerschmitt 109s had moved ahead, but for them the danger was more clear and more present. Even still, the British had no ground support airplane at all whereas the United States had the A-20, developed especially for that work and which was produced in thousands of copies all the way to the end of the war. Nor did the RAF have a four-engine heavy bomber in service until 1942, whereas the United States got its first one in 1935 and the second in 1938. Also, air development in our Navy was much more extensive and advanced than anywhere else save possibly Japan. So the point is that the glass was not completely empty, and the decisions the American airmen made with the information they had were not altogether without merit.

One of the great stimulants changing air superiority thinking was the progress of technology. The period between the Armistice and the Invasion of Poland was 20 years, during which time we changed from the SPAD XIII to the Spitfire. That period was shorter than the one since the F-15 first flew and now—and the F-22 is still not in the units in numbers—and the difference between the F-15 and the F-22 is much less than between the SPAD and the Spitfire. Also, the coming of radar was crucial, and that goes a long way to explain why the integrated air defense system (IADS) first developed in England. But the coming of Adolf Hitler was an important stimulus for that, and not even Hitler could have reasonably predicted Hitler.

In America, the context of the times should not be forgotten. It would have been difficult to explain to the jobless and hungry in America why we needed a new string of fighters when there was no plausible threat and when it would have taken a superhuman feat of imagination to predict the early arrival of radar. I was totally flabbergasted on Webster Avenue in the Bronx in 1941 when I first laid eyes on a television set showing the World Series while it was being played. I certainly was less amazed at the kerosene lanterns and outhouses on my grandfather's farm. So you could ask as easily how was it that we adjusted so fast rather than so slow. U.S. government policy was hard over on isolationism and no more foreign wars. That changed with blazing rapidity after Munich in September 1938—so that three years later when Pearl Harbor occurred, to cite but one example, we actually had seven aircraft carriers being built and eight battleships on the ways. Government policy is important in research and development decision making.

THE COURSE OF THE BATTLE OF BRITAIN

The Munich concessions that the British and French made to Hitler in the fall of 1938 only whetted his appetite. The following spring, when he took over the rest of Czechoslovakia, it became clear that his ambitions were not limited to the unification of German-speaking peoples in central Europe, and that war would have to come. Thus, the British gave a guarantee to Poland against invasion and in September 1939, Hitler marched. The *Luftwaffe* played a prominent part in the invasion, generally following a pattern now seen as typical in tactical air doctrine. Air superiority was quickly achieved, in that the Polish air force was flushed out of its main bases. The aircraft that were not destroyed in battle were recovered at auxiliary bases, where they could not be supported. With more or less complete air superiority, the *Luftwaffe* then turned to interdiction of the movements of the Polish army and finally lent some direct assistance to troops on the battlefield. Poland fell in a trice, but a period of relative inaction followed. As we have seen, in the spring of 1940 a last-minute change in the German plan of attack on the low countries and France succeeded well—perhaps well beyond their expectations. There again, the *Luftwaffe* operated in a pattern similar to that used over Poland. The British Royal Air Force in the battle had been active and perhaps held up the Germans long enough to enable the evacuation. However, the British did suffer serious losses in the fighting, and finally they refused further reinforcement of air units in France.[5]

After the British were driven off the Continent and France fell, another period of inactivity followed. The Germans hoped that the British would throw in the towel without a fight, and in any case they really did not have a plan for further action. Gradually, it dawned on them that Great Britain was not about to fall without a shove, and planning began for the continuation of the war. The scheme was to start with an air attack. First, it was to be over the English Channel and some of the British ports, hoping to lure the RAF away from its bases for destruction and the achievement of German air superiority. The RAF refused to fully engage over the Channel, conserving its forces for the fight over the homeland.[6]

Meanwhile, the German army and navy were planning for the invasion of Great Britain and gathering forces for the projected attempt. Neither service was enthusiastic for that project, for the doctrine and technologies for amphibious operations had not been developed in their forces.[7] Some authorities have argued that the whole thing was just another one of Hitler's bluffs; others point out that even if the *Luftwaffe* had won air superiority, the large numbers of the Royal Navy destroyers deployed to the area would have been certain to work mayhem among the invasion barges. One cannot really say what was in Hitler's mind, but in any event practically any scheme would have required starting with air superiority.

After the preliminary skirmishes over the Channel and the ports, the *Luftwaffe* began testing the air defenses by flying over land, and thereby gave the observers, radar operators, anti-aircraft gunners, and command and control personnel some very valuable training before the major assault began. In the process, the *Luftwaffe* employed its *Knickbein* electronic bomb aiming device and gave the British the opportunity to analyze it and develop countermeasures before the later-night bombing campaign began.[8]

Hermann Goering, head of the *Luftwaffe*, decided to commence the main attack in the middle of August 1940. He began it in an orthodox way with moves against the RAF airfields, radar installations, and the aircraft factories in the attempt to destroy the infrastructure. At the same time, he hoped to stimulate an air battle within the reach of his fighters in southern England that would help achieve command of the air. The Messerschmitt 109s could fly no farther than London, and the Me-110 with its two engines was too clumsy to even defend itself, much less the bombers. British intelligence about the *Luftwaffe* was far from perfect, but that of the Germans about the RAF was far worse and remained so through the battle. The British had the enormous advantages of being able to count the wrecks on the ground from both air forces, of reading the *Luftwaffe* signals through decryption, and by some prisoner interrogation.[9] It also had the even greater advantage of instant intelligence on the locations of incoming raids through the use of the new radar installations.

TECHNOLOGY

As we noted previously, Air Vice Marshal Hugh Dowding was in charge of RAF research and development in the mid-1930s, where he had a major role in the development of practical radar as well as in the just-in-time development of good fighters in the Hurricane and the Spitfire. A little later, he was put in charge of Fighter Command. There he built an integrated air defense system that included good fighters, ground observers, communications lines, radars, anti-aircraft units, barrage balloon units, and air operations centers. Again, although the timing was close, he managed to put it all together, develop a doctrine, and test and train his troops in its utilization. The Germans then cooperated by starting off with relatively small attacks for several weeks that gave some excellent combat training exercises for the entire system.[10]

TROOPS

Most of the RAF veterans of World War I flying were too old for fighter combat by 1940; yet many of them had not reached their dotage, and they had lived 20 years in a peacetime air force. Led by Air Chief Marshal Hugh Trenchard through the 1920s, a system of professional schools were developed and then attended by prospective commanders, and many of them received active command experience at various colonial stations in the Middle East and the Orient. Junior people were trained in some numbers not only in the regular forces but also under various reserve schemes, and they were available for the cockpit jobs. As it turned out, the *Luftwaffe* intelligence grossly underestimated the British capability to produce fighter aircraft, and airplanes were not limiting factors. However, the pilot supply was limited—but it proved just sufficient.[11]

Great Britain, like America (and Germany), was not far short of universal literacy. As an industrial society older than any other, she also enjoyed a supply of people with mechanical aptitude. Thus, the supplies of technicians for the maintenance of her air units were ample, as were those with the skills necessary to operate the observer and command and control systems.

The Versailles Treaty had limited the German capability to develop the personnel needed for an effective system. Until 1933, Germany was not permitted an air force, but she was able to get around that to some degree by training flyers and commanders in Russia in cooperation with the USSR. Also, she had developed a system of civilian flying clubs in the home country that at least gave young people some indoctrination into aviation via gliders. She was permitted an airline, *Lufthansa*, and developed a cadre of flyers and managers by those means.[12] The *Luftwaffe* was founded in 1933 after the rise of Hitler, and it made much technical and training progress in the ensuing eight years, but the loss of the thirteen years between the Armistice and then could not be completely compensated. For example, only a few of the officers had graduated from the professional military education schools by 1939. However, she was not as bad off in the matter of doctrine as one might assume because of the prescience of Hans von Seeckt, who headed her military forces just after World War I. He saw to it that even though Germany could not have much in the way of organized military force, she would nonetheless gather the information resulting from the combat experience of the war and develop the military doctrine—to include air doctrine—that arose from that experience. Notwithstanding that the Germans had given some thought to independent air operations, their geographical position as well as their military tradition guaranteed that tactical doctrine in support of the army would get major attention. That, along with Germany's economic limitations and lag in aircraft engine high-octane fuel development, made it highly probable that she would not have a strategic bombing force competent to the task when the Battle of Britain came up in 1940.[13]

PRELIMINARIES

After the moderate attacks during July and the first two weeks of August 1940, the *Luftwaffe* then turned to massive attacks on the RAF infrastructure that was within its reach in southern England. The losses on the ground and in the air were serious for the RAF, but it was not a cakewalk for the *Luftwaffe*. Some good results were had initially against the British radar stations, but Goering called off that part of the assault prematurely. The Spitfire proved equal to the Messerschmitt single-engine fighters and superior to all the other German aircraft. The Hurricane was not up to the former but could handle the twin-engine Messerschmitts and all of the other German planes. The battle in the air was more or less equal, but serious damage was being done to the air installations on the ground—possibly more serious than the Germans realized.[14] Most of the British command and control centers were above ground, and the *Luftwaffe* did not discover that fact, nor did they appreciate the degree to which the British were controlling their fighters from the ground. That and the radar system yielded information to the RAF flyers that was only minutes old; the less competent communications and command and control system of the *Luftwaffe* left its pilots dependent upon intelligence information that was at least three hours old.

The security of the German fighter pilots was not that bad but the bomber crews operating in daylight against radar-controlled fighters were at a huge disadvantage, lightly gunned as they were. Also, their bomb loads were so small and their accuracy so shaky that the damage per loss, had they even known what it was, was not commensurate with the price they were paying.[15]

To make the German situation worse, the *Luftwaffe* was highly dependent upon aircrew reports for the information needed for battle damage assessment. Since the beginning of time, aircrews have been highly prone to exaggerate their results when reporting back to the intelligence system, but it was worse in the German case than the British.[16] As the fight was over their homeland, the British had a better check on the accuracy of their aircrew reports—they could examine wreckage and were also able to get some information from decrypting *Luftwaffe* signals. When pilots were shot down, those of the RAF were prepared to fly again; those of the *Luftwaffe* were made POWs and interrogated. Not only was a way to verify aircrew reports not available to the Germans, but perhaps there was also a greater tendency to tell the boss what he wants to hear in the authoritarian Nazi society than among the English.

DECISIONS

One of the bad decisions of the *Luftwaffe* was made in response to the laments of the bomber crews, who felt they were sitting ducks.[17] Goering decided therefore that the fighters escorting the bombers had to use close escort methods—to fly within sight of the bombers in formation at their altitude and speed. Unhappily, that gave away the strong points of fighter aircraft: they would thus inevitably start the combat from a lower altitude and airspeed than the Spitfires and Hurricanes. It was a lesson to be relearned by the Americans in the dark winter of 1943–1944.

Even more serious was the change in objectives during the first week in September. The Germans were doing more damage than they knew to the RAF infrastructure but were becoming discouraged to find fresh English fighters opposing them day after day. That, and Hitler's fury over the bombing of Berlin, made them change the target from the air infrastructure to the city of London.[18] The time for an amphibious assault, if it ever really was contemplated, was disappearing because the fall weather in the Channel would prohibit the crossing of the barges. From the 7th of September onward, the population of London was suffering, to be sure, but the pressure on the RAF ground echelons was relieved just as it was reaching crisis proportions. The air battle reached its zenith on September 15th when the RAF imposed grievous losses on the *Luftwaffe*. The Germans called off the invasion and, for the most part, went over to night bombing of the city—with the same results that the RAF Bomber Command was getting over the Continent. The losses went down, but the targets could not be found and hit.

Reasons for the Outcome of the Battle of Britain

Radar is important and cannot be discounted but it was a part of an integrated system, and the command and control, communications, observers, anti-aircraft artillery, and airplanes were all a part of that system. The British had electronic identification means in their aircraft, and better air-to-ground and air-to-air communications.[19] They generally had an advantage in rate of fire but the German fighters had an edge in weight of fire.[20] The German bombers constituted either a bait or a hostage, depending on the viewpoint. The Germans made a tactical error by going over to close escort, which diminished the fighters' initiative capability. Distance from the base was another factor, now well understood but not so at the time. Although the numbers of British single-engine fighters were smaller, because they were fighting over their own base they each had much more time over the battle space. Also, they could be recycled and back into the fight in a much shorter time than the *Luftwaffe*. In effect, the margin was not as narrow as it is often made out to be in some of the British literature.[21] The English also had good public relations reasons for making it seem narrower than it really was. Even if air superiority had been lost, the RAF had a sanctuary into which they could have withdrawn their airpower to await the invasion so they could deliver their last best shot then. But even had they been unable to do that, if the Royal Navy were faced with a do-or-die situation and was prepared to sacrifice a number of destroyers, then the survivors could have worked a mayhem on the landing barges coming across. Clearly, the morale factor—both civilian and military—was heavily on the British side, fighting for the homeland.

Bad intelligence on both sides was a factor but it was even worse for the Germans, who did not have all the wrecks to count. This must have contributed to what many have labeled a mistake: the shifting of the target to London. Hitler seems to have ordered it on emotional grounds, but Albert Kesselring made a plausible operational argument for it that resembled in some ways Carl Spaatz's desire to continue going after the oil facilities in Germany in the spring of 1944. By then, airfield attack was not as promising as it seemed, and the oil facilities were the bait to draw the German fighters up and into combat. Spaatz knew this was so because of ULTRA, through which the Germans revealed the sensitivity to oil attack. Similarly, Kesselring thought the attack of London would make the British throw their last reserves into the fight, where the *Luftwaffe* could destroy them. Sometimes you find authors who speculate that the Battle of Britain was all just another one of Hitler's bluffs.[22] Some German authors say that it ended because the *Luftwaffe* had to pull back to prepare for Barbarossa. Maybe the Battle of Britain offers a caution for modern times. We have long thought the ICBM will always get through, and only the threat of a deadly nuclear counteroffensive could protect against it. But that is similar to the bomber always getting through, and the British response proved otherwise—or similar to our stealth fighters and bombers always getting through today. Maybe there are some defensive measures out there that could be effective against conventionally armed ballistic missiles or stealth aircraft, and we should at least be alert to the possibility.

DOES THE HISTORY OF THE BATTLE OF BRITAIN OFFER INSIGHTS TO THE MODERN LEADER?

The point I have been trying to make is that if we go back into history with the research question, "How could they have been so stupid?" we are sure to find answers aplenty. But keep in mind that the decision maker was operating with far fewer "knowns" than the historian has. Thus, it is essential that the planner do planning in abstract terms that will fit a wide variety of situations, no matter how history turns out. Decision theory teaches us that rational thought must be done in probabilities; when improbable things happen, like the invasion of Russia or Inchon or Pearl Harbor, then somebody is sure to be surprised. The odds were very high that none of those things were going to happen, and when they did, the folks who had been doing the abstract planning on a probability basis were bound to look foolish when the explicit facts became known, whether probable or not. Maybe a better research question would be, "How could they have done it better, notwithstanding the unknowns with which they were faced?" We should also allow for an answer that they, like you and me, were trying to do the best they could, and could not have done much better.

By now, there are so many technical and political surprises that we are somewhat used to them; thus, we can do more to expect them. One guide is, "Don't be surprised to be surprised;" that is the way that wars usually start. It was insane for the Japanese to attack Pearl Harbor and Yamamoto knew it—that is why it was so surprising.[23] It was insane for Hitler to undertake Barbarossa—that is why it so surprised Stalin, notwithstanding our advanced warning of the attack. Equally, given the early Russian explosion of the nuclear bomb, their orbiting of *Sputnik* before we could do it, the surprising capability of the MiG-15, and later the unanticipated end of the Cold War—when no one at all was predicting it—why in the world should we be amazed at being surprised at either technical or political or strategic events, no matter how radical? Michael Howard is correct when he says that our doctrines are certain to be wrong, and our duty is to try to make them less wrong than those of our adversaries and to make our system able to adapt to the lessons of combat more rapidly than can that of the adversary.

The dawn of the twenty-first century is a time when we are particularly likely to seek "lessons" of history to help us in the formulation of theories and doctrine for the exploration of space and its use in the pursuit of national security. The fact that movement in space, like aviation, is in the third dimension and that there is precious little history from which to draw generalizations make many people prone to drawing an analogy with the first years of aviation. Because the experts in airpower were a long way from having it right, as were the atomic scientists, I would be reluctant to say that the airpower experience has any firm "lessons" at all for space.[24] Even if you assume that strategic bombing doctrine and a separate air force and a Department of Defense were indeed logical and profitable, that is not an indication that a separate space force, the weaponization of space, and a space-Billy Mitchell will happen in the future. Only nonhistorians think that history repeats itself. National politics affected the development of airpower everywhere; it will and should control the way that space develops as well. The bureaucrats know that to increase their turf, they really must have an independent and growing mission. But what is good for the bureaucrat is not necessarily good for the United States. I would surely listen to the arguments of the people who are not experts on space, for some of their arguments may indeed be valid.[25]

As for technical development in space, I would not yet be wringing my hands. We have not done so badly, and we outclass the rest of the world. The Europeans are more worried that there never will be anyone able to catch up with the United States than that a peer competitor will appear. If we insist on becoming ever more threatening, we may be pursuing a self-fulfilling prophecy. Perfect security for us is zero security for France and everybody else. We may stimulate the formulation of the very coalitions and technological programs about which we are worried. Napoleon did a great deal to stimulate the formulation of cohesive coalitions; Hitler provided the motivation for the rapid development of the world's first IADS. Certainly, we should amply fund the basic science for space, but then in large part keep it on the shelf against the day we might need it. Some experts argue that just as the building of the *Luftwaffe* as an offensive instrument stimulated Great Britain into developing an elaborate air defense system, so too the American fielding of an offensive capability in space is likely to cause others to attempt to find ways to counter it.[26]

Generally, you cannot demand scientific ideas no matter how much money you are willing to spend; however, once the basic science is known it tends to become an engineering problem, and engineering does respond to money. You can certainly speed up the engineering and production programs with money much more easily than scientific discovery.[27] We outclass the world in airpower and seapower. Why should we hasten the end of that situation by stimulating the movement of international conflict to space? Could that be snatching poverty from the jaws of prosperity?[28] When Hitler invaded the rump of Czechoslovakia, the charade of merely gathering Germans into the Fatherland was exposed, and England gave a guarantee to Poland. She was unable to prevent the conquest of Poland but she did declare war, and the subsequent Battle of Britain was the first great check that the *Luftwaffe* and Hitler suffered. In the next chapter, we will explore the downfall of Hitler and his Axis allies and the United States' participation in that triumph.

5

American Airpower in World War II: Genesis of Precision-guided Weapons

The United States had observers watching the Battle of Britain and in the year that followed, and in effect she participated in the naval war against Germany. In this chapter, we shall briefly consider the American air experience in World War II in the Atlantic, North Africa, Europe, and in the Pacific and conclude with a brief treatment of the attempts to develop precision weapons during that conflict.

NAVAL AVIATION AS THE MAIN STRIKING FORCE

As we have seen previously, there was not general agreement that the main striking forces of navies were their carrier organizations, but Japan's Admiral Isoroku Yamamoto thought they might be. One of War Plan Orange's assumptions that went wrong at the last minute was that the Japanese Navy would wait on the far side of the Pacific for the US Navy to come to it for the climactic battle. It had been a sound assumption for a long time, but Admiral Yamamoto was reluctant to tackle America for good and sound reasons. He thought that if Japan were to have any chance at all in a war that his countrymen were insisting upon, it would have to open with a massive attack on the main strength of the U.S. Fleet. That would be intended to yield the time for the Japanese to consolidate their initial gains. It was a dim hope in Yamamoto's mind but it was the only way he could see that might yield enough time for war weariness to set in the United States to the point where she might accept a compromise peace.[1] He was wrong.

The Pacific War

Prewar

America generally favored the Japanese in their war against the Russians in 1904–1905, but the deterioration in relations started soon thereafter and grew much worse after the onset of the Great Depression and the resumption of Japanese imperialism. It is a perversion to make the United States the aggressor in this, and she did not react to the point of risking combat until the Japanese began to threaten her European allies.

Pearl Harbor

Many in the Japanese navy, including Yamamoto himself, did not favor war with the United States, but he persuaded the rest that if they were to have any chance at all they had to reject their traditional defensive strategy of waiting for the American navy in the western Pacific in favor of a preemptive strike on the fleet at its lair in Hawaii. In a narrow sense it succeeded, but they lost more than they gained.

Midway

Ever since June 1942, the battle has been considered the great turning point of the war against Japan, and certainly its carrier fleet was badly bent with the loss of the four of them exchanged for the *Yorktown*. But fewer Japanese carrier pilots than were then supposed went down with their ships.

Solomons

Beginning with Guadalcanal in the summer of 1942 and extending well into 1943, this campaign completed the work started at Midway by killing many of the remaining naval pilots and yielding a general air superiority for the rest of the struggle.

New Guinea to Philippines

From the dark hours of the spring of 1942, MacArthur's campaign complemented that of the Solomons into 1943, and then via a series of northwestward leaps up the coast and through the southern islands reached the Philippines in October 1944. Largely conducted with Kenney's land-based airpower, this story is particularly important to the modern airpower thinker.

Central Pacific

Admiral Nimitz did not get started on the Navy's traditional War Plan Orange until late because he had only avoided the loss of the command of the sea at Midway—too few flattops for any more. Near the end of 1943, he began to get the new *Essex*-class carriers and launched his thrust across the central Pacific, culminating in the great battles of the Philippine Sea and Leyte Gulf.

That yielded command of the sea for the American side and merged his thrust with MacArthur's in the Philippines.

Okinawa

Fulfilling Mahan's dream did not produce an easy road ahead because of the coming of the *kamikaze* threat, which in the spring of 1945 turned what was supposed to be the penultimate battle on and off Okinawa into the bloodiest of the war—and helped put the American leaders in a frame of mind to make the choice of dropping the atomic bomb into a non-decision.

Nuclear Weapons

It so happened that although some Army Air Force and Navy officers were thinking that Japan might be brought down without another bloody invasion of the home islands, in August 1945 the President nonetheless decided to use the nuclear weapons, precipitating the surrender that Churchill called the "Miracle of Deliverance."

There probably was more thought on the development of the aircraft carrier as the main striking force of the American Navy than was apparent to the outside observer; the absence of the carriers while the battleships were being sunk at Pearl Harbor made that development all the more probable. The offensive part of the deck loads was built up during the late 1930s in both quality and numbers, and dive bombing tactics were improved substantially.[2] A similar process was going on in the Japanese Navy, where level bombing was tried—with disappointing results—and that also led to developing dive bombing.[3] By 1941, the US Navy had a good dive bomber in the Dauntless but the torpedo plane, the Devastator, was lumbering and a relatively easy target. That fault was compounded by the facts that the U.S. torpedoes had much more stringent launching parameters than those of Japan, and they had important technical defects that worsened the problem. The fighters were Grumman Wildcats that were soon proved inferior to the Japanese fighters, especially in maneuverability and speed. The Japanese aircrews that fought at Pearl Harbor and Midway were beneficiaries of superior peacetime training, and many were seasoned in combat in China. Fortunately, the three American carriers then in the Pacific were not in port on December 7, 1941, having been sent on an aircraft delivery mission that kept them out of harm's way.[4]

As disastrous as was the attack on Pearl Harbor, there was a modicum of American luck involved. As noted, all the battleships that went down were the old ones, and the U.S. carriers were not there and survived for the crucial battles yet to come. Further, the Japanese opted against a re-attack that might have taken out the oil storage facilities in Hawaii, and that loss would have taken a good deal of time to repair. Finally, such isolationism as still existed in the United States was snuffed out in a trice.

Several hours after the attack on Pearl Harbor, and about four hours after Douglas MacArthur knew of it, the Japanese air assault on the Philippines severely dented airpower there. However, fortune was smiling on the other side. An early, small Japanese attack on Luzon flushed new American B-17 forces for their own protection, but fog on Formosa delayed the launching of the main Japanese air attack. When it did come, the Flying Fortresses were back on the ground in a most vulnerable condition. Many of them were destroyed, as were a large number of the new P-40 fighters. This was deemed a disaster at the time, for the leadership in Washington had an inflated idea of what a small force like that could have achieved. Its commander, Lewis Brereton, decided to use it against naval forces instead of airfields in any case, and America was yet to learn that high-flying bombers could seldom hit a moving naval target.[5]

The turning point in the naval war came much earlier than the United States had any right to expect, given the established "Germany First" strategy. The first great carrier episode came at the Battle of the Coral Sea in May, 1942, where the mighty *Lexington* went to the bottom and the *Yorktown* was severely damaged. The *Enterprise* and the *Hornet* were not in that fight because they had been sent on the Doolittle Raid against Tokyo. and that prevented them from arriving in time to turn the odds heavily in the favor of the USN.[6] Two of the Japanese fleet carriers were so badly damaged that neither was able to take part in the Battle of Midway the next month. For America, the consolation for the loss of the "*Lex*" was that the Japanese invasion of Port Moresby was called off. permitting us to advertise it as a strategic victory—the first time in the Pacific War that a Japanese mission was turned back short of its goal. It had been the first great naval battle in history wherein the ships had not come within eyesight of each other.[7]

The Japanese thought that the *Yorktown* had followed the *Lexington* to the bottom of the sea. That was among the factors that encouraged them to go through with the attack on Midway. However, Admiral Nimitz, now the commander at Pearl Harbor, had the benefit of superior intelligence arising in large part from decryption activity and he had the *Yorktown*, which he had ordered back to Hawaii at best speed. He had important insight to the Japanese plans and was ready to meet them after a remarkable repair effort on the carrier thought to have gone down at Coral Sea.[8]

On his return from the Doolittle Raid, Admiral William Halsey, who had been the task force commander, was hospitalized. On his recommendation, Nimitz chose Raymond Spruance (a non-aviator) to take over for the imminent battle. Internal Navy bureaucratic politics seemed to have fogged the issues associated with this battle and the subsequent ones at the Philippine Sea and Leyte Gulf.[9] The Navy fliers were discontent because although the battleships were nowhere in sight, the battleship sailors were still in charge. Much ink has been spilled over these things, but there is no denying that Midway was a great victory for the Americans, for the Japanese lost four of their best carriers, some of their superior peacetime-trained pilots, and the invasion had been turned back. Without taking anything away from the leadership of Nimitz and Spruance and the ingenuity and courage of the naval aviators and seamen, it is also true that the decryption yielded a very decisive advantage to the Americans—and just plain luck was also significant.[10] Also, the United States lost the *Yorktown* as the battle was winding down. One outcome was that there was not to be another great sea battle until two more years had passed, and by then the heart had been torn out of the Japanese flying forces.

But the U.S. victories at the Coral Sea and Midway did not halt the Japanese offensive in its tracks. During the subsequent months, they attempted to continue the southward thrust by land over the Kokoda Trail to take Port Moresby on the south coast of New Guinea. It was a brutal struggle, fought mainly by Australian troops assisted by airpower, and after the Japanese were turned back toward the north coast, an equally bloody campaign drove them out of Buna. Such air units as the Japanese were able to deploy to New Guinea were badly hurt in the process. Meanwhile, Allied intelligence was getting better and discovered a Japanese plan to launch a major convoy bringing troops from Rabaul, New Britain, to New Guinea to try again. By the winter of 1942–1943, the Fifth Air Force was well aware that high-altitude bombing could not work against moving naval targets and had been training for new, masthead-altitude attack techniques for some months. Some of its B-25s had been converted into forward-firing gunships, and their many guns could keep heads down on Japanese decks long enough to skip bombs into the vessels and then make their escapes. The Japanese convoy was composed of eight transport ships escorted by eight destroyers. All of the transports were sent to the bottom, as were half of the destroyers. The other half could manage to save only half of the troops embarked, and the Japanese never again tried a large deployment by transports in that region. That opened the way for MacArthur's farther advance northwestward along the New Guinea coast and later onward north to the Philippines, but only after more hard fighting.[11]

Another place where the Japanese air forces were bled mightily was in the Solomons. Soon after Midway, Admiral King was able to scrape up enough forces to send some to Guadalcanal to start an offensive on a small scale. That battle lasted for six months or so, resulting in some humiliating surface battles for our Navy, but in the end wore down the Japanese naval aviators to the point where they never recovered. Their precious naval air units were sent to Rabaul and points south to contest the American offensive, and once they were gone there would be no replacing them, while the U.S. training programs were grinding out good pilots by the tens of thousands. But War Plan Orange was in danger of becoming an historical artifact no more. There were two major offensives developing at the southern extremity of the Pacific Ocean, one by the Navy up the Solomons chain and one by the Army under MacArthur in the southwest Pacific, principally in New Guinea, for late 1942 and 1943. To some extent, both were pragmatic responses to the fortuitous events of a world war, and competed not only with War Plan Orange but also with the "Germany First" strategy.[12] Fortunately for the campaigns of MacArthur and Nimitz, the postponement of the Allied landings in France worked to release sea and air forces for use elsewhere. Some of these went to the North African campaign to help keep the USSR in the war. Others were sent inconspicuously to the Pacific to help with the assaults in the Solomons and up the coast of New Guinea.[13] Once the two thrusts cooperated to isolate Rabaul, Halsey's was terminated and it was possible to contemplate the use of his forces for the resurrection of War Plan Orange.

In the following months, two Pacific strategies competed. As noted, one championed by Douglas MacArthur called for a methodical offensive up the north coast of New Guinea, each hop being within the combat radius of land-based fighters, and thence through the islands back to Luzon. It would be an Army war with Navy support. That did not sit very well with Admiral Ernest King in Washington, and through his persistence the Orange scheme was pressed. Neither the Joint Chiefs of Staff nor the political leadership could or would impose a choice, and the outcome was that both strategies were implemented.

The Navy part of the war was resumed with the invasion of Tarawa during late 1943, and thence through the Marshalls and the Marianas through mid-1944. All those islands were small, and the bloody battles were blessedly short, at least until they got to the Marianas. It was during the latter invasion that the Japanese fleet, which had been hiding in the East Indies since Midway, finally decided to come out and fight.

The United States had advance information on the Japanese movement, this time in part from submarine reconnaissance. It posed a dilemma for Admiral Spruance, again in command of the Fifth Fleet after a stint ashore in Nimitz' headquarters. His mission was to protect the landing forces but the approach of the Japanese Fleet promised the great sea battle that would result in the command of the sea all navymen had dreamed of since Mahan. He chose to stick with his mission in spite of the urgings of his aviators to move to the west to enable our carrier forces to reach the core of the Japanese carrier fleet. Spruance refused to do so, and has been criticized for this conservative decision ever since.[14] Yet Admiral Frank Fletcher was harshly criticized then (and since) for taking his carriers out of harm's way in August 1942, and leaving the Marine landing force only half ashore at Guadalcanal without air cover. However, this time it resulted in the Marianas Turkey Shoot, which confirmed the inadequacy of the Japanese pilot training program. Although some of the enemy carriers did get away (three were sunk by American submarines) and although some American pilots were lost because of fuel starvation and darkness, so many Japanese pilots died that their navy never recovered. By then, the F6F Hellcat and the F4U Corsair were on the line in numbers, and the Zero no longer had the technical advantages it once enjoyed.

After the Marianas were taken in mid-1944, strategic choice was becoming an imperative. MacArthur was persisting in his preferences for Luzon, but there was feeling in the Navy that their central Pacific thrust might be better aimed at someplace further north, at perhaps Formosa (Taiwan) or the China Coast itself. In the end, the choice was made to merge the two thrusts in the attack on the Philippines, and then proceed on to Okinawa as the last stage before the assault on the Japanese home islands.

Associated with the landing in the Philippines was what has been called the greatest naval battle in history—greatest in size, perhaps, but the sides by then were not equal. Admiral William Halsey was in charge of the Third Fleet, assigned to protect the invasion force from enemy interference, just as the same ships as the Fifth Fleet under Spruance were assigned to protect the invaders of the Marianas. The Japanese Navy decided to give it one last shot, notwithstanding that it was practically devoid of airpower by then. In the subsequent Battle of Leyte Gulf (October 1944), they at least had the support of some surviving land-based airpower but it was far from adequate.

The Japanese plan called for a complex set of thrusts. There would be a decoy force of aircraft carriers in the north (without significant air groups), attempting to draw off Halsey's Third Fleet. Another force would come through the Surigao Straits south of the invasion area to join yet a third coming through the San Bernardino Straits north of it. They would form a pincer that would fall upon the amphibious forces and Admiral Thomas Kinkaid's supporting force of old battleships and escort carriers. Neither pincer had any carriers but the northern one included one of the two greatest battleships ever built, the *Musashi*, of 80,000 tons with 18-inch guns.[15]

Admiral Halsey's orders included an ambiguous provision that could be interpreted as direction to leave the protection mission behind if an opportunity came up for a great sea battle to destroy what remained of the Japanese navy. He received intelligence on the Japanese decoy force and went charging after it, leaving the San Bernardino Straits unguarded—after that pincer had been attacked, and (it was thought) it had turned around to a westerly course. This started a debate that continues in naval publications to this date.[16]

As it turned out, when it was found that the Japanese were indeed persisting in coming through the northern strait, the whole invasion force was at serious risk of decimation. The southern thrust was bashed by Admiral Kinkaid's Seventh Fleet, but the one on the north was opposed only by a few destroyers and some escort carriers. Halsey had turned around and was now steaming south at flank speed, but he was too far away. In one of the most stirring actions in American naval history, the destroyers and escort carriers reacted to the threat so aggressively that they might have built the perception in the Japanese admiral's mind that he was faced with a much more formidable force than was the case. In any event, he snatched defeat from the jaws of victory when he turned around and beat a retreat through the passage from which he had emerged.[17]

In the process, the *Musashi* was caught by American naval airpower completely devoid of her own air cover. This part of the action provided a footnote to both the Mitchell story and Pearl Harbor. Operating with complete impunity, it took the naval aviators 19 hits with torpedoes and 17 hits with bombs to put her to the bottom, showing that getting a battleship underway was not a simple task even at that late date (it was also caught in the straits without normal maneuvering room).[18]

That fall was a tough one. It was hard for the warfighters of the Arnhem offensive, the Battle of the Bulge, and the strategic bombers—then at the height of their rampage over Germany—to understand how the enemy could hang on, that victory had to be just around the corner. In the Pacific, it was the same. After the long agony in the Solomons and New Guinea, after the Turkey Shoot, after the debacle in the Philippines, after all that, how could the enemy possibly hope to last another winter? But just as the Battle of the Bulge blasted hopes of an early return home, a new scourge appeared on the Navy horizon in the Pacific—the *kamikazes*, unanticipated and hardly believable, starting in the Philippines and reaching their fury in the next phase, the invasion of Okinawa. The bomber offensive was building to its own fury out of the Marianas that winter, and there the P-51 was found to be an inadequate solution to the escort problem. Consequently, 6,000 Marines died to take a base for them halfway to the target on Iwo Jima. Then it was on to Okinawa, and the very ferocity of that campaign was on the minds of the decision makers just as they were making choices on the employment of nuclear weapons now on the horizon. Germany fell just then, and the revelations of the horrors of her concentration camps and gas chambers were also at the forefront. For one of the rare times in the Pacific War, just about as many sailors died in the Okinawa campaign as did soldiers and Marines ashore.[19]

About this time, there was increasing feeling among the admirals that War Plan Orange may work after all, that once the great sea battles were done and America commanded the sea, Japan would soon fall to the combined effects of blockade and bombing. In the decision to take the Marianas, General Arnold sided with Admiral King against General MacArthur in a rare sample of the AAF and Navy being in agreement on a strategic choice. Now sailors and airmen were voicing the opinion that the bloody invasion of the Japanese home islands might not be necessary after all.[20] A corollary among many of them was that perhaps the atom bomb need not be used because the collapse of Japan in the face of conventional incendiary raids and a crushing blockade was imminent. So declared the Army Air Forces' Curtis LeMay, for one.[21]

The choice to use the nuclear weapons was probably not a choice; in the total war context, one used whatever one had without much question if it might be expected to save even a few American lives. They were so used and precipitated the Japanese surrender and, after a while, a debate that goes on still.[22] The U.S. Strategic Bombing Survey (USSBS) concluded that the combination of the submarine blockade and bombing were decisive. It asserts that in all probability, they would have caused the collapse before the scheduled invasion of Kyushu on November 15, 1945.[23] Notwithstanding, the feeling was pretty strong in the Navy that the aircraft carriers with their airpower had been the decisive factor, and that part of the Navy would dominate the post-war world in spite of the coming of nuclear weapons. But whatever their feeling, their worldview was about to come unglued.

STANDOFF AND PRECISION IN THE BATTLE OF THE ATLANTIC

Returning now to the war on the other side of the world, even before Pearl Harbor and the great naval battles in the Pacific, the United States was gradually becoming involved in the naval war in the Atlantic. For all the talk about innovation in carrier aviation, the Battle of Britain, and the preparation of an amphibious capability, there had been mighty little in the area of anti-submarine warfare.[24]

The submarine struggle in the Second World War is a concern of modern air and space leaders for several reasons. One was that the application of airpower was one of the factors that first made the German underwater effort formidable, and then finally led to its defeat. Second, it provides an important precedent for the development of what we now call "information warfare." Third, to a large degree the submarine campaign was an effort on the part of the Germans to use stealth, standoff, and precision weapons to get around Allied naval superiority on the surface. Fourth, the story demonstrates the persistence of conventional theory in the face of contradictory evidence. Finally, like air and space, submarines operate in three dimensions and that experience might offer some useful analogs.

Alfred Thayer Mahan, the great American naval theorist, died in 1914. In the first decade and a half of the century, he was at the height of his influence. One of his great ideas was that if a state controls the sea through victory in a great sea battle between the heavy battleships of the opponents, then all else will follow.[25] We have seen previously how that theory influenced the initial development of naval aviation. We have also seen that in World War I, there was only one great battle like that: Jutland. Its results were indecisive, yet the Germans anchored their battleships and instead undertook a major campaign against British commerce through the use of submarines.

That would have been anathema to Mahan had he lived a little longer.[26] Those submarines came close to starving Great Britain then but were overcome through a combination of factors, including going over to an Allied convoy system. Another influence, even at that early stage, was the role of aviation that did not destroy the submarines but did force them to remain underwater for long periods. The U-boats also were a major cause of the United States' entry into the war on the Allied side. After the Armistice, the whole experience did not seem to have much influence on either the German or the Allied naval leaders. Admiral Eric Raeder at the head of the German navy persuaded Hitler that Mahan was still valid, and that Germany had to build a great surface fleet—inevitably at the expense of submarine warfare. A major element in both the British and American navies also still believed in Mahan, and was determined to sustain a great battle line and use aviation as an auxiliary to that—inevitably at the expense of an anti-submarine warfare capability.[27] Also, in spite of all Billy Mitchell's rhetoric about coastal defense, the men of the Air Corps did little or nothing to prepare for a role in any campaign against submarines.[28]

One of the reasons for the unpreparedness was the naval arms limitation movement. The Washington Conference of 1921–1922 outlawed submarine warfare against commerce, albeit Germany was not one of the signatories of the treaty. The Versailles Treaty, to which she had been a signatory, prohibited her possession of any submarines. Another factor in America was that submarine technology was not a major priority and was unreliable and downright dangerous.[29] There were several lost submarines during the interwar period, including the *Squalus* in 1939.[30] Also, the naval cultures in Germany, Great Britain and the United States all did not see either submarine or anti-submarine work as the road to success. Thus, the elite and the money tended to flow to the battleship force, or in the case of Japan and the United States, to the carriers to some extent. It so happened that when Germany went to war she had but 59 submarines, and the surviving anti-submarine ships in the United States were rusting in storage anchorages. The German submarines were really not much improved over the U-boats of the First World War. However, they were equipped with a superior torpedo that was propelled by an electric motor. The huge advantage is that the weapon did not leave a wake and could not be spotted early by defenders to either take evasive or offensive action.[31]

The submarine war got off to a slow start. It is true that there were grievous losses to British merchant shipping in the first couple of years, but not serious enough to threaten defeat. The German surface raiders did have some effect upon British commerce at first, but were finally swept from the seas. The Nazi surface combatants yielded some wonderful newspaper copy as with the scuttling of the *Graf Spee* off Latin America and the sinking of the *Bismarck* in May 1941. Hitler was shortly disenchanted with Raeder's vision of things, and thus swung to the theories of Admiral Karl Doenitz, a submariner veteran from World War I. As was the case with the Battle of Britain, the gradual mounting of the submarine offensive permitted the Allies the necessary time to develop technical, tactical, and organizational remedies. Also, by 1942 the experience level of the anti-submarine crews was increasing to acceptable levels.

The airmen in both the RAF and the USAAF were convinced that their attacks on the vital centers in metropolitan Germany would be decisive. They were most reluctant to release any of their four-engine bombers to any campaigns elsewhere—not to the Pacific, not to North Africa, and not to the middle of the Atlantic. There was a black hole in the middle of the North Atlantic that could not be reached by two-engine airplanes from Newfoundland, Iceland, or Great Britain; that became the hunting ground for the U-boats. Yet the four-engine airplanes did not start to roll out of British factories until 1942, and any serious reinforcements to the anti-submarine war would have to come from USAAF resources—principally from the Liberators because their range was longer than that of the Flying Fortress.[32] Also, the Battle of the Atlantic was competing with the Pacific theaters where the distances were so great that the preference was for Liberators.[33]

One of the things that was containing the losses on the sea line of communications was an information warfare advantage for the British. First, there was the ability to spot surfaced submarines with radar even in the dark. Unhappily, the Germans quickly developed a radar detector that gave them a chance to dive before the aircraft got within radar range. (The radar energy coming to the submarine only had to make a one-way trip, but that coming back to the receiver in the aircraft had to make a round-trip. That yielded only a very short time but it was enough in many cases.) Additionally, the British further developed a technology from World War I that helped locate the enemy submarines: radio direction finders. Admiral Doenitz had to live with this because his insistence on centralized control necessitated the transmission of information both ways by means of high-frequency radio, which could be intercepted by anybody.[34] Even when that information was in code, it still provided a bearing on the transmitting antenna, enabling triangulation of the submarine's position. Further, even in the absence of a usable bearing the mere analysis of the volume and addresses of the radio traffic gave hints as to the intentions of the German commanders. Atop that, in the early years of the war the British were successful in breaking the code produced by the German Enigma machine, with important assistance from the Polish. The Germans were also successful in breaking the British code but again and again, they refused to believe that their enemy had been competent enough to break theirs, even in the face of substantial circumstantial evidence to the contrary. To the latter part of 1941, on the whole the information advantage was on the side of the British.[35]

By the onset of 1942, the German shipyards were getting up to speed. They provided Doenitz with a formidable number of U-boats, and at times he was able to keep up to 100 of them at sea.[36] That winter, the Germans also changed their submarine code, and thus an important source of information for the Allies dried up for almost a year before the code was again broken. The competing demands of the Pacific War and the losses along the sea route to the USSR made the situation all the worse. The latter was particularly tough because of the long periods of daylight in the north and the ready availability of secure ports and bases for surviving German surface ships, submarines, and aircraft.[37] The preparations for the TORCH landings in North Africa required additional shipping just then, and the Russians were in desperate straits at the time. Here again, the last couple of years before Pearl Harbor were a godsend for America. Witnessing and then participating in an undeclared war in the North Atlantic got American attention. One of the reactions was to undertake a truly massive shipbuilding program that was ultimately able to replace the merchant ships sunk with new vessels faster than the losses were accumulating.[38]

That was also the winter of Pearl Harbor. Until that time, remembering the Kaiser's experience in World War I, Hitler had strictly forbidden his submariners from returning fire to American ships. Doenitz, who had been chafing at the bit in his eagerness to shoot back at American anti-submarine activities during the undeclared war, quickly grasped the opportunity. He redeployed what submarines he had available to the American Atlantic coast and thence to the Gulf of Mexico and the Caribbean. Though the United States had a merchant ship building program rolling, not much else had been done to prepare for fighting submarines off her shore. It was a navy responsibility and responding to the request for air assistance, the USAAF did send some bombers for coastal patrols. They were not the best planes available, and their crews had not been trained at all for anti-submarine operations, and they sank little or nothing.[39] All that contributed to making the first half of 1942 the worst period of the entire anti-submarine war.

The crisis came in the first three months of 1943. The British had long before captured a submarine, and the Germans did not know it. The captors kept it afloat long enough to remove the Enigma machine, the code books, and a large number of messages that had been sent to and fro.[40] That was a continuing asset. Happily, the British presently managed to again break the German submarine code. The anti-submarine forces were getting some four-engine aircraft that helped close the black hole in the center of the North Atlantic. The surface crews were being trained up to speed, and additional ships were coming on the line. The command and control system was improving. The Allied airplanes were being equipped with a new higher-frequency radar set that could not be detected by the German submarines.[41] It was a tough fight for the U-boat crews, and many of the best ones were killed. Before the year was over, the Mediterranean sea route was cleared, and that had the effect of increasing the shipping available by eliminating the long trip around the southern tip of Africa. March 1943 was a terrible month for the Allies but the days were getting longer, and by summer the U-boat losses were mounting to the point where Doenitz had to pull in his horns and deploy the survivors to less dangerous waters.[42] But they were hazardous everywhere, and although the Allied losses never stopped before the end of the war, the balance shifted in a major way. As with the jets in the *Luftwaffe*, the Germans too late came on with some technological improvements including snorkel (allowing the use of the diesel engines underwater) and the new higher-speed "Walter" boats.[43] But it was late in the day; now the shipping would be available for the support of both the bomber offensive and for the landing in France.

As with most great campaigns, the outcome was determined by multiple causes. Simple numbers made a difference: The American shipyards were booming. New radar helped. ULTRA intelligence was a major factor. The absorption of German airpower on the Russian front and in the Mediterranean was a factor; the FW-200 aircraft ceased cooperating with the U-boats in 1943. The growth in Allied experience and the attrition among the experienced submarine crews were factors. The bombing of the submarine pens and shipyards did not make much difference until after the crisis was past. Even in periods when the German codes could not be read, aerial reconnaissance and high-frequency direction finding helped fill the gap. The escort carriers came along late in the war to help fill the black hole in the center of the Atlantic. They also allowed a return to the offensive at the center of hunter-killer groups (one of which under Admiral Dan Gallery, USN, managed to capture and tow back to port a German submarine).[44] Torpedoes were developed that would home in on the sounds of submarine propellers, albeit they were not a major factor in the outcome. The focus on the destruction of submarine supply ships in 1943 met with great success and helped shorten the U-boat time on station. Perhaps most of all, Hitler's assumption that it would be a short war was wrong, and the German nation was simply worn down.[45]

It is not too much of a stretch to say that information warfare really began long before the twenty-first century, and the Battle of the Atlantic was only one of the later precedents. Also, the experience shows that there is more than one way to achieve standoff. Distance is fine; stealth below the waves is another. One of the reasons that airpower had an important effect was that it was less vulnerable to submarines than were merchant ships and escorts; its standoff came from altitude above the surface as well as the ability to speed away from surface fire. Precision fire was also a concern in the Battle of the Atlantic, as elsewhere. In a way, the submarines were able to hide in the limitless spaces of the ocean both below and on the surface. Achieving precision with gunfire and depth charges was a continuing problem, especially given the limitations of the sonar sensors that lost the returns as they passed over the U-boats. Forward-firing Hedgehog charges helped some and, as noted, toward the end of the war torpedoes were brought in that could home in on the sound of the submarine's propeller. The experience also helps explain why doctrine usually lags technology and tactics. The ideas of Mahan persisted in many minds surprisingly long. One of his notions was that a war on commerce was not decisive; only the destruction of the enemy main battle fleet and the achievement of command of the seas would enable it. But the wars on commerce against England in both the world wars were close-run things notwithstanding the Allied command of the seas, at least command of the surface of them. And in the Pacific, as we have noted, the submarine campaign combined with the bombing of the Japanese homeland was deemed decisive by the USSBS. Yet one of the finest naval scholars in America, Thomas Buell, brought up at Annapolis in the Mahanian tradition, written as late as 1989, that the Battle of the Atlantic proved Mahan right.[46] The command of the air and the command of the "cyberspace"[47] seemed to be at least as important as the command of the sea. Perhaps the idea that seapower theory and airpower theory can exist is a shaky proposition. Maybe only a theory of war can exist, and the command of any of the elements—even space—will be decisive in different ways at different times according to the extant situation.

THE AFRICAN AND MEDITERRANEAN CAMPAIGNS

As noted previously, the United States had the blessing of a couple of years to prepare for war. Hitler marched in September 1939, and Pearl Harbor did not come for more than two years. The initial efforts of the British Bomber Command were disastrous, and forced the RAF to go over to night bombing against area instead of precision targets.[48]

Thus it happened that the British were disposed to persuade the Americans to abandon their daylight precision bombing theory in favor of night operations. The first bomber units of the Eighth Air Force arrived in England in the summer of 1942 and did not get around to serious bombing of Germany proper until the summer of 1943. The numbers were much slower in coming than planned because of the competing demands for long-range aircraft everywhere. Thus, although the bomber forces were being badly bloodied by a radar-assisted air defense, the prayer was that when they were built up to sufficient numbers for large formations they would indeed be able to defend themselves. It came to a head at the Casablanca Conference in January 1943, but after arguing Churchill out of his opposition, the American airmen stuck with their favored approach.[49] As the pain was mounting, chin turrets were added and battleplanes completely laden with guns were tried. But the losses became simply too great by the Second Schweinfurt Raid of October 1943, and General Ira Eaker, then the commander of the Eighth Air Force, had to pull in his horns.[50] He and Secretary of War for Air Robert Lovett agreed months before that the development of long-range escort would be essential. Lovett went back to the United States in June 1943 to start a crash program for drop tanks[51] and to push the P-51 program along.[52]

Meanwhile, tactical airpower ideas that resided among the interwar air leaders were put to the test in the North African campaign (and in the Fifth Air Force campaign in New Guinea in 1942–1943). That caused a good deal of grief with the ground commanders in Africa. However, in the aftermath the Army Chief of Staff was prevailed upon to put his signature to Field Manual 100-20 in July 1943, notwithstanding that it was not coordinated through the Army Ground Forces. It became famous as the airmen's declaration of independence even though it really was not that. It did state principles for tactical air theory that are still present in USAF tactical air doctrine. First, air and ground are co-equal. Airpower must be controlled in a centralized way by an airman at the theater level. He should be co-located with the ground commander. In the usual conditions, the mission priorities would be air superiority, interdiction, close air support, reconnaissance, and tactical airlift. In a ground emergency, close air support could take the top priority.[53] Those elements of air doctrine have remained rather stable in USAF doctrine ever since. However, they were not accepted by the ground generals of the US Army at the outset of TORCH.

The Allied landings, called TORCH, occurred at three places in early November 1942. Two sites were inside the Mediterranean and one was on the Atlantic shore close to Casablanca. The march to the east was rapid, and although there were fiascoes aplenty, the French colonialists did not put up much of a fight and the Allies came close to cutting off Irwin Rommel's Axis ground forces by capturing Tunis early. However, the untrained US Army received a severe check at Kasserine Pass, and there was much recrimination about that. The air support of the ground troops was shaky, and there was much finger-pointing between the American soldiers and airmen. The airmen blamed the faulty application of air doctrine, but the logistic support was truly inadequate, as were the forward airfields, the air defense facilities, and the bad weather. Many of the air units sent to North Africa were taken from the body of the Eighth Air Force in England—units that were trained for strategic bombing and air defense, not support of ground troops.[54] As experience was gained in the school of hard knocks, these things were straightened out. The weather dried up, the British Eighth Army approached from the east, and the Axis forces were driven into an enclave around Tunis and Bizerte. Meanwhile, Allied airpower, with a big assist from ULTRA decryption, conducted one of its more successful interdiction campaigns against Rommel's sea line of communications across the central Mediterranean. By late spring, the African fight was over and although Rommel escaped, many of his *Afrika Korps* troops and Italian Allies did not.[55]

At the time, and frequently since then, historians have claimed that the hayseed Americans turned up in Africa with lots of airplanes and flyers but not much sophistication in doctrinal matters. Having recent experience with Rommel, the RAF (it is alleged) taught the neophytes what tactical war is all about. That had an element of truth insofar as the American wartime temporary help was concerned, and also insofar as the ground generals of the US Army were involved. As the writings of the 1920s of Mitchell and others, the teachings in the Attack course at ACTS, and the application of the same principles by Kenney in the southwest Pacific in 1942–1943 show, the Air Corps heavyweights already had the main ideas firmly in mind. The British may have had a role in developing these notions among the American airmen but, if so, it came from the association in World War I, not North Africa. Both George Kenney and Carl Spaatz were deeply involved in France then, and certainly picked up some of the ideas in that war. What seems to have happened in North Africa is that the American airmen were unable to persuade their own ground generals of the validity of their set of ideas. They were happy to have RAF Air Marshal Arthur Coningham and Field Marshal Bernard Montgomery persuade the American infantry leaders of the necessity of centralized control, air superiority, and the rest—coming as the British did on the prestige of their victory at El Alemein.[56]

Just as the strategic campaign against Germany was beginning to gather steam, the political leadership decided that there had to be a 1942 campaign in North Africa. The Russians were under attack in a bad way by the Germans, and the President and British Prime Minister decided that the ground forces had to engage the Germans soon, if for no other reason than to offer encouragement to the Russians. Albeit the deployment to Africa retarded the buildup of the strategic bombing forces and allowed the Germans some respite to prepare their air defense systems, it did afford important seasoning for American forces. There is no way of really knowing whether there was any chance of the Russians making a separate peace with Hitler.[57] But the African campaign did draw considerable German air forces from the Russian front at a critical time—Stalingrad was under siege during TORCH. Also, at the same time the anti-submarine campaign in the Atlantic was in crisis. By the time of the Sicily invasion the problem was coming under control, and long-range aircraft had a role in solving it. That diversion also helped.

The story was similar in Sicily and Italy, where new invasions were mounted in 1943. The Axis forces managed to save major units from Sicily and fought a terrific defensive battle in Italy (with inadequate air cover) under Field Marshal Albert Kesselring. In the end, it failed and the Allies entered Rome at the time of OVERLORD, which was also the time of the invasion of the Marianas. As we have seen, another benefit of the success of the Mediterranean campaigns was that it opened the shipping route through Suez, saving so much time for goods going to and coming from the Middle East and the Indian Ocean that it was a major benefit for the anti-submarine effort. Finally, toward the end of 1943 the USAAF was able to open new bases in Italy for the Fifteenth Air Force bombers to pose a new threat from another direction in the strategic bombing campaign against Hitler.

THE REVIVAL OF THE STRATEGIC ATTACK ON GERMANY

We have seen that Robert Lovett returned to the United States about the time of the Sicily invasion to undertake a crash program to develop drop tanks and the long-range escort fighter. The P-51s became operational in England in January 1944. In the meantime, the *Luftwaffe* had certainly not been given a free ride. Although it was difficult to see from England or a Fortress cockpit over Schweinfurt, the German fighter pilot experience level was rapidly declining because of huge attrition being suffered everywhere.[58] Also, by the spring of 1944 the bomber raids were nearing a force of 1,000 strike airplanes with escort fighters all the way to Berlin. The combination caused a turn of the tide. After about May, the attrition declined to the point where crew members could hope to have a better than even chance to survive their tours—the unescorted raid against Schweinfurt in October 1943 had around 300 bombers and no escorts for much of the trip, and it suffered an attrition of about 20 percent. By the summer of 1944, the rate was reduced to about 1 percent of sorties launched.

Generals Dwight Eisenhower and Carl Spaatz were in Africa but returned to England at the onset of 1944. However, the attack on the vital industrial targets in Germany could not be immediately resumed. If air superiority over the French coast was not won by June, then the OVERLORD invasion would not be possible. The air situation seemed desperate because at that moment, fewer than one quarter of the bomber crews were making it through their 25-mission tours. But through ULTRA, Spaatz was reading many *Luftwaffe* messages and knew the Germans were suffering, too. Further, the first P-51 Mustang units were coming on line, and were able to escort the bombers all the way to Berlin and back. During the first months of 1944, the remaining heart was torn out of the German air defense forces (although the anti-aircraft artillery units remained a serious threat until nearly the end) and we have seen that the U.S. bomber loss rate was much diminished by May. Air superiority was won, and the invasion of France went on as scheduled.[59]

Although the Eighth Air Force Fortresses and Liberators were sent against many targets in direct or indirect support of the ground forces during the summer of 1944, some effort was allowed against targets in Germany. The most vital of these was the petroleum industry, and especially the synthetic gasoline plants. The results of that part of the attack were substantial.[60] During the fall, a strategic attack against the German railroads was undertaken so that both the transportation system and the coal industry were in shambles by the end of the year.[61] Not only did this aid the march of the ground forces, it also contributed to the maintenance of air superiority in an important way. All this was examined by the USSBS near the end of the war, with the conclusion that no advanced industrial power could ever afford the loss of air superiority over its homeland. Clearly, strategic bombing had not won the war by itself, but it was a substantial contributor to victory.[62]

According to the USSBS, that was even more true in the Pacific War, where the campaign was mounted later but increased in intensity more rapidly than it had in Germany. One of the main purposes for the invasion of the Marianas was to provide bases for the new B-29s for the bombing of the Japanese homeland, and that reached its fury in the incendiary attack on Tokyo on March 9, 1945. As noted, the Survey concluded that the combination of the submarine blockade and the strategic bombing attack were decisive and would have caused the surrender of Japan by November 1945, even in the absence of the atom bomb or an invasion of the home islands. That conclusion has been contested vigorously, but many of the highest-ranking officers of the Air Force and some in the Navy at the time subscribed to the notion.[63]

THE TACTICAL CAMPAIGN IN FRANCE

The Landings

Much of the air contribution to OVERLORD was accomplished before D-Day. Air superiority was an essential prerequisite, and that was achieved in a variety of ways: attacks on German petroleum, their aircraft industry, and attrition against their flying forces by the guns of the bombers and the fighters of the Eighth Air Force, Ninth Air Force, the RAF, and the Red Air Force. The landings were bloody to be sure, but almost none of the damage was done by the *Luftwaffe*. Also, there was a major controversy regarding the isolation of the Normandy battlefield. Some believed it would be best achieved through employing the heavy bombers of the Eighth Air Force and Bomber Command against the French rail yards; others argued that the best effects would be had by low-level attack by fighter bombers against the bridges across the Seine and Loire Rivers. As it happened, both were undertaken and the military traffic through the rail yards was never halted, but the traffic across the rivers was seriously impeded. Clearly, the interdiction campaign was a success and the Germans simply could not reinforce their units around the bridgehead soon enough to prevent it.[64]

Falaise Gap

The Allies were stalled in the bridgehead for a time, and a plan was conceived to use the heavy and medium bombers to saturate the German defenses in front of Omar Bradley's forces to the point where the Americans could march through. Thus, the Saint-Lô Breakout was preceded by a massive bombardment in front of the Americans, and it led to many recriminations for fratricide claiming the lives of 300 Americans, including that of General Leslie McNair, the commanding general of the Army Ground Forces. However, the Breakout did succeed, and the American armies on the right flank charged southward along the coast and then eastward.[65] Hitler then launched the Mortain Offensive and marched into a pocket between the Americans on the south and the British in the north. An attempt was made to close the pocket at Falaise, but it did not succeed in time, albeit the Allied Air Forces had a field day beating up the German forces retreating through the gap—and losing a substantial portion of their combat vehicles in the process.

The Charge to the German Border

While all that was happening, the Marianas were taken after much blood was shed, and a tough battle was fought against the Japanese Navy at Leyte and against its *kamikazes*. By this time, the Ninth Air Force and the RAF Second Tactical Air Force had their logistics and combat engineering well under control and were building new airfields in the wake of their armies. The Germans were under a severe handicap because the *Luftwaffe* was a shadow of its former self and the Americans and British enjoyed a general air superiority over the front. The Allies marched swiftly to the German border, and there were hopes that the boys would be coming home for Christmas 1944. Unhappily, that was not to be.

The Battle of the Bulge

For a long time, our enemies enjoyed the sanctuaries of darkness and bad weather that protected them from American air attack. Few on the Allied side thought for a moment that the Germans had another offensive in them. However, the *Wehrmacht* planned on using one of those sanctuaries for one last best shot in the west. They hoped to hit at the hinge of the American and British armies with a drive through the Ardennes that would again wind up on the coast, splitting their enemies. In the process, they hoped to capture Allied fuel supplies sufficient to overcome the shortages imposed on them by the bombing and the Russian capture of the Ploesti oil fields. They keyed their start date to the beginning of a forecast for very bad December weather that would keep the Allied air forces on the ground and somewhat equalize the odds. For a time, the scheme worked.[66] The Allies had a very bad hour, and the Germans almost reached the Meuse River—but not quite. Commanding the Third Army to the south of the salient, General Patton made a rapid left turn and came in on the left flank of the bulge. The forces surrounded at Bastogne held out under severe punishment, although they were receiving some aerial resupply. Unfortunately for the Germans, Patton's march from the south and clearing weather conspired to ruin the plan. Not only was Bastogne relieved by the Third Army but the Germans never captured the fuel and had to leave many vehicles on the battlefield out of gas.[67]

Also, once the weather cleared the Allied air forces had another field day thrashing the fleeing Germans. By mid-January, the crisis was over and the strategic bombing campaign against downtown Germany was reaching its full effect. The defenses were gone and the economy was grinding to a complete halt. The Allied standoff was longer than in World War I, but not enough to prevent the loss of hundreds of thousands of lives. The American-advertised precision of the 1930s was not so precise over Europe in the bad weather and in the presence of the angry *Luftwaffe*, and the damage was done more by the volume of fire than its precision.

The Results

The USSBS declared in 1947 that airpower was decisive against Germany. Most combatants granted that tactical airpower was a huge advantage for the Allies, and some outside the air forces did grant that strategic airpower had important effects, although it did not eliminate the need for the ground campaign. Practically everyone granted that air superiority was essential. The European states and Japan were so weakened by the war in general that the locus of international power migrated outward to Washington and Moscow.[68] World War II was also the time of the first truly successful employment of precision-guided munitions in actual combat, albeit on a very small scale.

SMART WEAPONS AND UAVs IN WORLD WAR II

The desire for accuracy and standoff in weapons is about as ancient as warfare itself; the story of David versus Goliath is evidence enough for that. The first really successful use of precision weapons guided from afar after launch came in September 1943, off the Italian Peninsula. The Italians were about to abandon their alliance with Germany and their fleet was attempting to sail to Allied ports for surrender. The British and Americans were already so superior at sea that the Germans certainly did not want to see that enhanced with the Italian ships. They got wind of the defection and were prepared.

The *Luftwaffe* already developed a guided bomb that could be directed in both range and azimuth from afar through a radio link from an airplane, the Dornier 17. The guided bomb was called the "Fritz." It was stabilized by a gyro to prevent rotation, and the bombardier watched the flare in its tail and gave it left/right and range corrections through a joystick in the cockpit. A *Luftwaffe* crew at 17,000 feet spotted the Italian battleship *Roma* en route to a sanctuary port. Two bombs were released and both hit the ship. One went all the way through and exploded on the bottom of the sea, but the other appeared to have detonated inside the *Roma's* bowels, near the magazine. She went down with most of her crew. The Allies anticipated the development to the point where they had a ship equipped to jam the radio link before the winter was gone—and the German technicians in turn anticipated that measure by providing a wire-guided version of the Fritz, not dissimilar to the guidance on the modern TOW missile still in use.[69]

Meanwhile, in America similar development programs had long been afoot. The Fritz truly was a precision-guided munition, a weapon whose trajectory can be directed remotely after it was launched. The United States developed the AZON and the RAZON during the war, although only the first got into combat. Both had guidance systems very similar in principle to that of the Germans, but the former was guided in azimuth only whereas the latter could be directed both right and left and in range as well. Some AZONs were used in Italy but the airmen there did not deem them very successful; better results were had in the China-Burma-India theater in bombing bridges. Against them and other long targets, the absence of a range capability did not matter so much as the azimuth capability, and many spans used by the Japanese were brought down with much less effort (and fewer losses) than would have been required using "dumb" bombs. However, the Japanese soon learned that the bombers had to fly a relatively straight track during the fall of the bomb, and that made them more vulnerable to anti-aircraft fire. The USAAF found a work-around in the "Droop Snoot P-38," normally a single-seat fighter. The armament was removed from its nose and a bombardier's cockpit was fabricated. The bombers would release their weapons and then immediately break away. Meanwhile, the Droop Snoot would be flying high above, unbothered by Japanese ground fire, directing the flight of the weapons during their freefall.[70] Several other types of guidance were under development before the war ended but none was brought to operational status.[71]

Unmanned aerial vehicles (UAV) were developed even before World War II.[72] They are similar to precision-guided munitions in that they receive their guidance through remote means; they differ in that they are intended for repeated use, whereas the precision munitions are used only once. Thus, the guidance system is lost with each precision-guided munition round, but in a UAV it can be used over and over again. Further, the UAV differs from a cruise missile, albeit that its guidance system is very similar. The cruise missile is also used only once and no recovery system is required for it. The larger UAVs today generally have a launch and recovery team (often deployed), a guidance and employment team that handles the guidance during the mission (sometimes located back in the United States), and a logistics team for supply, maintenance, and security. The pre-World War II UAVs generally were guided by means similar to RAZON (and to radio-controlled airplane models of the 1930s) but were most often used as practice targets for shipboard anti-aircraft crews.

Those in use during the war probably would be more properly described as cruise missiles. "Weary Willies" were worn-out bombers that had ended their useful lives in the normal configuration.[73] They were provided with remote guidance systems that were located in a "mother" ship. A human aircrew would take the Weary Willie off, climb to altitude and set the autopilot. They would then bail out over friendly territory and the mother ship would guide the UAV into the intended target using a radio data link as in Fritz—sometimes into the intended target. The operator kept track of the Weary Willie visually, or later through a television camera in the cockpit of Willie. The guidance systems of the day were neither accurate nor reliable, and the airmen in Europe soon decided that their potential was not worth the effort.[74]

Meanwhile, in the United States development programs were afoot at Eglin Field in Florida for more than just radio-controlled freefall bombs. Glide bombs and pure gravity weapons were designed using infrared guidance and preset autopilots. Radar guidance was experimented with and the Navy actually got such a weapon into combat in the Pacific—the Bat. In addition to its radar guidance, it had a lock-on feature that made it into a launch-and-leave weapon. That is to say, the radar could be locked on to the target and once that was achieved, the weapon would guide itself automatically. That would leave the aircrew free to flee the area to avoid the surface fire of an irate enemy. The Bat actually achieved about 20 ship kills before the war was over. It was a bit of a cumbersome weapon, and had a host of vacuum tubes that made it less reliable than it might have been, and perhaps difficult to test and maintain.[75] Those were common impediments to the development of economical and effective precision-guided munitions and UAVs prior to the coming of solid-state technologies and miniaturized electronics making possible small processors capable of handling huge amounts of data.

As World War II was nearing its end, the commanding general of the Army Air Forces, Henry Arnold, was fully alive to the implications of the huge technological advances that were made during the war, and that were showing no signs of abating. Thus, he convened a substantial force of scientific leaders under Theodore von Karman that was known as the Scientific Advisory Group. It resulted in a huge and prescient report that foresaw, among other things, intercontinental ballistic weapons and various types of missiles that have since come to pass.[76] The euphoria that gripped all

Americans in August 1945 was great indeed but it did not last very long. Huge political changes were in the offing because of the weakening of the states of Europe and Japan, and technical changes were on the immediate horizon that were revolutionary—nuclear science, jet travel, missiles, electronics, computers, and much more. We shall turn to those subjects in the next chapter.

6

The Coming of the Balance of Terror: Heyday of the SAC Bombers

Bernard Brodie has written that World War II exposed the defects in Douhet's theories, but that the coming of nuclear weapons made his mistakes irrelevant.[1] The new weapons were so fearsome that bombing accuracy no longer mattered so much. They were so destructive that any war would be bound to be over in a day or two. That war would be so short that Schweinfurt-like attrition would not be disabling because crews would not have to fly anywhere near 25 missions. Anyway, the improvement of aircraft radar would permit them to fly those few in the darkness and still find their targets. Those radars will give much better precision than theretofore, and the new bombers would fly higher and further than ever, yielding even more standoff. Besides, America had a monopoly on nuclear weapons and a firm commitment to peace in the world, so the crews would probably not have to fly any at all. Those were popular ideas but were not universally shared by military leaders—nor by the air leaders.[2]

The fight for "unification" and a separate air force was in the offing. Few in the Army and Navy thought that the nukes and strategic bombing would be decisive—and anyway their use on cities would be too immoral for the United States.[3] Neither were the Air Force officers completely unified on the subject of strategic bombing. Rather, many of them came away from the war with a conviction that "balanced" air forces were the key to victory. The bread-and-butter mission justifying a separate air force would have to be strategic bombing for sure. But that was not enough: The requirements for "balance" demanded interceptors, tactical bombers, and day fighters for theater air superiority. It also required transports for air unit mobility, surface forces logistical support, and air assault operations with paratroopers and their equipment. Even before the war was over, the airmen were arguing that this balance could be achieved only with an air force of 70 groups or more. The Air Force four-star generals met in an Air Board and then an Aircraft and Weapons Board at about six-month intervals for the first couple of years after the war.[4] Their consistent force proposals asked for such a balanced force, albeit the strategic bombing assets were to be the core strength.[5]

But again, the traditional American demobilization approach was followed with a vengeance. The Army Air Forces discharged over 400,000 airmen in the month of October 1945 alone—greater than its total end strength in the spring of 1947 (and its strength in 2007).[6] It was almost inevitable that this huge drawdown would stimulate interservice rivalry, for the Navy was suffering as much or more. It did lead to a bitter fight over the Unification Act, and it was intensified by the coming of the Cold War, the Berlin Blockade, and then the Soviet detonation of its nuclear device years earlier than had been anticipated by the most pessimistic of the American leaders.

President Truman was a firm advocate of a separate air force under a unified department of defense, as were George C. Marshall and Dwight D. Eisenhower.[7] But Truman especially was deeply concerned with the economic health of the United States. One of the great appeals of a separate air force armed with strategic bombers and nuclear weapons was its perceived economy. Instead of huge conventional ground and naval forces that could fight long but debilitating wars, there would be a mostly strategic air force that would finish a war in just a day or two—or perhaps deter one altogether. This scheme had no place for a 70-group balanced air force. To get the federal budget balanced and to start paying down the debts incurred by World War II, that air force would have to be capped at 48 groups. The only independent operations that could justify a separate air force were strategic bombing and strategic defense. Thus, the units that would fall out of the program in reducing it from 70 groups to 48 would inevitably be the ones that could have given that force "balance."[8] The transports, troop carriers, day fighters, and tactical bombers would have to go. The point is that although the air leadership no doubt favored the strategic attack mission, if they had their way they would not have neglected the others. The common notion that they were obsessed with strategic bombing is too strong.

The late 1940s was a period of rapid technological evolution, to say the least. Nuclear weapons seemed to make for eternal peace because this time, the weapon was so powerful and economical that it surely would dissuade aggressors everywhere. Missile development was in its infancy. The Theodore von Karman report anticipated intercontinental ballistic missiles (ICBMs).[9] Electronic development was moving rapidly. The technological changes were even more than Douhet and Mitchell could have anticipated. The doctrine and theory shift from airpower as a supporting force to an autonomous striking force with a strategic attack mission was partially accepted. The organizational implications were imperfectly recognized in 1947 when a separate US Air Force was created, and at the time it thought it had a monopoly on the nuclear strategic bombing mission. It was little dreamed that the nuclear weapons would be so miniaturized within ten years that Navy fighters or Army artillery tubes would be able to handle them. In 1946, a dedicated strategic attack organization was created with the Strategic Air Command (SAC). Support for the Air Force as the new first line of defense was strong in both Congress and the media.[10] But neither Generals "Hap" Arnold nor Carl Spaatz had any notion that the airmen had routed their adversaries in the great unification war.[11] The US Navy was especially loath to accept those notions. However, it no longer had the Japanese Navy to plan against—it had been too successful at achieving command of the sea in the Pacific. At that point, it could not justify itself based on the Soviet Navy, for that was a mere coastal defense force and no threat to command of the sea.[12] In any event, the USSR was not at all dependent upon overseas markets or sources of raw materials. Therefore, blockade was not a consideration.

THE BERLIN BLOCKADE AND KOREA

Though it was little recognized at the time, the Berlin Blockade marks the turning of the tide. The movement of two B-29 groups with their supposed atomic capability (they really were not nuclear capable) to England did not result in the immediate resolution of the crisis. Rather, it seemed to have been resolved in large part by the use of airlift and diplomacy. The Blockade began only a few months after the foundation of the USAF and dragged on for more than a year. A surprising portion of the supplies necessary to sustain the city through the winter were brought in by airlift from the Western powers—the United States, Great Britain, and France.[13]

The incipient recognition of the limits of nuclear bombing's power was reinforced by the Korean War experience, though few of the leaders made an issue of it at the time. Rather, their revulsion at the Korean experience drove them back in the direction of reliance on nuclear strike forces as the pillar of peace and security. There just did not seem to be any vital targets worth a nuclear weapon in Korea. Rather, there was a healthy fear of escalation to World War III, and the conventional strategic bombers found very little in the way of nodal points in an industrial web upon which they could shower their conventional weapons.[14] The rationalization was that the strategic bombing theory was sound but that the vital centers in the industrial web were across the Yalu River in Communist China and the USSR. Thus, whatever the operation had been in Korea, it was not strategic bombing and therefore was not a valid test of the theory.[15] Although President Eisenhower himself recognized at the time that the nuclear hegemony could not last forever, the huge American lead in delivery systems enabled the United States to go on a while longer with the nuclear-centric strategy. Meanwhile, the USAF cobbled together tactical forces for the Korean War using much leftover equipment from World War II, plus some early generation jets. The experience may have led to complacency on the air superiority mission, uneasiness on the losses suffered and the inaccuracy of weapons in the ground support missions, and defensiveness regarding the apparent limitations of interdiction. Also, among the USAF flyers there was much angst over the unfulfilled hope for the unified control of airpower by an airman at the theater level.[16]

This fear was accompanied by the notion that at the end of the war, Eisenhower made a nuclear threat against the People's Republic of China, and that caused them to agree to a truce.[17] The combination caused a return to something like the Truman national security policy. The new name was "massive retaliation," but it looked to economical security through the reliance on the USAF nuclear attack of vital targets at places of our choice. That would enable limiting tactical air force, naval, and ground force funding and permit a balanced federal budget.[18] Atop that, in the late 1940s the Strategic Air Command got off to a slow start under General George Kenney,[19] and in the middle of the Berlin Airlift Curtis LeMay was brought back to the United States to take over. In the aftermath of the unification debate, it was a bureaucratic imperative that SAC succeed and, given the massive retaliation doctrine, a strategic necessity as well.

Vannevar Bush, one of America's most distinguished scientists, in 1949 suggested that the notion that we might see ICBMs in our lifetimes was a fantasy,[20] and that reinforced a huge focus on long-range strategic bombers and their supporting tankers during both Eisenhower Administrations.

Strategic Attack: Theory and Doctrine

World War II Background

In spite of the utter decisiveness of Allied victory, there was no consensus on the impact of strategic air attack on the outcome—notwithstanding the nuclear weapons that the pioneer theorist of the nuclear age, Bernard Brodie, asserted had corrected the mistakes of Giulio Douhet. Led by Bernard Baruch, the United States made an ineffective stab at establishing nuclear arms control in 1946, and SAC was then established.

The Era of American Monopoly

American leaders little doubted that nuclear technology would spread, but thought it would take longer than it did. President Harry S. Truman wanted to overcome the economic bite of World War II by using the nuclear monopoly to escape the high costs of conventional military power and thus balance the budget and pay the national debt—and avoid the depression Moscow said was imminent. But the 1949, the Soviet nuclear explosion and the Korean War ended that hope.

The Eisenhower Massive Retaliation Hegemony

America came out of Korea much disillusioned with the idea that the demise of Nazism and Japanese imperialism plus the coming of nuclear weapons would guarantee "One World Built on a Firm Foundation of Peace" forevermore—and with the outcome of the Korean War, which it vowed never to repeat. Notwithstanding the Soviet nuclear explosion, the United States still had an enormous lead in delivery systems that it hoped would deter future Koreas, or at least terminate them in the incipient stages through nuclear attacks on the Communist heartland. SAC was transformed from the "hollow threat" of the B-29s to the fearsomeness of a B-52 retaliation force—security and a balanced budget.

Approaching Parity: The Kennedy/Johnson Balance of Terror

Many in Europe and the US Army argued that massive retaliation would not survive the coming of full-fledged Soviet nuclear power, and the Kennedy administration agreed. It added flexible response and renewed pressure for ICBM and nuclear weapon development to the national strategy to reassure NATO that the nuclear guarantee extended across the spectrum of conflict, and made some hesitant steps toward a renewed quest for arms control. Some have argued that the Cuban Missile Crisis was a trauma that convinced the Kennedy men that graduated military threats work and the Khrushchev men that they had to close their nuclear missile gap to avoid future humiliations. They did close it, and the balance of terror was fully matured. What was called "strategic attack" in Vietnam used only conventional weapons.

The Hesitant Dawn of Nuclear Parity

Vietnam disillusioned America in many ways, but it was not free for the other side of the bipolar world. That was one of many things conducive to a moderation of the Cold War and the revival of the prospects of nuclear arms control. One result was détente and the ratification of the SALT I arms control agreements by both sides. The future seemed brighter but Watergate and Afghanistan made it look like a false dawn to both. The Senate refused to ratify SALT II, but Afghanistan and many other things (it now appears) were badly tearing the USSR's social and economic fabric. In the United States, they said the "Fighter Mafia" unseated the "Bomber Barons."

The Twilight of Nuclear Parity

The Reagan administration undertook a massive expansion of U.S. military power and more elaborate arms control agreements ensued, followed by the collapse of the Communist empire. Again, cause and effect were debated endlessly but the disappearance of the bipolar world was clear enough—although whether the replacement was to be unipolar or multipolar was debatable. Many feared that at the end of the day, nuclear proliferation would bring on the holocaust so long denied. Some would say Cold War deterrence worked; flexible response in Vietnam did not.

The Dawn of a New Era of Human Conflict?

Still, the yearned-for "One World Built on a Firm Foundation of Peace" seemed as far away as ever. Some argued that Desert Storm was the last of the old-style wars, that the drug cartels and potential Mao Tse-tungs would learn from Saddam Hussein's experience and return to less direct efforts to undermine the security, prosperity, and balanced budgets of Western civilization. Others asserted that Desert Storm proved that the various high-tech dimensions of airpower, if properly understood, would indeed be the foundation of one more century of peace and prosperity—a Pax Americana in place of the ancient Pax Britannica.

Still, the Tactical Air Command (TAC) survived throughout. The development of guided weapons languished before 1950 for the want of funding. However, during the Korean War RAZON was resurrected for a fairly comprehensive combat test. Good results were had in terms of accuracy but the reliability of the components was still too low. A much larger version called TARZON was also employed for a short time, and when the 12,000-pound weapons hit a bridge, the structure was destroyed. But it was cumbersome to use and after two accidents occurred, one with the loss of the entire crew, the effort was suspended.

A string of new tactical fighters and some conventional weapons (Mark 80 series of bombs, M-61 Gatling Gun, AIM-9 and AIM-7 missiles, and C-130s) were developed after Korea. Some unmanned weapons—like Bomarc, Mace, and Regulus—were developed during that time but today they would be classified SAMs or cruise missiles. The limits on their navigational accuracy and the unreliability of vacuum tube-based control systems prevented their acceptance as main line weapons. Thus, there is no doubt that the heavy emphasis was on bombers and nuclear weapons. In fact, TAC was so hell-bent to develop a tactical nuclear weapon capability of its own that training in conventional air-to-ground bombing and in air-to-air fighting was not at the forefront of its program.[21] As noted, from the beginning Eisenhower knew that the U.S. monopoly and then hegemony of nuclear war fighting could not last, but the implications were slow to be recognized.

The Berlin Blockade and the Korean War both raised a modicum of doubt that strategic bombing even with nuclear weapons could solve the problems of security and war. The rapid USSR development of atomic weapons and then apparently of ICBMs concerned both Europeans and some Americans. One of the rationales for the development of tactical nuclear weapons was that they could offer a coupling of the security of the European Allies with the nuclear umbrella of SAC. An argument was that no American president could be expected to invite a nuclear attack on New York or Washington merely to keep the Soviets out of Berlin or Paris. If the forces in Europe had nuclear weapons of their own, then the hope was that they would automatically tie the defense of Europe to the defense of the United States itself. But then the thought arose that the choices still facing the leaders were deterrence to fail were still pretty limited. Even before the end of the Eisenhower administration, some important people like Generals Maxwell Taylor of the Army and Lauris Norstad of the Air Force were saying that the president had to have a greater variety of strategic choices to make deterrence and defense viable. Some of those choices had to be short of the nuclear firebreak.[22] That logic was also complicated by the imperatives of domestic politics in both the United States and Europe. One of the complications was that the opposition party in the United States was howling that the Soviets were approaching parity in nuclear power, and even had opened a "Missile Gap" over the United States that would lead to the downfall of NATO.

The Strategic Air Command was near its zenith in strength when the Eisenhower tenure ended, but its theoretical basis was eroding. It seemed that a nuclear stalemate was approaching, if it had not already arrived. Strategic bombing or attack with nuclear weapons seemed to have lost any utility in the active sense of helping to solve international conflict. Its only utility seemed to be a passive one: deterrence. The Kennedy administration came in with a new national security policy, "flexible response," which portended good things for the prospects of both tactical and unconventional warfare forces.[23]

AN INTERREGNUM AND THE US NAVY

My memory stretches back to before the election of 1932. The most euphoric recollection I have in all of that time was the day of the Japanese surrender. The world was good and was to become better. The First World War had not been the "War to End all Wars," to be sure, but this time the United Nations would do it right. This time, Congress would unite behind the President to join the other great nations of the Grand Alliance to impose world peace forever more. Two or three months after the United Nations was founded in San Francisco, our class song at our high school graduation was "One World Built on a Firm Foundation of Peace." Further, poverty was on the way out. Nuclear power would make energy so cheap that everybody the world over would be rich, or at least middle class. All that was to be conducive to equality and freedom for everybody.

Meanwhile, redefining a new mission for the US Navy was an organizational imperative of the first order.[24] It was altogether more so because the Army Air Forces came out of the Second World War with an increased array of partisans in the press and in Congress. Further, it was allied with the US Army behind the old Mitchell program for an independent third service under a unified department of defense.

At that point, the Secretary of the Navy was James Forrestal, himself a former aviator and the champion of naval aviation within the sea service's bureaucracy. In a brilliant piece of bureaucratic politics, he did not confront the Army and AAF positions (supported as they were by President Truman) head on. Rather, he contrived an in-house committee headed by Ferdinand Eberstadt that took the indirect approach that would only modify the proposals of the bureaucratic adversaries in such a way as to leave the Navy in an exceedingly strong position. For example, the new Secretary of Defense was not to have directive powers but rather only the coordination function, and his staff was to be limited by law to 100 people. The separate air force was taken as inevitable and that became law, but the unified defense department was much, much weaker than had been envisioned by Billy Mitchell, George Marshall, Henry Arnold, and President Truman himself.[25]

As noted, Forrestal's program was a bureaucratic defensive action of the first order, but it did not solve the Navy's problem. The prerogatives of the USMC were preserved in law and those of naval aviation were left largely intact.[26] But the absence of a clearly defined mission in an atomic age was still a difficulty. In an ironic twist, Forrestal became the first Secretary of Defense and soon was victim of the downside of the limitations the Navy had succeeded in imposing on the new office.

One thing was working in favor of the Navy in its quest for a new mission: the Soviets were cooperating. Although they did not have an overseas commerce to speak of and although they had no blue water navy at all, they had grabbed substantial numbers of German submarines and the technology to go with them. Unhappily, that suggested the building up of an American anti-submarine warfare capability—a traditional backwater of destroyers and escort carriers not much favored by the Navy's inner core. At that point, technology mandated that anti-submarine warfare be done mainly from surface ships and the air. One consequence was that as the new supercarriers came on the line in the 1950s and 1960s, some of the old *Essex*-class were not retired; rather, they were converted to anti-submarine work. As time went on, new methods were developed that submarines became more effective in anti-submarine work, and the old carriers were gradually phased out.

Since about 1947, the growing hostility between East and West had been increasing pressure for improved military security measures of various types. President Truman had been holding the budgetary line until the Korean War came along. As we have seen, the Air Force, with a big assist from the President's Air Policy Commission of 1947 (Finletter Commission), was fighting a good fight for the 70-group Air Force with the B-36 as its interim centerpiece until the B-47 and B-52 could be developed along with a tanker force to support them. The Navy was working hard to get a prototype flush-deck aircraft carrier capable of operating airplanes large enough to carry the atom bomb, then thought to be at an irreducible 10,000 pounds. A few within the Navy, like Rear Admiral Dan Gallery, advocated these things for the sake of taking over the Air Force strategic bombing mission on the grounds that the Navy could do it better.[27] The Navy main line based the case on the proposition that the Soviets were indeed building up a formidable submarine threat, and the best place to counter that was through atomic attack in their home ports.

After many bloody skirmishes such as the Key West and Newport Conferences on roles and missions in 1948, it all came to a head after Forrestal resigned and President Truman appointed Louis Johnson as his successor.[28] One of Johnson's very first acts was to cancel the Navy's pride and joy, the *United States* flush deck carrier (the absence of an "island" would permit launching and recovery of airplanes with enough wingspread to haul a 10,000-pound bomb a long distance).[29] In turn, this led to the "Admirals Revolt" of 1949, during which the Chief of Naval Operations (CNO) himself, Louis Denfeld, was removed and succeeded by Admiral Forrest Sherman, the first naval aviator to hold that office.[30] Sherman had been at Nimitz' right hand during much of the Pacific War, and had coauthored the compromise (with General Lauris Norstad, USAAF) that cleared the way for the National Defense Act of 1947. That helped calm the waters some, but there still was much discontent among all the ranks in the Navy.

POSTWAR POWER PROJECTION ASHORE

Just a few months later, quite by surprise the North Koreans invaded the south. Perhaps equally surprising, the United States reacted in a military way and soon had the backing of the United Nations. The war went badly in the early months in part because of weak air support from the USAF for the unprepared ground forces rushed to the Peninsula.

The principal USAF units engaged in the early days were equipped with an early jet, the F-80 Shooting Star. They were trained for the air defense of Japan, and neither their training nor their aircraft and its weapons were well-suited to the ground support mission. There were no fields in Korea capable of handling the long-takeoff run jets of the day, and in flying all the way from Japan the F-80 was so short on fuel that it had precious little time over the target area in which to identify the mark and make a pass on it. Clearly, there was a fortuitous gap for the naval aviators to step in, which did much to restore their fortunes.[31]

In the years between the wars, one new class of aircraft carriers had come on the line as a result of wartime programs: the *Midway,* the *Coral Sea,* and the *Franklin D. Roosevelt.* They were the first in America with steel flight decks (weight and stability considerations caused all earlier U.S. carriers to come with wooden decks atop), and they had half again the displacement of the *Essex* class. As we have seen, the British carriers in the closing campaigns in the Pacific had shown the desirability of such decks under *kamikaze* attacks.[32] Carrier and jet engine design limits caused the Navy transition to jets to lag that of the Air Force, which worked out to the mariners' benefit in the Korean War. The longer takeoff rolls of jets was one problem; another, perhaps more serious, was the slow throttle response of jet engines—watching F9F Panther operations aboard the *Franklin D. Roosevelt* was quite a thrill for me and other spectators, never mind the crews themselves—and wave offs were frequent.

One consequence was that the standard deck loads for the carriers of the Korean War vintage included both F4U Corsair fighter bombers and AD1 Skyraiders, both of which were propeller driven and happened to be better for ground support in a permissive environment than were the early jets. (In the end, the jets did have the advantage of less maintenance, a higher sortie rate, and less warning to the enemy because of their greater speeds. Also, their greater speed and lack of a need for an engine warm up enabled them to get to the battlefield faster than the propeller airplanes.) The lack of long fields on the Peninsula put a further premium on the aircraft carriers, even though only the *Essex*-class and smaller carriers were used there. The *Midway* class ships were too broad in the beam to fit through the Panama Canal, so they were kept in the Atlantic.

Thus, it happened that the Navy was awakened to a not-so-new mission that was plausible even in the absence of any possible deep-water adversary suitable for a great Trafalgar-like battle in the Mahanian tradition: power projection ashore.[33] Among the things done during and shortly after the Korean War to facilitate that role was the adaptation of two British ideas: the canted deck carrier and the steam catapult, both of which gradually helped carrier aviation to get more fully into the jet age. The former reduced the danger of a slow throttle response resulting in a crash and holocaust among the previously recovered aircraft on the foredeck; the latter helped speed up the launch rate and facilitate increasing both range and payload capabilities of the jets.

The Navy did not much participate in the air superiority battle over Korea but suffered more losses than it liked to surface fire. That stimulated some development work in precision-guided munitions afterward to reduce the number of passes required for a given amount of destruction and, perhaps, also reduce vulnerability by developing a little standoff range. The Bullpup (visually tracked and radio guided, rocket powered but with guidance similar to "Fritz" and RAZON) and Walleye (electro-optical, primitive television guidance with launch-and-leave capability) weapons were the result. All were still dependent upon vacuum tube technology, and components had not yet been miniaturized.[34] None were yet built in a modular way as are modern laser-guided bombs. That modularity was to greatly increase flexibility and at the same time simplify logistics and safety problems.

It was also during the 1950s that the Navy led the way in air-to-air precision-guided munitions: the (AIM-9) Sidewinder and the (AIM-7) Sparrow. Developed at the Navy's China Lake research and development facility, the former was infrared guided and the latter was directed by semi-active radar.[35] The Sidewinder depended upon sensors that would identify the enemy's hot jet exhaust against a cooler sky, and it had the very great virtues of simplicity and self-guidance after launch. The Sparrow was a longer-range weapon that had its own radar receiver that would home on reflections of the radar energy directed at the target by the attacking aircraft's radar transmitter. Unhappily, it was much more complex, less reliable, larger, and more expensive than the Sidewinder. The latter got history's first air-to-air missile kill from a Chinese Nationalist F-86 against a Chinese Communist MiG-15 in the 1958 Quemoy-Matsu Crisis.[36] Both missiles yielded longer standoff than guns. Until then, practically all the air-to-air kills had been done by guns or unguided rockets.

As soon as he was elected, President-elect Eisenhower traveled to Korea to try to make peace between the United Nations and the Communists. About as soon as he took office, he also moved to make peace between the Navy and the Air Force—perhaps in a way the final act in the Admirals' Revolt. He appointed Admiral Arthur Radford as Chairman of the Joint Chiefs of Staff, and Radford had been one of the most active bureaucratic fighters in the unification debate. It was a symbolic gesture of the first order as Eisenhower himself as Army Chief of Staff had been foursquare behind the separate air force and a strong department of defense.[37] However, by 1954 the good Admiral became an advocate of strategic bombing to the degree that would have pleased Douhet himself:

> History has shown that military action produces decisive results when it destroys a nation's military forces and his (sic) fundamental war-making capacity upon which his forces depend. The destruction which can now be wreaked upon an enemy's military forces, and upon the enemy's war industries, with nuclear weapons, makes such weapons the future decisive factor in warfare.[38]

In addition, partly as a result of Korea, the Navy finally got its supercarrier in 1955.[39] The first was the *Forrestal*, which at 60,000 tons was more than double the displacement of the *Essex* class that had done most of the fighting in the Korean War. Shortly after, the first nuclear carrier, the *Enterprise*, was authorized (at 75,000 tons, nearly three times the size of the *Essex*) and it entered service in 1961 at the onset of the Kennedy administration.[40] For a while thereafter, the high initial cost of the nuclear-powered carriers caused us to build yet another class of oil-fired vessels, the *Kitty Hawks*. Soon after, the Navy went over to nuclear-powered carriers for good with the *Nimitz* class, which was the standard for all subsequent carriers at about 80,000 tons. Through it all, the number of aircraft in a deckload remained fairly constant (about 80), although the size of the individual aircraft was far bigger than its World War II ancestors. The Carrier Air Wing also came to include a greater number and variety of support aircraft as well. The virtue of the oil-fired carriers was a lower acquisition cost; the benefit of the nuclear carriers was more endurance, a higher sustained speed, greater storage for aircraft fuel and weapons, and lower life-cycle cost because of the infrequency of the requirement for refueling.[41]

By the late 1950s, the Navy was pretty well over its identity crisis and had a fairly well-defined mission carved out for its carrier forces. The Cold War was stabilized, and the principal naval threat was still in the Soviet submarine fleet. With the coming of a nuclear capability to the Communist world, there were growing thoughts that there would be a stalemate at the nuclear level and there might be a conventional war on the northern European plain after all. It was perceived as one that would last longer than the Douhet one-day conflict, and perhaps long enough for the transatlantic line of communications with NATO to make a difference.[42] There were thoughts that the carriers might be used to make nuclear attacks on the adversary submarine bases (such weapons had been miniaturized in the mid-1950s so that the Navy could use them aboard smaller aircraft and still retain islands on their new carriers).[43]

Elsewhere in the world, there would be the Korea-like power projection missions to justify a fleet of carriers in the western Pacific, for example. The aviators were firmly in command at the heights of the Navy, the submariners were few in number and not yet very powerful, and the battleship era was becoming a dim memory.

THE DAWN OF THE SPACE AGE

Precedents

The miniaturization of nuclear warheads benefitted more than naval aviation. At about the same time, in 1955 the first nuclear-powered submarine, the *USS Nautilus* went to sea—a capability far, far greater than the World War II U-boats, as it could remain submerged almost indefinitely. The new, smaller nuclear warheads made thinkable missiles small enough to be put aboard submarines and yet with enough range to make a serious contribution to the strategic attack mission. The first ICBMs were liquid fueled, but that propellant was much too volatile to be used aboard ship. Rather, solid propellants were developed for the USAF Minuteman and the USN Polaris that were a huge improvement over the liquid fuels. The solid propellants were storable, and thus they could be held inside of the missiles without the need for preflight fueling. That radically increased safety and reduced the time for launching, much to the advantage of the notion of the submarine-launched ballistic missile (SLBM).[44] The strategic significance of that was only to grow in reaction to Soviet moves in the late 1950s and early 1960s.

Ever since the German launching of the V-2 missiles against London and Antwerp in 1944 and 1945, the services had been arguing as to which of them would be in charge of the missile business. For a short while, a compromise was imposed that assigned ballistic missiles to the Army and those dependent upon aerodynamic lift to the US Army Air Forces.[45] That arrangement held for about ten years before the Eisenhower administration decided that the Air Force would have jurisdiction over the intermediate range ballistic missiles as well as the land-based ICBMs.[46]

In the meantime, the Air Force established the Western Development Division (WDD) in California with the explicit mission of creating an intercontinental ballistic missile as soon as possible. That was done in 1954, and Brigadier General Bernard Schriever was made its commander a month later. About a year and a half later, the WDD was also assigned the responsibility for developing space equipment. Before the end of the decade, the Atlas Missile was brought to operational status at Vandenberg AFB, and the Titan and Minuteman Missiles followed in 1962 and 1963, respectively.[47]

All that occurred when the Cold War was in its most virulent phase. The Soviet explosion of a nuclear device in 1949 came years ahead of most anticipations;[48] their detonation of a hydrogen bomb came in 1953, hardly a year after the United States developed one. The USSR interned some B-29 crews toward the end of the Pacific War, and although the men were returned, the airplanes were not. Rather, in a remarkable reverse-engineering project, they quickly built their own versions thought to be a threat to the U.S. bases overseas, if not the North American homeland. But the USSR decided to skip the strategic bomber phase and quickly develop the ICBM to equalize the strategic balance with the United States. At first, this did not generate a panic in the United States, and American missile programs were carried on in a deliberate way.

Sputnik

The early USSR detonations of atomic and hydrogen bombs were unhappy surprises for Americans. But the United States developed both technologies before the Russians and actually used nuclear weapons in combat over Japan. Although RAND researchers and Air Force people both suggested the possibility of orbiting a satellite at an earlier time, the Soviets did it first with a spectacular impact on American and world opinion. The secretive nature of the USSR made the impact all the greater, for imaginations made their lead all the more radical than it really was. Truly, the lead was in time more than in any across-the-board technological superiority, but that was not easy to see in 1957 and in the next two or three years. When Soviet Yuri Gagarin was the first human in space, the effect was only magnified.[49]

The U.S. Reaction

A couple of years before *Sputnik* went up, the United States tried to reduce the unknowns regarding the Soviet military capability with the U-2 reconnaissance plane. It flew so high that the Soviet air defenses were unable to reach it. The Russians knew that the Americans were flying across their territory with impunity but apparently decided not to make an issue of it because of the loss of prestige that would have been involved in the admission they were unable to do anything about it. The flights were indeed a clear violation of international law, and their continuation was making the American political leadership distinctly uneasy—the President himself insisted on clearing each flight beforehand. But the imperatives of national security and the strategy of deterrence demanded some knowledge of the target complexes in the Soviet homeland,[50] so the flights proceeded.

When *Sputnik* went up, the reaction in the United States was strong. The ICBM programs received additional impetus that resulted in the early fielding of those under development. So too with the Polaris missile and the nuclear submarine programs. New emphasis on math and science was developed in American educational programs at all levels. The airborne part of the Strategic Air Command was nearing its zenith, and major portions of the bomber and tanker forces were kept on alert. An election was in the offing after two terms of Republican rule, and knowledge was a sort of a disadvantage in the campaign. The President and others in the administration knew from the U-2 flights that there really was no missile gap. However, that knowledge was so highly classified that it could not be exploited in the campaign. The opposition was not privy to the knowledge, and consequently was free to make an issue of the supposed American inferiority. It was one of the closest presidential campaigns in our history, and when John Kennedy and his new Secretary of Defense came to office, they quickly learned the truth.[51]

When Gary Powers was shot down in the U-2, it was a substantial embarrassment. Eisenhower was ready to promise the Soviets that the U-2 flights would stop but that did not appease Nikita Khrushchev, who caused the collapse of the Summit Conference in the aftermath. However, the President was able to face that with a certain amount of equanimity for several reasons. One was that he knew that if there was any missile gap, it was in favor of the United States, and she still held a huge advantage in bombers as well. Secondly, his Open Skies proposal and the Soviet launching of *Sputnik* without any request for permission for overflight of U.S. territory were promising to become good assets. Only months after the downing of Powers, an alternative source of information about the Soviet interior began to come to the United States. The first images from a Discoverer satellite were in our hands in August 1960, and there could be no objection to that overflight since *Sputnik* had set the precedent of the freedom of space. So just about the same time the ICBMs were becoming operational in numbers, a new and secure source of data was also coming from space in a way that could not be denied.[52] Attack warning was improving rapidly, the building of silos for the land-based ICBMs reduced their vulnerability, and the commissioning of SLBMs so increased the problems of surprise attack that it seemed impossible to eliminate an enemy's capability for a nuclear "second strike." That was the basis for the so-called Balance of Terror. That tended to put the settling of international conflict between the superpowers by direct confrontation out of the question. It magnified the tendency for such differences to be tried in conflicts between clients of the USSR and the United States, and yet reduced the chances that such conflicts would be decisive. It tended to reflect the stalemate at the strategic level down into contests among regional powers, as in Vietnam. We now turn to that subject in our next chapter.

7

Vietnam and the Coming of the Smart Weapon Age

NUCLEAR PARITY AND FLEXIBLE RESPONSE: RETURN OF THE FIGHTERS

During the 1960s, as the Soviets increased their nuclear capability and approached parity with the United States, the nuclear bombers and ICBMs were ever more confined to the passive role of deterrence. The nuclear standoff seemed to be ever more stable, and if there was to be combat at all, it would be among conventional—not nuclear—forces, and then probably among the superpower clients, not directly between the USSR and the United States. One result was renewed vigor for tactical and special operations forces.[1]

A START ON UNCONVENTIONAL WARFARE AND TACTICAL AIR BEFORE VIETNAM

As noted, there were stirrings among military and political leaders before the Kennedy administration toward a lesser reliance on strategic nuclear forces. There had been a few conventional weapons development efforts and some huge air transport programs for army support during the 1950s. It really did not take long for the services to recognize the way the wind was blowing once Kennedy became president. The Army quickly mounted a campaign for air mobility helicopters that got the support of the new Secretary of Defense, Robert McNamara.[2]

Since 1947, not everyone in the Army agreed with George Marshall and Dwight Eisenhower that there ought to be a separate Air Force. The Korean experience demonstrated the great value of helicopters for casualty evacuation from the battlefield. It was but a short step from that to the notion that the Army could compensate for inferior numbers by the increased mobility that choppers could give to healthy soldiers. There were folks down at the Aviation Center at Fort Rucker, Alabama, who were straining to take Army aviation beyond mere battlefield mobility. But the trauma of 1947 was in recent memory, and the heavyweights from that fight were still alive and most reluctant to resume the bureaucratic battle. But once McNamara came aboard, the obstacles to escalating the helicopter mission disappeared. The mission increased from mobility to armed escort of assault forces, to cavalry functions of armed reconnaissance, thence to organized helicopter units for close air support, and finally to creating organizations of them as main maneuver elements of combat divisions. Helicopters were no longer mere support forces. But these things were highly conducive to turf battles with the Air Force and still in the future in 1961.[3]

Both the Army and the Air Force established unconventional warfare centers at Fort Bragg and Eglin AFB almost immediately after the inauguration in 1961. The Air Force also founded a Tactical Air Warfare Center on Eglin at about the same time.[4] The laser-guided bomb (LGB) program was started there soon afterwards, and the side-firing gunship development also commenced by 1964.[5] The point is that both the services and the administration began to move beyond massive retaliation before the difficulties in Vietnam forced them to do so.

THE AIR WAR IN VIETNAM

There were really several air wars in Southeast Asia from 1945 to 1975. First, there was the French effort against the Viet Minh, culminating in the latter's victory at Dien Bien Phu. As it turned out, the enclave there could not be sustained by aerial re-supply alone. On the whole, it had been what we would call a tactical effort using conventional weapons and airlift. Much of the money and air equipment used by the French was supplied by the United States, not so much as an effort against the Communists there as it was a part of the effort to shore up the French as a key element of the NATO alliance. Notwithstanding the advantages in the air, the French were simply unable to overcome the forces of Vietnamese nationalism, supported as it was by outside Communist assistance.[6]

After the French departed and a short interregnum in the late 1950s was past, the struggle was resumed. At first, for the United States there was a special operations air war in South Vietnam conducted through Air Commando advisers, who were not supposed to be involved in combat. Old World War II aircraft were supplied to the Air Commandos and to the

South Vietnamese air force. That was not enough to defeat the rising insurgency of the Viet Cong assisted by the North Vietnamese. After the assassination of President Diem (and President Kennedy), the escalation continued so that by 1965, two new air wars emerged. First, there was the tactical effort in support of U.S. and South Vietnamese ground forces south of the demilitarized zone (DMZ). Simultaneously, there was also what has often been described as a strategic effort over North Vietnam aimed at causing the Communists there to discontinue their support of the insurgency in the south.

The air war in the south was mostly conducted by second-line aircraft in the close air support, interdiction, reconnaissance, and airlift modes. Many older aircraft were still used, such as the C-47, AC-47, AD Skyraiders, F-100s, and others, some built in the 1950s. Albeit that all the enemy air defense effort was ground based, and usually done by sabotage, small arms, and automatic weapons, the U.S. and Vietnamese air losses were substantial. The use of helicopters by the Army and Marines grew by leaps and bounds and although it yielded important mobility, fire support, and medical evacuation advantages, there were many losses there as well. Yet on the whole, the Viet Cong and their North Vietnamese allies suffered heavily and the friendly ground forces benefited greatly, although there were some complaints about the air support.[7]

As always, the insurgency depended upon avoiding major battles and making attacks along the ground lines of communications. To a large extent, moving the American and South Vietnamese line of communications into the air with helicopters and fixed-wing aircraft drastically weakened that dimension of the insurgent effort. Also, such movement greatly sped up the pace of redeployments at both the tactical and operational levels (battlefield and theater levels, that is). Until very late in the war, most of the weaponry used by the friendly forces was conventional, sometimes World War II bombs and guns. New bombs and guns had been developed in the 1950s, but it was economical to use up old stocks in the south when the last increment of effectiveness was not required. As had always been the case, there were jurisdictional disputes over the control of air operations for both lethal and nonlethal units. Generally, the ground commands always desired decentralized control for the sake of immediate responsiveness; air forces still preferred centralized control for the sake of capitalizing on air flexibility and the ability to bring mass to bear quickly anywhere in the theater.[8]

It is sometimes argued that the most effective weapons arise from new combinations of mature technologies. So it was with Spooky, the initial version of the side-firing gunship. The Browning M-2 and M-3 machine guns that were standard in World War II were among the most effective weapons ever developed (some are in use still today). However, because of the heat limits of barrels they just about reached the ultimate limit on rate of fire. In the late 1940s and 1950s, the Army researchers started a program that revived an old idea from the Civil War era: the Gatling gun. The idea was to use a single action to feed multiple rotating barrels that would share the generated heat among them. The ultimate aircraft gun result was the 20-mm M-61, still standard in most American fighters. By the middle of the Vietnam War, the Gatling gun design was scaled down to the rifle caliber size and three them were mounted to fire from the side windows of the AC-47. That yielded a huge firepower capability in an economical airplane that could loiter for long periods over base camps at night. Spooky quickly became a favorite among the ground forces, and later versions are still in service at some places in the world.[9]

Some of the latest technology was tested in the southern air war. Radio, infrared, and radar bomb guidance was tried in World War II and Korea, but the principle behind laser guidance was not discovered until the late 1950s. Starting with development with the Army as a possible asset against tanks, the effort was turned over to the Air Force in the early 1960s in part because of the absence of enemy tanks in Vietnam. By 1967, the technology was adapted to bomb guidance and tested upon Air Force ranges. Late that year, it was ready for combat testing and during the winter, a team was deployed to South Vietnam. Just about that time, the bombing halt was declared against the north and all the testing work had to be completed in the south. The initial generation of weapons, known as PAVEWAY I, was beautiful for its simplicity, which gave both economy and reliability. They yielded unprecedented accuracy and aircraft survivability as well—precision and standoff. The team returned to the homeland with some sensible recommendations for further improvements that were implemented during the next four years. Little notice was taken of the success at that point because of the bombing halt and the political distractions in the United States.[10]

The air war in the north generated much more conflict on the matters of strategy and control. Although operations there were the responsibility of the Pacific Command leader, Admiral U.S. Grant Sharp, units from the Air Force in Thailand and in South Vietnam participated. Navy units flew from the carriers on Yankee Station. Late in the war, Strategic Air Command bombers had a role. Its tankers had a role in supporting the fighters throughout. Generally, the latest generations of aircraft and weapons were assigned to the war in the north.

A good deal of ink has been spilled over the disappointments with the air superiority war over the north. Although the success of the MiGs in the air-to-air battle was not all that great, it was so much better than it had been in the Korean War that it was a shock. There were greater losses to the ground defenses over the north, including the surface-to-air missiles (SAM) and the anti-aircraft artillery (AAA). The whole array was assisted by relatively new radar technology and a very competent command and control system that integrated its three elements: MiGs, SAMs, and AAA. The SAMs of the day were a particular threat at medium and high altitudes. The defense against them was to make a radical turn toward them and to dive. Often that would evade the missile but at the same time, the crew would wind up at an altitude so low that it was in the range of a wide variety of AAA weapons, often radar-guided with huge rates of fire. Atop that dilemma, the crews had to worry about several generations of MiGs coming from below or behind, competently directed by radar operators below.[11]

Many of the American fighters involved in the air superiority battle did not have guns, only the Sidewinder and the Sparrow. In the case of the Sidewinder, an American aircraft had to get itself into a narrow cone behind the enemy—difficult to do with our larger, heavier aircraft, sometimes loaded down with external bombs. The Sparrow could be fired from the forward hemisphere,[12] but at the time it required a two-place airplane and the rules of engagement prohibited firing it before a visual identification of the target had been made. That visual contact requirement gave away the range advantage of the Sparrow, but the United States simply could not afford to shoot down a peaceful airliner or a friendly aircraft by mistake. Meanwhile, most of the MiGs were equipped only with guns until very late in the war. Also, all MiG versions were lighter and more agile than the American aircraft, if only because they were operating close to their own bases and did not have to save a lot of fuel to get home. Nor were they burdened with external bomb loads. True, the range of their weapons was short, but in the case of the American fighters not equipped with guns, they had not only a maximum launch range but also a minimum. Inside the latter, the MiGs had a real advantage.[13]

The Navy fighters had a better kill ratio than those of the USAF. There were several reasons for that: The principal Air Force air-to-air fighter was the F-4C, and it was designed by the Navy. The Navy F-4B was essentially the same airplane, and neither had a gun. The airplane was designed for fleet defense against incoming, nonmaneuvering Soviet bombers at long ranges (out of gun range). But in Vietnam, it was applied against maneuvering, very agile air defense fighters. Generally, the Navy fighters came from offshore and did not spend very much time over enemy territory vulnerable to SAMs and AAA. The Air Force fighters were coming from Thailand and had to spend a much longer time over enemy territory. Also, the enemy usually employed the latest-generation MiG-21 in those regions assigned to the Air Force, but he used the older MiG-17 and MiG-19 in the coastal regions assigned to the Navy. There is no denying that some Navy fighter units were better trained than the Air Force counterparts. The most successful among them were those flying the Vought F-8 Crusader. That airplane was equipped with 20-mm guns and only the Sidewinder—no Sparrows. In the end, the record for Sidewinders was nearly two kills for every ten shots; the record for Sparrows was only about one out of ten. The Crusader was a single-seater and had no ground attack mission. Thus, all of its training was done for air-to-air fighting. Finally, the NATO strategy long demanded a low-level penetrating nuclear attack capability among USAF fighters, and much of the training was for that mission. That had no application against North Vietnam. The disappointments led to the foundations of the Navy's Top Gun and later the Air Force's Red Flag training programs, both of which had positive results as the war was ending.[14]

Still, the ratio of losses favored the United States, for both services. The disappointment was that they were not nearly as good as they seemed in the Korean War. It is also clear that the Communist airmen came a long way since then, as had the Soviet air defense systems that now were deployed to help them.

As there was no ground battle in the north, there has been a temptation to classify all those operations as "strategic." That was an annoyance to the World War II generation of airmen who asserted that whatever it was, it was not that. The argument was again that all of the "strategic" targets were beyond the borders of Vietnam in the People's Republic of China and the USSR, as had been the case in Korea. Thus, the basic industries and sources of raw materials were almost wholly out of bounds, and everything done in the north was really in the nature of tactical interdiction directly or indirectly related to the battle on the ground. It was the attempt to disrupt the movement of troops and finished goods en route to the battlefield, even as they came ashore in Haiphong Harbor.

In early 1972, the North Vietnamese thought their hour had come. The American troops were gone, and they decided to enter what Mao Tse-tung described as the last phase, the conventional attack. Thus, their army marched south into Quang Tri Province. That was a mistake. President Richard Nixon was able to rapidly deploy large air units for the Linebacker I Campaign to assist the South Vietnamese Army in defeating the invasion. The terrain in the northern end of South Vietnam favored the air effort. It is relatively open and the rivers run across the North Vietnamese line of march, and that required many bridges. The LGB now came into its own. Numerous bridges in front of the marching units were downed by few airplanes operating at altitude above the ground fire. That caused the marching units to stack up against the broken bridges, making them highly vulnerable even to aircraft with less accurate weapons.[15] The contrast with what was to come in 1975 was striking.

One of the most impressive uses of precision-guided munitions that spring was against the Thanh Hoa Bridge. American forces had been trying to eliminate it for many years, and had lost 11 airplanes against it in a futile effort. The bridge was one of the most stoutly built in Vietnam, and it was so heavily surrounded with ground defenses it was a virtual trap for the U.S. airmen. But in the spring of 1972, the USAF permanently removed it from the war with just two missions. They used LGBs and early versions of optically guided bombs to achieve numerous direct hits with 2,000- and 3,000-pound bombs to achieve the result. No aircraft was lost on those two missions.[16]

At any rate, the Communists were checked and negotiations continued through the summer. However, the Americans began to lose patience, thinking that the enemy was not serious hoping that the upcoming elections in the United States would yield a more pliable administration in Washington. That was one time the enemy analysis of our culture seemed faulty, and the sweep in the elections instead freed the President's hand for even more offensive measures during Linebacker II that December (1972).

The result was an 11-day air offensive over the Christmas Season. For the first time, the B-52s were sent to the north and the harbor at Haiphong was mined. The United States did lose 15 B-52s in the operation, and the LGBs were not as useful as they had been in the spring because the operations were at night and we did not yet have an extensive night target designation capability. (The AC-130s could then do it using their night sensors with a laser beam slaved to them, but that airplane could not be used in the high-threat areas).[17]

We have seen that much of the bureaucratic conflict among the services was over the locus of command and control—centralized or decentralized. That argument applied in the north as well as the south, but on another plane the services were united in their chagrin: the micromanagement of the war in the north. The politicians, including the President himself and the Secretary of Defense, involved themselves in the minute details of targeting and the rules of engagement. Both the admirals and generals thought this was an invasion of the province of the military. Some civilians saw that as a new stab-in-the-back effort to escape the blame for the failure; others saw it as micromanagement by people not well versed in either the technical military dimensions nor in the details of the North Vietnamese culture and psychology. Still others argued that the Vietnamese defeated us not on the battlefield but rather in the contest for world opinion. In any event, neither the economy of North Vietnam nor the re-supply effort for its forces was defeated in spite of our major air effort. The external support from the USSR and the People's Republic of China was substantial; the dedication and ingenuity of the enemy was impressive.

Another dimension of the debate was the gradualism of the attack; that was in accord with the theories of Thomas Schelling of the University of Maryland. He long argued that war in a limited context was a game of bargaining. The best way was to destroy enough to persuade the enemy of the capability to do more, but leave him enough that he still has something more to lose if the air forces decide to go all out. Many of the political staffers in Washington took their recent success in the Cuban Missile Crisis of 1962 as proof of the theory and they sold the idea to the leadership. Many of the military leaders, brought up on a diet of the "Principles of War," believed that those of the offensive and mass both demanded a maximum effort from the outset. They thought that would provide the maximum shock to the enemy, and at the same time deny him the time to develop his defenses at his leisure. They argued that the contrasting experiences against Germany and Japan in the strategic bombing of World War II proved the point. They also argued that a comparison of the Rolling Thunder campaign from 1965–1968 with the Linebacker campaigns of 1972 repeated the lesson.[18] As always, military history can be used to "prove" the opposite sides of practically every question.

Unhappily, the Watergate scandal soon followed, and the political disarray in the United States gave the Communists yet another chance. They again entered Mao's last phase, and this time they marched down the whole length of South Vietnam in a matter of days. President Nixon resigned the previous summer, and this time there could be no Linebacker III (assuming that the earlier ones had some decisive effects on North Vietnamese thinking).[19] Saigon fell that spring, and for the most part all that airpower could do was assist in the evacuation of the capital city—ending up with helicopter evacuations to an aircraft carrier off the coast with some Thailand-based fixed-wing aircraft giving them top cover.[20]

The last act came a few weeks later off the Cambodian coast. Phnom Penh fell shortly after Saigon, and Southeast Asia was in turmoil. The *SS Mayagüez*, a U.S. container ship loaded with post-exchange goods, was heading northwestward through the Gulf of Siam toward U-Tapao. Cambodian gunboats came out to capture the ship even though it was proceeding in accord with international law. They took it to an anchorage just north of Koh Tang Island, set anchor, and removed the crew (although the U.S. authorities did not know the location of the crew at the time). This caught the United States in an exceedingly downcast mood as a result of the fall of Saigon and Phnom Penh, perhaps the worst humiliations in our military history. The capture may well have provoked a reaction highly surprising to the new Cambodian authorities.

The *Mayagüez* was soon located by a Navy patrol plane, and in the ensuing days the USAF units in Thailand were able to keep a substantial air cover over the anchored ship, night and day. The orders were to prevent boat traffic between Koh Tang and the mainland and to report developments. The aircraft involved were F-4Es, A-7s, F-111s, AC-130s, OV-10s, and both rescue and special operations helicopters. Several of the gunboats were sunk in the following hours, and the ship and island were under constant surveillance. C-141s brought a U.S. Marine invasion force down from Okinawa to U-Tapao while the helicopter forces were being gathered and prepared. Meanwhile, the aircraft carrier *USS Coral Sea* was nearing Australia, about 700 miles away. She was diverted to the Gulf of Siam, but the Marine invasion was mounted in helicopters before she arrived. The helicopter assault landed just about 20 minutes before the *Mayagüez* crew was discovered embarked in a Thai fishing boat and heading back to Koh Tang, having been released earlier. Shortly after 0700 that Thursday, the crew was back aboard a U.S. warship, and although the attack from the *Coral Sea* had not yet started, it was not called off until bombs fell on Kom Pong

Som Harbor. Americans did not really know what caused the Cambodian authorities to change their minds and release the crew, but it seems highly improbable that either the landing or the mainland bombing had anything to do with it, given the timing of both. Unhappily, numerous Marines and airmen died during the landings and evacuations. It seemed like a victory in a very dark hour for the United States, whatever the cause of the decision.[21]

THE IMPACT OF VIETNAM ON AIR THEORY AND DOCTRINE

As we have seen, Stephen Rosen correctly asserts that disaster in war is not essential to real military reform or innovation. He uses the cases of USN carrier development and USMC creation of amphibious doctrine and technology in the absence of defeat to illustrate the point.[22] But it is clear that such disasters are conducive to reform. The Prussian experience after Jena-Auerstadt, where Napoleon demolished them, or those of the Germans after the end of the First World War, are examples enough. Certainly, the United States' defeat in Vietnam stimulated a major reconsideration of our air doctrine, technology, and organization.

Air Superiority

The Korean War did not stimulate much concern over American air superiority doctrine. The kill ratios were highly in favor of the United States, and although we were a bit surprised at the competitive design of the MiG-15, it was not enough to provoke major change. Perhaps the ratios were conducive to complacency. The restraint exercised by Stalin on his air forces skewed interpretations some, and the B-29 bombing effort against Communist work to build fighter fields closer to the battle area get much less publicity than the air battle in MiG Alley—even though both those things had an important impact on the air superiority campaign.[23] During the following decade, because of the combination of the focus on tactical nuclear delivery and concerns over the horrendous accident rates from about 1945 to 1955, not as much was done with realistic air-to-air training as was possible. The great improvement in Communist air defense systems after Korea resulted in a synergy among their air-to-air fighters, SAM systems, and AAA that came as a partial surprise to the tactical portions of our air forces. This was all the more so because those enemy elements were integrated in a competent command and control system. Thus, although the kill ratios in Vietnam still favored the United States, the margin was much less than it had seemed in Korea, and that was a major cause of concern.

The USAF and the USN came away from Vietnam as firmly convinced as ever that air superiority was a prerequisite for everything else, but the definition expanded some to include the ground elements of the defense systems. The need for a capability to suppress enemy air defenses (SEAD) was escalated into doctrine. It was not immediately clear whether that was to be best accomplished by lethal or electronic means, or a combination. Nor was it clear whether SEAD ought to be done by dedicated platforms or merely added to the functions of fighter-bombers.[24]

Also, the unreliability of air-to-air missiles was a disappointment, and technical solutions to those problems became a high priority. Earlier, there were some theories that the day of the gun and the dogfight had passed, but the aircrews came away from Vietnam thoroughly disabused of that notion.[25] Notwithstanding that the missiles were much improved by the year 2000, the new F-22 design provides for a gun, as does the one for the F-35.

Finally, airmen were still frustrated at the end of the Vietnam War in their hope that airpower would be centrally controlled at the theater level by an airman. That was as important in the air battle as in any of the other airpower roles, but nothing was permanently settled in Vietnam.[26]

Strategic Bombing

The idea of strategic bombing was further tarnished in the minds of political leaders, scholars, some airmen, and many officers of the other services. The bombing of the scanty industrial resources of North Vietnam did not seem to have any worthwhile results. Although there was plenty of noise in the media about population bombing, the civilian deaths in North Vietnam were microscopic by the standards of earlier wars. Nor was there a credible case that they were deliberately targeted. Defenders of that use of airpower again were to assert that whatever it had been, it was not strategic bombing.[27] The vital centers of the industrial web that supported the Communist war again were all in the USSR or the People's Republic of China.

In the years that had passed since World War II, some confusion crept into the vocabulary of strategic bombing. Sometimes it seemed to mean bombing done by large airplanes. Sometimes it was identified with nuclear weapons. Sometimes it seemed to be identified with the operations of the Strategic Air Command. Some people tended to call it anything that was not Close Air Support on the battlefield. Vietnam may have clarified that somewhat. The B-52s were used in close air support operations at places like Khe Sanh, and the fighters went so often against targets like oil storage facilities that a movement occurred shortly after the end of the war to clarify the concept. The notion was that strategic bombing was to be identified solely by the nature of the target effects, not by the weapons used, the length of the route, nor the size of the airplane.[28]

Close Air Support

The work we call close air support today has been a rub between the airmen and the soldiers since World War I. Close air support is thought of as operations in such proximity to friendly surface forces as to require direct coordination with the ground commanders. This is necessary to reduce the hazards of fratricide—both ways. However, in Vietnam the vast majority of senior officers in the Army came away believing that they were very well served by the USAF on that score. The traditional complaint of the ground officers was that airpower was insufficiently responsive. In Vietnam, the average time between the initial request and the arrival of the fighter was 20 minutes, in the case of a plane diverted from another mission, and 40 minutes with those launched from an alert posture on the ground. Airfields were plenty, and no spot in South Vietnam was further than perhaps 15 minutes flying time from one of them.[29]

But there was also some tendency to confusion in the vocabulary of tactical airpower. Traditionally, everything done in direct or indirect support of the ground battle had been termed "tactical." That included interdiction of the flow of materiel to the battle as well as the reduction of the mobility of enemy ground units en route to the battle, or laterally near the battle. In Vietnam, there was a tendency among soldiers and civilians to call everything done within South Vietnam as close air support, and everything else as independent operations.[30] Then there was also confusion of the terms "independent" and "strategic."[31] So cutting off some ammunition between Tay Ninh and Saigon would be termed close air support even in the absence of a battle. But cutting off the same load of ammunition in Cambodia a few miles away from Tay Ninh would be termed independent operations and then confused with strategic bombing. However, a purist brought up on air doctrine would have called the destruction or delay of finished ammunition on a train coming down the railroad from China or into Haiphong Harbor aboard a ship as tactical interdiction. It also would have been so described along the Ho Chi Minh Trail in Cambodia, or on the road from Tay Ninh to Saigon. At the very least, this confusion in categories increased the difficulty of post-war analysis and the generation of new doctrine.

Interdiction

My definition of "interdiction" would be to degrade the enemy's mobility or supply capability by interfering with movement. If it is related to the battle on the surface and is moving ready military units or finished goods, then it is tactical interdiction; if not, then it is strategic interdiction. At least back to the battles in Tunis in 1942–1943, the rub between the surface forces and the airmen was over the former's demands for close air support and the latter's general preference for interdiction. Vietnam did nothing to resolve that controversy. Notwithstanding that the USAF claimed to have greatly reduced the goods coming down the Ho Chi Minh trail,[32] many soldiers and political leaders were frustrated in that its results could not be decisive in the guerrilla war in South Vietnam. The outcomes were much more satisfactory in Linebacker I in the spring of 1972, aided as they were by the first large use of LGBs. Still, even then the impact of interdiction was only temporary.

Air Mobility

Perhaps the one unblemished success story for the USAF in Vietnam was air mobility. The tactical airlift was everywhere. There were two wings of twin-engine airlifters deployed to South Vietnam itself, and three more wings of C-130 four-engine tactical airlifters on the offshore islands serving the needs of the war in Southeast Asia. Few airborne operations were tried, and they were in no way decisive. The logistical work of those wings was massive, and many special forces camps could not have existed without them—and even the larger installations saved both time and lives by means of the airlifters flying between them. There were important aerial re-supply operations, as in the A Shau Valley in the spring of 1968 and the more spectacular work at Khe Sanh earlier that year, which is widely held to be decisive in sustaining the garrison there.[33] The infrequency of airborne and aerial re-supply missions caused some analysts to imply that the logistical mission is basic and should therefore command a funding priority.[34] However, it is probably not possible to assert that a consensus exists there. The US Army still maintains substantial paratrooper formations, and the USAF also gives a good deal of training effort to the aerial delivery of both troops and materiel.

The chief airlift doctrinal issue of the Vietnam War revolved around the command and control of airlift forces and dated from World War II. The argument was between consolidation for efficiency or decentralization for responsiveness. The ground perspective was usually similar to that on close air support cited previously. The local ground commanders needed control of airlift resources so that they would be immediately responsive to tactical needs. The Air Force position was usually that the airlift resources should be controlled by an airman at the theater level collocated with the theater commander. That way, it could be rapidly massed at the point where it was needed, and capability would not be wasted in areas where the demands were low. The Military Airlift Command argument was usually that efficiency demanded the management of like functions by a single manager to benefit from the economies of scale and the efficiencies of specialized expertise. A 1966 Army-Air Force agreement got the Army out of the fixed-wing airlift business, albeit with a price to be paid in conceding most helicopter roles and missions to the Army. In 1976, the other end of the debate was temporarily resolved when all the C-130 forces were transferred from the Tactical Air Forces (TAC, Pacific Air Forces, US Air Forces, Europe) into the Military Airlift Command.[35] By 2007, the Army-Air Force agreement of 1966 seemed to have receded into history in that both services were now involved in a joint program to develop a new two-engine aircraft for tactical airlift purposes that would be flown by both services.

The air refueling function was developed in the late 1940s to enable the Air Force to go over to jet bombers that would have a better chance of safely penetrating Soviet air defenses. Only in the mid-1950s was the capability applied to fighters in a substantial way, and then only for the sake of transoceanic deployment. That was important, for it greatly improved the responsiveness of fighter forces and reduced the number that got bogged down for maintenance at the en route bases. But the idea was greatly expanded in connection with Vietnam. Not only was air refueling more widely used for fighter deployments, its tactical use also became an essential part of strike operations. The fighters were enabled to get off the ground with larger ordnance payloads and to reach farther into the combat zone. Further, refueling outbound from the target helped on the range and sometimes was a factor in saving combat-damaged aircraft that otherwise would have gone down. Even before the Vietnam War was over, the airlift to Israel in the Yom Kippur War was so hampered by the denial of overflight and landing rights that the air refueling capability was later retrofitted into the C-141 fleet, and even the AC-130s (airlifters configured as gunships with 20-mm, 40-mm, and 105-mm cannons, and lately with 25-mm Gatling guns) for similar reasons.[36] By the end of the Vietnam War, the air refueling function was much less specialized to the strategic air attack role and was spread across most of the roles and missions of the Air Force.

At the end of the Vietnam War, the status of air theory and doctrine seemed to be:

- Air superiority was still paramount but now was much more complicated than heretofore, and the American air forces no longer enjoyed the hegemony they had in Korea.
- Strategic bombing theory and doctrine were tarnished, and many doubted their effectiveness.
- The soundness of interdiction was seriously questioned because of the disappointing results on the Ho Chi Minh Trail.
- Close air support with service by forward air controllers was satisfying to the Army, but a dedicated platform and better munitions were desired.
- Tactical airlift was successful and much in demand.
- Air refueling was accepted as an integral part of the tactical roles and missions.

The ideal of unified control by an airman at the theater level was still not accepted by the Army, and especially the Navy and Marines. We have repeatedly asserted that defeat, although not essential to military reform, is nonetheless conducive to change. In our next chapter, we will explore that subject in the wake of our defeat in Vietnam.

8

Reaction to Vietnam: Air and Space Theory and Doctrine, Technology, and Organization

EMERGENT CHANGES

Air leaders everywhere emerged from the Vietnam War with a variety of reasons for our failure there, but there was none who was content with the outcome. As we have repeatedly noted, Professor Rosen has shown that defeat is not necessary to real reform, but it is conducive to change. So Benjamin Lambeth aptly termed the years after Vietnam, "The Transformation of American Air Power."

DOCTRINE AND A NEW GENERATION OF AIRCRAFT AND WEAPONS

As noted, one of the outcomes of the Vietnam War was deemed a reaffirmation of the necessity of air superiority. By then, it was clear enough that the struggle consisted of more than the air-to-air battle. Also, the idea that the design of at least some of the aircraft for the air-to-air battle could not be compromised to meet the requirements for other functions of airpower. The air superiority struggle requires a viable doctrine, good training, a sufficient force structure, competent organization, reliable weapons, and good aircraft. Multiple-purpose aircraft were sometimes desirable because of cost-effectiveness, but the post-Vietnam generation concentrated on the optimization of the fighters for the air superiority role in the F-15C and the F-14. Further, the dual-purpose F-16 was developed with the air fighting role as the main consideration. Further, the A-10 was added as a specialized airframe optimized for ground support, particularly close air support. The entire design revolved around the newly-developed GAU-8 gun and its specially designed 30-mm ammunition optimized for killing tanks.

Finally, the F-117 was secretly developed in the aftermath of Vietnam, promising an alternative way of overcoming the synergies of radar, SAM, AAA, and air interceptors. By greatly reducing the visibility of attacking aircraft to radar, the old "bomber will always get through" notion was given new life. An aircraft invisible (or nearly so) to radar would not need the enormous force packages used to protect the bombers over Hanoi, and that led to economies of force of very great proportions—which were multiplied by the use of precision-guided munitions, especially in their smaller versions. Atop that, communications and command and control systems were so enhanced by the application of space technology that the advantage was further magnified, and the pendulum swung back in the direction of the air and space offensive very decisively.[1]

We have seen that relatively simple radio-controlled precision-guided munitions were in use since World War II in weapons like the Fritz, the RAZON, and after Korea in the Bullpup. During Vietnam, the LGBs were developed using monochromatic laser light. A beam of such light was aimed at the target and reflected off it for substantial distances. The precision-guided munition was equipped with a sensor that could detect that light and its direction from the weapon. A relatively simple device generated a signal to correct the trajectory so as to cause the fins on the bomb or missile to fly it toward the target. The Maverick missile was developed shortly after the Vietnam War, and one version of it came with laser guidance. Extreme precision was possible with both the LGBs and the Mavericks. The latter also came in versions using infrared and electro-optical guidance seekers in the same airframe with the same warheads. The warheads on Mavericks were much smaller than in the LGBs. The advantage of laser guidance is that it is relatively cheap, yields great precision, and permits the attacking aircraft to remain at a relatively high altitude. The disadvantage is that someone must keep the beam of laser light pointed at the target during the entire time of flight of the weapon. Infrared and electro-optical (similar to television) guidance systems have the advantage of being usable at night (in the case of infrared) and of having precision similar to the LGB. Both come in launch-and-leave versions that permit the weapons to be "locked on" to the target, and therefore requiring no further assistance from the aircrew—in other words, self-guiding, permitting the crew to begin their escape immediately. The disadvantage of infrared and electro-optical weapons is that they are much more expensive than LGBs, and like the latter they require some visibility to work. All those guidance systems were fully developed and ready for action in time for the First Gulf War of 1991. Most of these weapons yielded more standoff than unguided bombs. The LGBs could be dropped from altitudes above the range of much of the ground-based defense, but someone had to be close enough to the target to hold a beam of laser light on it. The infrared weapons yielded the standoff of darkness to the attacker, but that was limited to some degree by distance and obscurants to visibility. Similarly, the electro-optical weapons at first required that someone get close enough to the target in daylight to acquire it, again limiting the standoff there. Some of these limits have been improved by adding autopilots to provide midcourse guidance until the sensors are within range of the target yet permitting more standoff to the crews. That also requires a data link, and those devices add expense and potential failure points. Also at additional expense were folding glider wings to extend the reach and even rocket motors to the weapons for even more standoff. The addition of inertial guidance with GPS updating to the autopilots yield precision at ever greater distances, and if the location of the target is precisely known in advance the sensor can be dispensed with altogether—as in the joint direct attack munitions system (JDAM).

The rising importance of ordnance, especially precision-guided munitions, led to dedicated organizations for their development and testing at China Lake, California, in the case of the Navy, and Eglin AFB, Florida, in the case of the Air Force. The former, known as the Naval Ordnance Test Station and then the Naval Weapons Center, long led the world in the development of air-to-air and anti-radiation missiles. The later, for a time known as the Armament Division and then the Munitions Systems Division, both of the Air Force Systems Command, was largely responsible for the creation and improvement of LGBs.[2] Both have enormous live-fire ranges with extensive laboratories and instrumentation second to none.

SMART WEAPONS, UAVs, THEORY, AND DOCTRINE

At least a part of the technological change that in turn stimulated post-Vietnam doctrinal and organizational improvements was the growth of precision-guided munitions in variety, quality, and numbers. The use of UAVs in Vietnam was neither extensive enough nor public enough to yet stimulate great changes in doctrine and organization. The Vietnam disappointments led to major improvements in both the radar AIM-7 Sparrows and the infrared AIM-9 Sidewinders. The reliability of both was greatly enhanced by the increased use of solid-state circuitry and miniaturization, and the infrared weapon was so improved that it had practically become an all-aspect missile by the time of the Falklands War of 1982. As we saw, during the Vietnam War the infrared Sidewinder missiles had to be fired from a narrow and moving cone behind the target aircraft; the new versions could be launched from nearly any aspect—that is to say, from nearly any direction. This was vitally important because ever since the First World War, the odds were very highly in favor of the fighter crew taking the first shot.

Maneuvering to get a tail shot used up time that increased the chances of detection before an attack could be consummated.

Additionally, the remaining limitations of the AIM-7 Sparrow were overcome by an entirely new missile, the AIM-120 advanced medium-range air-to-air missile (AMRAAM), which is a radar weapon with its own transmitter, making it capable of autonomous operation.[3] Although developed at Eglin AFB, like the Sparrow and the Sidewinder it is used by all the services and some of the American allies. It has an autonomous mode of operation because it has its own transmitter as well as a radar receiver. As we have seen, the Sparrow has only a receiver and depends upon the radar pulses sent out of the attacking aircraft's radar for the guiding energy. Thus, that aircraft must keep its nose pointed at the target during the time the missile was flying, but AMRAAM could depend on its own radar pulses, and thus the aircrew could begin its evasive action or go on to another target soon after launch—another huge advantage. It is simpler in operation than the Sparrow as well, making it usable by a wider variety of aircraft. One of the latter is the F-16, which is flying in large numbers in the USAF and in many Allied air forces as well. AMRAAM has thus greatly expanded the West's capability to dominate the air-to-air battle.[4]

By now, all those weapons were the beneficiaries of miniaturization, solid-state technology, and substantial growth in the capability of small computer processors. Their reliability and accuracy was greatly improved, and the size and weight of weapons for a given amount of destructive capability much reduced. This was to have an impact on naval airpower in ways even greater than that of the Air Force. In Vietnam, the limits on it had arisen largely from the low sortie rate, limited sortie payloads, and short time on station. After three or four days of operations, the carriers would have to retire to their replenishment ships for re-supply. The advances in accuracy and low weight greatly reduced those handicaps. Similar results were had by Air Force airpower. The necessity of large numbers of support airplanes in the strike force mattered less in that the lethal aircraft had much better accuracy, more weapons in the payloads, and longer standoff. In the case of the stealth fighter, the difference was even greater, for it could get by with nothing—or much less—in the way of supporting airplanes.

The Development of Smart Weapons

The Era of Converted Guns and Shells

For many years after the Wright brothers first flew, air forces simply adapted the weapons of ground warfare for use in the air. This is probably not all that remarkable, given the maturity of gun and explosive technologies, common for hundreds of years. Airframe and internal combustion-engine technologies absorbed about all the energy and money that airmen could muster.

Thus, both the flexible and fixed guns of the Great War were designed for war on the ground, and the first bombs were merely rejected artillery shells with tail fins attached. These practices continued well into World War II and beyond. The standard American gun was the 1917 Browning, and bombs differed little in principle from those of World War I.

The World War II Catalyst

The second great war in a generation provided the impetus for original thinking about weapons on both sides of the Atlantic, although standard weapons used in war often did not reflect those ideas. The Germans experimented with a variety of guided bombs and even air-to-air missiles, and the US Navy and US Army Air Forces had programs on all of the guided-weapons technologies that have since come into use, except the technology for the laser-guided bomb (LGB). On top of that, the United States reaped a great harvest of German ideas about aerial technology with its foresighted Operation Paperclip at the end of the war. The Bat, an autonomous radar-guided glide bomb, actually got some ship kills in the Pacific before the war ended.

The Morning Twilight of the Guided-weapons Age

During the huge drawdown after the war, nuclear weapons, new electronics, and jets largely absorbed the available energy and money, leaving little for the development of conventional weapons. The Berlin airlift and Korean War demonstrated that all conflicts might not become nuclear and, even in those years, the Navy and Air Force proceeded with developing air-to-air guided missiles. Some of the World War II guided-bomb technologies were resurrected for the Korean War, and the Navy and Air Force's losses to ground fire stirred a modicum of new interest in guided weapons that would yield both accuracy and standoff for crews. This brought air-to-air missiles into standard use by 1956, and the Sidewinder got its first kill in 1958.

Disappointments of the Fight above Vietnam

The Korean War also led to the development of the Bullpup standoff air-to-surface missile, which proved unsatisfactory in several respects. The Sidewinder infrared and Sparrow radar missiles did not live up to their great expectations for several reasons. However, toward the end of the Vietnam War electro-optical bombs and especially LGBs proved successful and instrumental in checking the North Vietnamese army in Linebacker I. We made a beginning toward penetrating the sanctuary of darkness, and the efficiency of precision-guided munitions also tended to swing the pendulum away from surface-to-air missiles and anti-aircraft artillery back in favor of the aerial offensive.

The Maturation of Precision Guidance at Century's End

As the century waned, the Gulf War and Kosovo demonstrated that the night had indeed become the friend of the aerial offensive and that the enemy had lost the sanctuary of darkness. Laser, infrared, radar, and global positioning system (GPS) guidance systems all helped achieve efficiencies that would enable parallel (as opposed to sequential) attack and greatly reduce friendly casualties. Some people began to talk about deterrence via conventional precision-guided munitions instead of nuclear weapons. The advances in miniaturization and solid-state circuitry greatly improved the reliability and envelopes of both Sparrow and Sidewinder, and the fielding of the new advanced medium-range air-to-air missile (AMRAAM) permitted the West to dominate the air battle as well.

Implications for the Future

The longed-for collapse of the Soviet Union did not free us of security worries. On the contrary, it made the future less ponderable than it had been since the 1930s. The threat was perhaps less forbidding but also much less well-defined, making it difficult to predict what the improvement in precision-guided munitions might mean for the future. Many people argued that the West so dominated conventional warfare that all thinking adversaries would seek asymmetric means to overcome that advantage. Guerrilla warfare and terrorism were only two of the possible methods. Also, air forces seem to have become victims of their own successes. Precision-guided munitions seemingly led to such rapid and bloodless victories that airmen worried that the expectations had now become unreasonably high, enough to paralyze the use of airpower. But others argued that the new precision allowed us to use conventional warheads to achieve objectives formerly possible only with nuclear weapons. Thus, these weapons might underwrite deterrence more effectively in that the deterred parties could not count on the president's humanitarian reluctance to use them, as they could in the case of nuclear weapons. The First Gulf War demonstrated that the sanctuary of darkness was gone for the defenders; the Second Gulf War showed that GPS/INS weapons had eroded their sanctuary of bad weather.

Precision air-to-ground weapons were used extensively in Vietnam, and they generated great enthusiasm there for they promised to overcome the difficulties entailed with the addition of many support aircraft to strike packages. The hope was that you could get many more direct hits from a smaller number of shooter sorties, thus compensating for the growth in SEAD and escort requirements. Paveway II and III laser-guided bombs improved the original weapons by allowing greater loadouts* on a single sortie, simplifying the delivery procedures, enhancing the reliability, and developing more delivery options. Follow-on programs for the electro-optical bombs used in Vietnam (GBU-15 and AGM-130) enhanced the reliability, increased the standoff ranges, and provided both a television and infrared guidance option for day and night. As noted, unlike the LGBs they did have a mode of operation that allowed a launch-and-leave delivery or they could be steered into the target by the aircrew. But those two weapons were significantly more expensive than the LGBs. Like the LGBs, they also could not be used in adverse weather. Finally, the anti-radiation missiles of the Vietnam era were superseded by the high-speed anti-radiation missile (HARM) that helped cope with the ground-based defenses. In Vietnam, the radar operators had a few seconds to turn off their radar before a missile arrived in the vicinity; the HARM moves so fast that that time is much reduced.[5]

As we noted, there was a synergy among the new platforms and weapons that tended to ease the problem of winning command of the air, and at the same time increasing the effectiveness of strike sorties. This helped swing the pendulum back in the direction of the aerial offensive.[6] But the American air forces still had only a limited capability in bad weather.

Another effort to reduce aircrew vulnerability and enhance airpower effectiveness was the use in Vietnam of unmanned aerial vehicles (UAV). By that time, space satellites were entering the picture and yielding much better weather forecasting than had been the case in Korea. But the images coming down could not have the resolution needed for reconnaissance, and satellites did not have the flexibility in scheduling and routing enjoyed by airplanes. Some of the airplane work had to be done at very low altitudes and through highly defended zones. So the UAVs were brought on line to take on some of the most dangerous missions. As they did not need to accommodate a pilot, nor have all the redundant systems for the sake of aircrew safety, they could be made smaller and less expensive than reconnaissance airplanes. Thus, they were less detectable by radar and visual means, more expendable, and could be used in more dangerous missions than could airplanes. Mother ships were developed on C-130 airplanes to launch the UAVs and direct them during the missions. Once the flights were complete, the UAV would deploy a parachute and a helicopter was assigned to snatch it in flight before it hit the sea. Thus, after refurbishment they could be reused.[7]

The UAVs gained their most fame in connection with the attempt to rescue prisoners from the Son Tay camp in North Vietnam. Unhappily, it was not a successful operation. The UAV was sent over the camp for

* The awkward size of the tail structure on the original LGBs limited the number of weapons that could fit onto the pylons; installing folding fins permitted a greater loadout (more bombs) on a single airplane.

a last-minute look before the very dangerous aerial raid was launched. A programming error made it turn a fraction of a minute too soon, and thus it did not bring back the imagery that would have revealed that the Son Tay camp had been emptied. The mission was executed with an enviable precision only to find an empty camp. But the UAVs were to come a long way in the next couple of decades.

TOP GUN AND RED FLAG

The definition of air superiority, having been changed by Vietnam to include dominance over the ground-based air defenses, and the disappointing results in the air-to-air battle over Hanoi also entailed major changes in training. The Navy led the way at first with the establishment of its "Top Gun" program at NAS Miramar even before the war was over. That program was focused on the air-to-air battle. The USAF soon followed with its "Red Flag" training program on the ranges of Nellis AFB. That syllabus included more than just the air-to-air battle. A multitude of ground defenses were set up on the ranges to simulate the electronic and SAM threats typically found in the USSR and many Third World countries. The fighting units were periodically rotated through Red Flag, where they trained in practically all of the USAF roles: air-to-air, air-to-ground, SEAD, special operations, search and rescue, and even airlift. All the air maneuvering is recorded, and that yields a video depiction of the simulated battles. That depiction is employed in the post-mission analysis and training that greatly enhances the value of the experience—and reduces the arguments about who shot down whom in the simulated air battles.[8]

The Air Force supplemented the Red Flag training with the development of Air Combat Maneuvering Instrumentation (ACMI). This was not as elaborate as the installations at Red Flag, but it was possible to provide several sites throughout the world for the training in air combat with fighter units not far from their home stations. The ACMI includes the sensors, the communications, and the recording capability that yields a post-mission debriefing with accurate three-dimensional images.

The great recriminations over the outcome in Vietnam, the doctrinal implications, the subsequent end of the Cold War, and the continuing march of space and smart weapon technology all stimulated great change in America's outlook on national security. Our next chapter will explore some of the U.S. reactions to those events.

9

Reorganization for the Era of Smart Weapons and Unmanned Aerial Vehicles

The great standing military forces at the outset of the Gulf War were untypical of the American military tradition. They were built largely in reaction to the outcomes of World War II and the onset of the Cold War. The frustrations of Vietnam stimulated some pressure for organizational change. The large standing forces had come to be seen as traditional after nearly a half century, but when the USSR and the Warsaw Pact disappeared, continued reorganization and drawdown became practically inevitable.

REORGANIZATION: THE GOLDWATER-NICHOLS ACT, 1986

There was plenty of recrimination to go around in the wake of Vietnam, and the defeat not only stimulated technological solutions but also some important organizational changes. Interservice rivalry was alive and well after the war, and Congress moved to reduce some of its negative impacts with the Goldwater-Nichols Act of 1986. In part, this Act aimed to improve the unity of command of operations by strengthening the role of the Secretary of Defense, the Chairman of the Joint Chiefs of Staff, and the Geographical Joint Force Commanders, by 2007 known as Combatant Commanders (COCOMS). In part, it moved to confine the service chiefs to the world of organizing, training, and equipping forces for employment by the geographic commanders.[1] The Chairman would no longer be confined to presenting advice based on the unanimous decisions of the Joint Chiefs of Staff, which was usually watered down to the lowest common denominator.

Entailed in the legislation was a provision that enabled but did not require the geographic commanders to appoint their own Joint Force Air Component Commanders (JFACC). When implemented, this seemed to be the realization of the airman's dream since the days of Billy Mitchell: the unified control of all airpower at the theater level. There was no requirement that such appointee be a USAF officer; rather, the Act suggested that he be an officer of the service providing the preponderance of airpower for the theater commander's employment.[2]

Further, the legislation moved to improve strategic and contingency planning. One of the problems facing military planners throughout our history has been a lack of prescribed political objectives. Thus, they often had to define them for themselves through assumptions. The Goldwater-Nichols Act removed the services from the business of strategic and contingency planning. It required the president to issue a national security strategy at regular intervals and made contingency planning the province of the geographic Commanders-in-Chief. Further, it moved to make joint service more attractive to officers and to improve joint training in professional military education institutions. The Act also made a stab at improving the business practices of the services and the defense agencies, but the results there were not as promising as they were in the operational world.[3]

Meanwhile, another major organizational change was in the offing, and that was only partly driven by changing technology. The greater impetus came from the ending of the Cold War. Since shortly after Hiroshima, the ultimate pillar of U.S. national security was the long-range nuclear capability, at first solely an Air Force responsibility carried out with bombers and large atomic weapons. Later, this evolved into the "Triad" made up of USAF bombers, USAF ICBMs, and USN submarine-launched ballistic missiles (SLBM). The principal target—and almost the only target—was the USSR and its satellites. When the USSR and the Warsaw Pact collapsed, SAC bombers, the SLBM force, and the ICBMs largely lost their reason for being. So before Desert Storm (the first war with Iraq in 1991), major organizational changes were being stimulated by political factors.[4] Those changes will be discussed in more detail later.

STRATEGIC REACTIONS TO THE VIETNAM DEFEAT

As noted, there was a general revulsion to the Southeast Asia experience in America and in her military. One result was a renewed attention to a potential conflict with the Warsaw Pact on the northern European plain. In the Army based in America, the resulting new scheme was called the Air/Land Battle (ALB). In the NATO context, a similar notion was termed the Follow-on Forces Attack (FOFA). Both were an answer to fighting outnumbered and hoping to win nonetheless. The idea was to hold the forces immediately to the front of NATO formations and attack the reinforcing enemy units en route to the battlefield. The major difference seemed to be that the ALB was focused on the corps only, whereas the FOFA was a theater-wide concept.[5] At first, the idea had some appeal to some airmen in that it suggested that the soldiers were finally coming to appreciate the value of interdiction—and for the present, the deep attack was to be performed by air forces. However, other airmen soon wondered about the soundness of these schemes. It became clear that the new Army enthusiasm was based in part on new ground force technologies yielding longer range for their fires and thus an expansion of the soldiers' turf into what had traditionally been airmen's territory. Further, in the case of ALB, the focus at the corps level and the implication that the corps commander would have complete control flew in the face of traditional air theory and doctrine that asserted that an airman at the theater level should have centralized control.[6] The Warsaw Pact went away, but the ALB and FOFA ideas lingered on long afterward to cause interservice conflict during and after the Gulf War.

MICROMANAGEMENT

The improvement of communications technology since the 1950s made micromanagement ever easier and ever a greater temptation. Combined with a complex command structure, at times it led to mass confusion at the lower levels.[7] After Vietnam, the coming of computers, miniaturization, space communications, and many other technologies further increased the hazards as the end of the Cold War and the crisis in the Persian Gulf approached. As noted, some critics wondered how much of that was due to technological advance, how much to low confidence among the political leaders, and how much to an incipient stab-in-the-back legend by the airmen attempting to dissociate themselves with the defeat in Vietnam.

THE COURSE OF THE FIRST GULF WAR

The test came with the onset of Desert Storm. Reacting to Saddam Hussein's invasion of Kuwait in August 1990, the United States built a coalition designed to eject him from that country. The preparatory phase, required because of the enormous distance from the United States to the theater, lasted for several months and was named Desert Shield. The active combat phase began in early 1991 under the name of Desert Storm. For several weeks, the fighting was confined to air and naval units.

Air superiority was quickly established over the Iraqi Air Force. It was established in large part through air-to-air kills but also with air-to-ground assault on the integrated air defense system (IADS), with both lethal and electronic means. Also, airfield attack was conducted in the opening hours by bombing runways, but the targeting shifted to aircraft shelters once it was decided that the Iraqi Air Force was not going to fly. The aircraft losses of the Coalition were minimal, and possibly only one was downed by air-to-air means.[8] The idea that command of the air is an enabler for all other operations certainly seemed to be reinforced, but the battle was so unequal that it did not constitute valid evidence supporting either change or continuity in the other dimensions of air superiority theory and doctrine.

Some of the major planners contributing to the air campaign strategy along with post-war analysts, including Colonel John Warden, came away feeling that the experience reinforced the notion that strategic attack can be successful and, in some cases, even an air-alone effort might achieve control.[9] However, many others are reluctant to draw that conclusion, and perhaps the preponderance is in favor of the idea that the attack on fielded forces was a greater influence on Saddam Hussein's thought.[10]

Extensive interdiction was done between Iraq and the battle area, and much was also conducted within Kuwait and in the immediate area of the front. As many of the POWs seemed to indicate that the shortage of food and water in the front line units was the major cause for surrender, there is evidence that the interdiction was successful. As there was no ground battle going on for by far the greater part of the campaign, those air attacks on the fielded forces on the front and in the rear were described as battlefield preparation. It seems that they were enormously successful, so much so that the ground campaign was over in four days and the total losses amounted to 148 Coalition personnel killed.[11] The Battle of Khafji is difficult to categorize in conventional terms. Airpower assaulted the Iraqi formations moving toward a battle, but for the most part no major Coalition ground units were engaged. The Iraqi forces were decimated and forced into retreat almost wholly by air attack. I suppose it would fall under the category of interdiction inasmuch as the enemy forces were en route to the town when the Coalition air units caught them in the open. It seems that the Gulf War experience yielded some evidence in favor of the notion that interdiction can be effective, and perhaps even that it is to be preferred over close air support except in the case of a ground emergency.

It was rather clear in the Gulf War that the enemy could no longer count on the sanctuary of night. In fact, the night now belonged to the air offensive. Technical measures preserved the stealth of the F-117 from electronic and infrared sensors. Flying in darkness protected it from optical observation.[12] However, at least one more sanctuary remained for the defenders: weather. The LGB required that someone see the target and hold the laser light spot on it. Thus, it was limited by any weather obscuration. At the time, the F-117 and the F-111F both were equipped with infrared devices that could view the area below and ahead at night. Laser designators could be slaved to them, enabling the use of the LGBs even at night. Both the infrared and television sensors of the gravity bomb GBU-15, its rocket-powered version AGM-130, and the Maverick missile required some visibility to work properly. The infrared versions of all three could be used at night, and the Maverick came in a laser-guided version as well that was used by the Marines. Thus, bad weather during the Gulf War did limit the effectiveness of the air-to-ground units. The B-52s and F-15Es could use their own radars for bombing through the weather, but the high concern for fratricide and collateral damage or enemy civilian deaths inhibited such use.[13]

As we have seen, side-firing gunships were developed during the Vietnam War. First on line were the C-47 Spookies, equipped with three Gatling guns firing to the left through the airplane's windows. The guns were of rifle caliber, and the fire was directed visually. The first time I saw one was at night during the Tet Offensive at Saigon (January 1968). Used at night their tracer streams looked like huge, red waterfalls. The effectiveness of Spooky led to demands from the Army and others for larger and even more effective gunships. Before that war was over, the concept evolved into AC-130 Spectre gunships, about six times the size of the Spookies. Spectre could direct fire visually but it was equipped with a suite of the most advanced avionics, sensors, and processors in the world to enable extremely accurate fire at night and even in partially obscured weather conditions. The sensors included infrared, radar, and low light level televisions. The guns were much bigger than those of Spooky (20-mm, 40-mm, and 105-mm cannons) and both the endurance and ammunition supply were substantially greater as well. Spectre was in high demand, especially for interdiction on the Ho Chi Minh Trail, during the latter phases of Vietnam, the *Mayagüez* Rescue Operation (1975), and even more so during Desert Storm.

By the time of the Gulf War, the AC-130s were further improved and were in great demand by the ground forces. Built upon cargo airframes, they could not be used in high-threat areas but where the enemy ground defenses were suppressed, they could deliver precision fire at night. They also had to fuel to loiter in areas where fleeting targets might appear to yield a quick reaction in either close air support or interdiction missions, and they could be refueled in flight. The latest versions have trainable guns and can attack two targets at one time. Also, they are now pressurized so that they can use the improved guns at greater altitudes, above more of the threat from ground defenses. The new AC-130U has the same radar as the F-15E and can therefore fire through the clouds at targets on the ground.[14] However, manned by a crew of 14 the loss of one was a very serious matter, and several went down during the later phases of the Vietnam War. In the Gulf War, one of the gunship crews was preoccupied working targets in direct support of troops on the ground when daylight approached. It became vulnerable as the dawn came along and it was lost to a visually directed missile, with its entire crew killed.[15] Another was lost off the Somali coast later to an accident. But the side-firing gunships continued to deliver such yeoman service in the Gulf War and beyond that the new version was developed, this one with a 25-mm Gatling gun in place of the 20-mm weapons in the older models.

UAVs AND THE GULF WAR

The development of UAVs continued at a modest pace after the Vietnam War. The Israelis had some and used them with great effect in the Bekaa Valley fighting in 1982 at more than just reconnaissance missions. Of course, that use continued and others were used for decoys for the ground defenses, target acquisition, and monitoring enemy airfield activities for extended periods with little or no danger to Air Force personnel. This experience generated additional support for UAV development programs in the United States.[16] At the time of the Gulf War, the United States had no organized dedicated UAV organizations. Such vehicles were put to use in the fighting. One successful example was the use of television on Pioneer UAVs by our battleship crews off the Kuwati coast to help with spotting the fall of shot from their 16-inch guns. UAVs were also used in that war by the Marines and the Army for reconnaissance with good results. The experience was encouraging enough to cause the Department of Defense to spend $3 billion on various UAV programs during the 1990s.[17]

SPACE AND THE GULF WAR

The UAVs at the time of the Gulf War were controlled from within the theater. However, the progress that was soon to be made with Global Hawk and Predator in the 1990s was dependent in large part on space communications. The development of such a capability enabled over-the-horizon control of such vehicles, and the return of information in large quantities for the sake of identifying targets, designating them, and reporting the battle damage. Much of that was still to come. Even at the time, space yielded a huge advantage to the Coalition. Albeit the global positioning system (GPS) constellation was not yet complete, it was far enough along to support precise navigation through the desert wastes of the region, which was important in carrying off the famous “Left Hook” of the four-day ground campaign. The soldiers in the field had not yet been fully equipped with government GPS receivers, and many thousands were acquired from commercial sources to help the troops keep track of where they were and of the location of other friendly units. By 1991, the progress in weather satellites continued from the time of Vietnam, and the Coalition had a great edge in this area. The regional weather was atypically bad during Desert Storm, and at the very least the superior awareness prevented the waste of sorties against targets with unsuitable weather. At the time, the GPS/inertial bombs were not yet available, so any bombing through the clouds had to be done by radar aboard B-52s and F-15Es with unguided bombs. The Defense Support Program (DSP) satellites were designed for strategic warning of ICBM launch, not warning of the SCUD theater ballistic missiles that did not burn as long or as hot as ICBMs. However, there was sufficient flexibility in the DSP system to permit the warning of SCUD launches in time to allow some reaction.[18]

The database of the Gulf War is insufficient to support any inferences about close air support. There simply was not much demand for such support, as the Army forces were amply supplied with artillery and attack helicopters. They provided about all the fire support that could be desired. Although plenty more was available from air forces, there was little need of it. Air Force General Charles Horner had such ample supplies of combat airplanes that he instituted something called "Push" air support. Air-to-ground fighters were launched in a steady stream and directed to report to controllers in the forward area. If those controllers did not have a target to which to direct the fighters, then they flew on to designated "boxes" on a type of an armed reconnaissance mission against whatever enemy targets they could find.[19] Although this assured a quick response to any ground requests for support, there was no guarantee that the responder would have the appropriate ordnance aboard. Further, such a procedure would have been questionable to airmen in the 1943 North African campaign because it was a type of a rolling air patrol against undetermined targets. In World War II days, this would have been deemed highly wasteful.

By all reports, the Gulf War experience offered only confirmation for tactical airlift doctrine. In general, tactical airlift refers to the movement of supplies, troops, and patients within the theater; strategic airlift describes movement of the same things from the United States or between theaters and their return. The theater airlifters did yeoman work in helping with the unit moves associated with the famous "Left Hook," and their logistical work during Desert Shield and on into Desert Storm stimulated few complaints. Strategic airlift was also efficiently accomplished, and it was so massive and timely that it earned widespread praise, even though one C-5 was lost in an accident in Germany en route to the theater.[20] The traditional argument over command and control of airlift forces did not cause its usual trouble. Rather, a Commander of Airlift Forces (COMALF) was appointed to serve under the theater commander, but he was chosen from Military Airlift Command resources. He was charged to coordinate the strategic and tactical operations and manage the theater airlift in detail; these things were done with little difficulty.[21] The most notorious flaw arose from the incompatibility of supply and air transport software systems. Because of that, "in-transit visibility" of cargo was lost, so that generated a good deal of confusion in the freight yards at the various unloading airfields in the theater.[22]

The tanker part of air mobility was still under the Strategic Air Command and worked well enough that there was little impetus for doctrinal change in the aftermath. The airbridge from the United States to the theater was efficiently managed, and the tactical employment of the tankers was as it had been in Vietnam. Air superiority was such that it was possible even to move some of the air refueling control points into Iraq itself. The chief flaw in all of this had to do with Navy complaints that it did not get its fair share of air refueling.[23] The response from General Horner's Air Operations Center was that the air refueling was assigned to produce the greatest possible numbers of bombs on the target. In some cases, the Navy carriers were so far from the target areas that greater combat power was generated by using the available refueling assets to support a greater number of more heavily loaded combat sorties out of the fields closer to the targets.[24]

The Gulf War

Ancient Times

Sophisticated civilizations developed in what is now Iraq, Iran, and Egypt 4,000 years before Christ, which causes many people from that region to look upon confident Americans as arrogant Johnny-come-latelies.

Modernity

Western civilization got its start much later, and for a long time was enshrouded in backwardness. However, by the nineteenth century it passed the older cultures, especially in military technology. This enabled it to start a new wave of imperialism that imposed European rule over much of the Middle East and Africa in that century.

World War I

The Great War was a turning point in imperial history in many ways. The great Russian, German, and Habsburg empires collapsed, but the winners were really the prime colonial powers. However, they were so severely weakened by that war that they never were able to recover their former greatness, although Great Britain and France temporarily gained League of Nation mandates in the Middle East.

Internal Combustion Engines and Oil

An energy revolution started with the development of internal combustion engines earlier, but the massive interwar conversion of ships, land vehicles, and home heating to oil greatly increased the strategic importance of the Middle East.

World War II

This world war completed the process of setting the great French and British colonial empires on the road to oblivion. It also marked the transition of the United States from the first of the colonial powers to break away to the main champion of the fading imperialists—and thus it became an enemy of many in the Third World.

Palestine and Israel

Creation of the Israeli state soon after World War II further weakened the U.S. position in the Middle East. We became the only guarantor of the survival of the Jewish state on land that, for many years, had belonged to the Palestinians. Therefore, the United States became the "great Satan" not only to the Arabs but also to the whole world of Islam.

British Withdrawal

U.S. security long depended in part on the relationship of the United States with Great Britain. That began to weaken soon after World War II, when a lack of resources no longer permitted the British to maintain stability in the world between Singapore and Gibraltar. Gradually, the United States began to assume part of that role.

The Nixon Doctrine

America further alienated large parts of the anti-colonial world in its apparent assumption of the French role in Vietnam, really as a part of its containment policy. But the Third World did not see it that way, and the American defeat in Vietnam led to a new policy whereby the United States would supply the seapower, airpower, and some economic power but local counterrevolutionaries would have to fight their own war on the ground.

The Fall of the Shah

The first test of the Nixon Doctrine failed because Iran, the pillar of the Persian Gulf region, collapsed to an Islamic fundamentalist revolution. The Shah fled his homeland and died in exile.

The Soviets, Afghanistan, and the Horn

For a time after Vietnam, there was a period of détente in the Cold War but it disappeared in the late 1970s. The Russians got into their war in Afghanistan, and it was not immediately clear that they would lose it. Also, they were soon promoting instability in noncontiguous areas like the Horn of Africa, and that seemed to flank the Persian Gulf's oil lifeline on both sides.

The Iran-Iraq War

After the Shah, Saddam Hussein grasped the opportunity that he thought arose from the instability, starting a war with Iran that lasted for most of the 1980s. Although he won, he was drastically weakened from the long fight. The United States, alienated from Iran by the seizure of its embassy there, slightly tilted toward Iraq in that war but did so with restraint because Saddam remained a Soviet client.

The Osirak Reactor

Saddam showed himself capable of using weapons of mass destruction (WMD) by attacking his own people with chemical weapons. Because the Israelis could not tolerate the nuclear development program he had undertaken, they launched a preemptive air attack on the facilities of Osirak in 1981 that set back his effort but did not kill it.

The Invasion of Kuwait

Early in August 1990, Saddam attempted to restore his economy by taking over Kuwait, asserting that it was only a province of Iraq. This diminished the already tenuous stability of the Gulf region, and some observers saw this aggression as an intermediate step toward taking over Saudi Arabia, a rich country that nevertheless lacked the human resources to offer much military resistance to Saddam's army.

The Gulf War: Deployment and Combat

Permitting Saddam to dominate Gulf oil would have amounted to giving him dictatorial powers over the developed world. The entire world economy depended heavily on Gulf oil, especially that of the NATO allies and Japan, so the United States immediately decided to take military action. Although the first requirement called for setting up a credible defense, U.S. forces had to deploy halfway around the world. Inexplicably, Saddam permitted the United States several months to assemble a coalition and deploy overwhelming force to the region. The Coalition's offensive against Iraq did not launch until after the onset of 1991, and then it included an air-only phase that lasted several weeks. The air campaign began with a strategic attack at the center of Iraqi power, seeking to achieve air superiority, undermine Iraqi command and control (C^2), and neutralize Saddam's WMD capabilities. The abundance of airpower permitted an almost simultaneous conduct of the later phases, which sought to gain control of the air over Kuwait and then prepare the battlefield. That done, the ground war commenced with a turning movement around Iraq's western flank, and airpower then began to support the ground operation, which lasted four days.

Outcomes and Implications

The Coalition quickly attained all of its declared objectives at a very low cost in casualties and with minimal collateral damage to Iraqi civilians. Space capabilities, information assets, and precision weapons technology received high marks, as did airlift, air refueling, and transportation systems. Many people thought the experience implied that, in the future, air forces would increasingly become the supported elements whereas ground and sea forces would provide support.

The Attack on the World Trade Towers

In September 2001, Islamic terrorists attacked the American homeland by hijacking four airliners and killing about 3,000 Americans. The immediate U.S. and her allies' reaction was an attack on Al Qaeda and the Taliban in Afghanistan, followed by a quick victory there. Soon after in 2003, in part for some of the same reasons and for fear of Iraqi weapons of mass destruction programs, the United States attacked Iraq again with quick military results but stimulating an insurgency that is still underway.

The Joint Forces Air Component Commander (JFACC) Lieutenant-General Charles Horner declared that the traditional unity of command problem for tactical airpower has been solved.[25] He argued that he had sufficient control over the air assets of the several services to efficiently fulfill all his requirements. Because there was a huge number of aircraft available, some critics have questioned whether the problem has really been solved because that abundance made it unnecessary to answer the really difficult questions that would arise where there is a scarcity of airpower. Others have questioned it because the Navy and Marine Corps were required to give control over only their "excess" sorties, and they themselves defined those that were excess.[26] Also, the Army helicopters were defined out of the problem in that those flying at 500 feet and below were not required to be under the control of the JFACC nor listed on the Air Tasking Order (ATO). The huge drawdown that the services went through in the years after Desert Storm worried those critics in that they wondered whether the ample supplies of airplanes would ever again be available.

The doctrinal consequences of the Gulf War included a reaffirmation of the necessity and great utility of air superiority. It was done with a combination of the air battle and ground attack, and practically all the air-to-air kills were with missiles. Like Vietnam, the Gulf War did not do much to resolve the debate over the efficacy of strategic bombing. The interdiction efforts were a mixed success, and so did not stimulate any great change in its doctrine. Notwithstanding the ease of the ground campaign, there was some Army and Marine grumbling about the low priority of air support. Air mobility functions were efficiently performed, and thus there was little impetus for doctrinal change there. The ideal of centralized control of airpower at the theater level by an airman gave little trouble because of the personalities of the leaders and the great abundance of airpower available, so there was not much new that was resolved on that issue.

As for naval airpower, it came away with some disappointments. It was not able to participate in the air-to-air battle as much as it liked because it was not up to the requirements with two positive identifications of the target before weapons release. Also, it had not stayed abreast with the development of theater command and control systems, and its capabilities were such that copies of the ATO could not be electronically transmitted to the carriers, no matter how much bandwidth was available. Rather, the ATO had to be flown out to the fleet every day. Finally, the Navy itself decided that it had not moved briskly enough to equip all its attack force for the delivery of precision-guided munitions. That along with the other concerns were vigorously addressed in the few years that followed so that the problems were overcome by the time of Operation Iraqi Freedom.[27]

The quick and relatively cheap victory in the war against Iraq gave renewed steam to the usual debates on airpower theory and doctrine. It had both internal (to the USAF) and external dimensions. In the euphoria immediately following the war, some airpower advocates took a chest-thumping attitude, saying that the air-only campaign had finally come of age. Those of the ground and naval forces were quick to express their doubt, and even some airmen were loath to claim too much. Many asserted that "boots on the turf" remained essential to victory.[28]

The short-term feedback was ambiguous, and Secretary of the Air Force Donald Rice constituted a Gulf War Airpower Survey (GWAPS) reminiscent of the World War II USSBS. However, that had to be even more ambiguous than USSBS was, if only in that at the time it could have access to neither the enemy archives nor interviews with the defeated leaders. Thus, the implications for air theory and doctrine were necessarily uncertain. Not all was uncertain, though: There was widespread agreement that information warfare was a great success and would only become more important. Space was a part of that, and that effort also got great accolades. Finally, as noted the use of UAVs received high marks and seemed destined for great things.

TWIXT DESERT STORM AND ALLIED FORCE

The next eight years were a time of great change in national security affairs. The nearly simultaneous collapse of the USSR and the Warsaw Pact and the decisive victory in the Persian Gulf War made that practically inevitable.

DRAWDOWN

The natural result was a severe drawdown of all the services. At the height of the Vietnam War, USAF strength was something above one million. In 2007, it was lower than at any time since the Korean War, down to about where it was after the World War II demobilization. This time, the demobilization was more orderly and there was some success in retaining the best people and the newest equipment (although it was not so new by the standards of 1947). The other services were similarly diminished, although the USMC did manage to hang on to its three divisions and three air wings.

INTERSERVICE RIVALRY

There is little doubt that there is a correlation between declining force structure and funding and the intensity of the competition among the services. The Mitchell court-martial took place in the aftermath of World War I; the Admirals Revolt happened in the wake of World War II. So it is no surprise that such rivalry should reappear immediately after the Gulf War, and especially after the end of the Cold War. To some degree, such conditions are stimulants of change. Organizationally, in the first instance the Navy organized the Bureau of Aeronautics and the Army the Air Service, which evolved into the Air Corps. In the second, the United States organized a Department of Defense and a separate air force. In the third, the Air Force abolished the Strategic Air Command and created the Air Combat Command from its remaining units and those of the Tactical Air Command. It also merged the Air Research and Development Command with the Air Force Logistics Command to form the Air Materiel Command. The United States established a new joint functional command, U.S. Strategic Command, to take SAC's place in charge of the strategic forces. The tankers in SAC were left without a home, so they were merged with the airlifters of the Military Airlift Command under the new name of the Air Mobility Command. In part, these organizational changes emerged from the imperatives of the drawdown but some of them had deeper roots. In all three postwar periods, a case could be made for the notion that they were also times of extraordinary technological change.

NAVAL AIRPOWER IN THE TWILIGHT OF THE TWENTIETH CENTURY

As we have seen, in many ways for the Navy Vietnam was a replay of Korea. This time, some of the larger carriers were a part of the Pacific Fleet, and naval aviation was heavily engaged in the war up north, with a lesser involvement in the struggle within the borders of South Vietnam. There was a more-or-less constant presence on Yankee Station and an occasional deployment at Dixie Station down south. By far, the greater number of the air-to-ground weapons employed were dumb bombs (usually Mk-82,500 pounders), although both Bullpup and Walleye precision-guided weapons were used against the Thanh Hoa Bridge as early as 1967. The Sidewinder and the Sparrow were used in large numbers in the air battle up north with success but somewhat disappointing results. Although the Navy had not much participated in the air superiority battle over Korea, this time it was heavily engaged and, as we noted, had kill ratios that compared favorably with Air Force results—partly because of the Navy training program and partly because of geography.

Meanwhile, the hegemony of the aviators in the Navy was being quietly diluted by technological developments and by the powerful activities of Admiral Hyman Rickover. Up through the Korean War, all line submarines were not submarines (in any Navy); rather, they were surface ships that could submerge temporarily. But a new world opened up in 1955 when the first nuclear submarine, the *Nautilus*, went to sea. It was a true submarine in that it was completely independent of the surface for as long as the crew could stand it. The carriers had never really been able to take over a significant part of the Air Force's strategic attack mission. But as we have seen, with the rise of a Soviet nuclear threat the bomber bases and missile installations were becoming increasingly vulnerable to surprise attack, which tended to undermine the stability of deterrence. If the retaliatory forces are vulnerable, that is deemed to be a strong incentive for a first strike; if not, they will always be available for a second strike, making a first strike suicidal for the instigator.

Not long after the coming of nuclear power to submarines, the idea of installing nuclear missiles aboard them to yield a completely invulnerable weapons system came to the fore. The Polaris missiles could not be deemed a first-strike capability* in the Kremlin because they were not accurate enough for that—but clearly they could "bust" a city, and their launching apparatus could not be found under the sea. Thus, a secure retaliatory capability guaranteed the second strike, which was said to be stabilizing in the deterrent equations in both Washington and Moscow.[29]

The Kennedy Administration embraced the concept fully, and while the Navy's aviators were away fighting from Yankee Station, the submarine infrastructure and bureaucracy was growing by leaps and bounds. According to some authorities, the submarine community became dominant in the 1970s and 1980s. Its stature was founded upon a primary role in nuclear deterrence and on the fact that the Soviets were building their own SLBM force and a blue water navy—with a major counter to both being the nuclear-powered attack submarine.

Unhappily for the Navy, again the threat underwriting its most favored programs went away, not overtaken by technology this time but rather by the political and economic collapse of the Soviet Union. The USSR was almost the entire threat against which the whole post-Vietnam "Maritime Strategy" had been built, even to the point of projecting naval attacks on the flanks of a westbound Red Army bent on marching to the English Channel.[30] All of this was particularly difficult for the submarine community, as both its attack force and SLBM force were justified on the grounds of the threat of the USSR. The carrier force could more easily be swung to conventional operations in other parts of the world. In Afghanistan, the attack carrier

* To qualify for a first-strike weapon, the missile would have to be accurate enough to dig out enemy missiles from their silos at a rate that would make the enemy's second strike impossible.

USS Kitty Hawk deployed with special forces aboard rather then her usual load of jets.[31] The brown-water navy, its amphibious force, never really had a serious role in the possible war against the Warsaw Pact,[32] so now it was back in the game. The new concept passed from the "Maritime Strategy" to the "From the Sea" vision.

TECHNOLOGICAL CHANGE AFTER DESERT STORM

There was much excitement about the applications of technology in the Gulf War, especially those related to space and to precision-guided munitions. However, there was more in the offing in the few years after the war. One of the limitations on the application of smart weapons to combat that was proven diminished but not eliminated in the Gulf War was adverse weather. As we noted, the laser-guided weapons required a visual line of sight between the designator and the target, and both the television and infrared sensors could not work if there was excessive obscurant in the air. Neither the air-launched cruise missiles nor the Tomahawks were bothered much by weather in their mid-course phases while they were usually guided by inertial means internal to the missile, but they did require some visibility in the target area for their terminal phases. The smoke and unusual bad weather of the Gulf War demonstrated these handicaps.[33]

A developmental program was afoot at Eglin AFB even before Desert Storm that promised to reduce these limitations. It aimed at accurate delivery of weapons (as opposed to precise, something on the order of 30 meters CEP rather than 10) and was dubbed the Inertially Aided Munitions Program. (The circular error probable, or CEP, is the radius of a circle around a target into which 50 percent of the projectiles or bombs can be expected to fall.) The initial application was seen as removing wind effects from the fall of submunition dispensers so as to enable higher and safer delivery altitudes.[34] But along the way, a capability to update the inertial measurement unit (IMU) with corrections from the Global Positioning System (GPS) was incorporated so as to make the combination even more accurate. The system did depend upon advance knowledge of precise target coordinates but did not necessarily include an expensive sensor with its associated processing requirements. Nor did it depend upon clear weather as a visual target acquisition was not required: the drop was made upon target coordinates through the clouds.[35] The INS/GPS technology was quickly incorporated into a new guidance kit for the inventory of conventional bombs and called the Joint Direct Attack Munition (JDAM). Applied first to the 2,000-pound Mark 84 warhead, it yielded great accuracy at costs far below those of the precision weapons and, most importantly, it could be used with no visibility provided that the target coordinates were accurately known. When the first versions were a success, the idea of applying the technology first to 500 pounders and then to an entirely new weapon, the 250 pounder, quickly gained support.

The appeal here arose from the fact that the destructiveness of a weapon varies only directly with the size of its explosive charge, but it varies inversely with the cube of the miss distance. That is to say, if you double the warhead weight you only double its impact; if you double its accuracy, you increase its destructiveness by a factor of eight. Thus, a much smaller bomb could yield the same destructiveness as a large one if it were delivered accurately. Not only did that enable the carrying of many more bombs on each flight and thus multiplying the number of targets that could be destroyed, it also reduced rather dramatically the dangers of collateral damage and fratricide. It could be delivered much closer to cultural monuments without destroying them and yet still take out military targets hiding in their shadows. Also, in an expeditionary air force the use of smaller bombs and fewer of them, because of their precision, greatly reduces the logistical tail and helps speed up deployments and ease re-supply.[36] The services have made continual efforts to improve inventory weapons. Among the ideas for the small diameter bomb (SDB)[37] was the creation of an inexpensive set of diamond-shaped expanding wings. Once the weapon leaves the airplane, the wings spring open, adding a considerable distance to its range at no cost in accuracy. Some of the SDBs are to be produced with a composite (instead of a steel) casing to reduce the fragmentation hazards and further limit collateral damage. The weapon is now being provided to the tactical units. The standoff is something over 40 miles, and its GPS/INS guidance delivers the same accuracy as the JDAM.[38] Yet another improvement effort is to add an inexpensive laser seeker to the JDAM kit to add precision in cases where there is someone available beneath the clouds to designate the target with laser light.[39] In fact, the Predator UAV is equipped with a laser designator so it can do the job without risking an aircrew.

The GPS/INS combination proved so successful that it was quickly expanded to other applications. One was the Joint Standoff Weapon (JSOW), a glide bomb with folding wings that deploy on release. Using the new guidance, it can deliver the same accuracy as JDAM from a much greater distance, and do so without the expense and complication of including an engine. Also, the absence of an engine makes the weapon less detectable than, say, a cruise missile.[40]

Both JDAMs and JSOW were deployed before the coming of the air campaign against Serbia in 1999, but they had not been certified for carriage on all the aircraft in the inventory. JDAMs were certified first aboard the B-2, and combined with a stealthy platform were such a spectacular success in Allied Force that they stimulated a broad expansion of the capability.[41] Not only did this weapon promise for the first time accurate delivery through the clouds from medium altitudes for fighter aircraft but, as noted, it was also much cheaper than other guidance systems and therefore could be bought in great numbers. Both JDAMs and JSOW can be handled on single-seat aircraft.

The latest weapon to utilize the GPS/INS technology for guidance is the Joint Air-to-Surface Standoff Missile (JASSM), coming on the line in 2006. Although the design is not fully stealthy, the weapon is much smaller than an airplane and therefore much less detectable—2,250 pounds. Like the JSOW, it has folding wings but it also has an engine. In the first version, that yields a range of about 200 miles, well outside most defenses. Because of that engine, it is more expensive than the JSOW but it would be used on the initial days of a campaign before the enemy air defense system had been taken down—against radar, command and control, and SAM sites and the like. That will enable the attacking force to later use the JSOW and JDAMs in far greater numbers when the shooters can move in closer, less vulnerable to the defenses. Improvement efforts are underway to produce an extended range version of JASSM that will yield even greater benefits in standoff with no loss in accuracy.[42]

Another application of the technology was to retrofit it to other older weapons in the precision-guided munitions inventory. We said that such weapons as the infrared and television bombs require some visibility to work. By adding a relatively inexpensive GPS/INS kit to such bombs and missiles, they can be guided to the vicinity of the target through low clouds. Once beneath the cloud deck, the guidance can be shifted to the television/infrared mode to deliver precision on hard targets without risking the aircrew and plane in low-level penetrations in bad weather. By the time of the Second Gulf War (Operation Iraqi Freedom), continued advances in precision-guided munitions further enhanced the prospects of the air offensive. But at the same time, UAVs were also being improved to the point where they not only enhanced the operations of older weapons systems but also became able to take on offensive missions of their own.

There were many UAVs in development here and in other countries in the decade after the First Gulf War. The two new American systems nearest operational status were the Predator and the Global Hawk. The first was envisioned as a tactical system to be used at the theater level, and the latter could be used at intercontinental distances. The Predator was developed first as a reconnaissance system, and it functioned very well in both Afghanistan and Iraq—so well, in fact, that the idea of using it to designate targets with a laser beam was obvious and soon accomplished. It is much smaller and generates much less heat than an airplane; thus, it is much less detectable by enemy radar and infrared systems. Yet it can loiter for long periods, carrying a television sensor above the battlefield. A laser designator was slaved to that sensor so that the Predator can fly—and has flown—in low while the bomb delivery airplane is at a much higher altitude and at a greater and safer standoff distance. The Predator finds a target with its sensor and holds the laser beam on it. It feeds back its video to the operations center or even to an aircraft, and then the LGB can be released for precise delivery. Thus, LGBs could be used in Afghanistan and Iraq through the clouds even if not equipped with an INS/GPS kit, provided a Predator was available to find and designate the target. The Predator could also prowl about the battlefield looking for targets for the JDAM or the JSOW.[43] In early March 2002, during Operation Anaconda a single Predator discovered a substantial group of enemies headed toward the battle zone. Using the feedback from the UAV, the ground controllers were able to direct aircraft to the scene before contact was made, and the enemy troops were decimated. Predator can either find the coordinates for such targets and relay them back to the operations center for use by attack aircraft under the latter's control or use its designator to project laser light onto the target to enable precision attack by other airplanes.[44]

It was but a short step from the idea of using Predator for target designation to using it for an attack system.[45] The first models did not have the payload capacity to handle standard bombs, but the Army was employing a lighter weapon, the Hellfire Missile, from helicopters for a long time. It is laser guided and the Air Force adapted it to be carried (in pairs) on the Predator, and it actually has designated targets for itself and achieved combat kills—always with the weapons release being ordered only by an in-the-loop human in the operations center.[46] A larger model of the Predator is being deployed now, and two fighter-sized and stealthy UAVs (the X-45 and X-47) designed specifically for combat are also in development and flying.[47] The Predator must be carried overseas but the Global Hawk is much bigger and is self-deploying. It is envisioned as a replacement for the manned U-2, which has been on the line since the 1950s.[48] This has led to thoughts of developing an aerial refueling capability for Predator and its follow-on UAV, the Reaper. If that proves feasible, those systems could be self-deployed overseas without consuming scarce and expensive airlift.[49]

Global Hawk is a high-altitude system that has been extensively used over Iraq and Afghanistan. It is designed for reconnaissance and surveillance and, although not really stealthy, it is not easy to detect at the high altitudes it uses. Space satellites operate at much higher altitudes, it is true, and also do reconnaissance. However, they cannot as easily be moved to new orbits nor directed to targets at different times—they are highly useful, to be sure, but they are not as flexible as is Global Hawk. Additionally, the Global Hawk is much cheaper and more quickly launched and sent to a new target area. Its mission can be easily changed en route, and it can be recovered back in the continental United States. It and the Predator can be economically stored when not required for operations, and much more of the crew training can be done on simulators than has so far been the case with air crews. Because its operations and support personnel remain back in the United States, its "footprint" in the combat theater is very small. Not only does that reduce costs in an expeditionary situation, as well as hold down the stress on the airlift and air refueling forces, it also has some political benefits in some situations.[50]

For a long time, the USAF led the way in UAV development. However, the march of technology and war has made it clear that such vehicles have so much utility for the ground forces and so much future promise that a bureaucratic battle for their control was sure to ensue. Their increased use has led to many hazardous situations above Iraq because of uncertain deconfliction of air traffic.[51] The USAF made a bid in 2007 to be made the executive agency in the acquisition of UAVs that operate above 3,500 feet, but the Army and Marine Corps protested that move vigorously and the decision went against the Air Force.[52]

DOCTRINAL IMPLICATIONS

The disappearance of the Soviet Union and the Warsaw Pact caused major doctrinal changes among all of the U.S. services. The threat of immediate annihilation as the result of a war between two superpowers or two great alliance systems was much diminished. Those superpowers and other things in the Cold War period had a dampening effect on the antagonisms existing among their allies and protégés. Once the Cold War was over, many of the ethnic and religious conflicts that had been repressed were released for new battles. In place of a well-defined immediate threat to survival, the West found a much more diffuse and ill-defined threat to stability and peace. All this imposed two requirements. First was a huge drawdown for all the armed services because of the less immediate threat to survival. Second, because of the uncertainty of the locus and methods of future combat, a redeployment of the remaining forces from forward locations to their homelands was needed.[53] There they could be maintained more cheaply and more easily deployed again to wherever new threats emerged. Through most of the Cold War, the United States followed a "threat-based" planning scheme; now, because of the uncertainties ahead, there has been a shift to "capabilities-based" planning in the hope of being able to meet a wide variety of threats.[54]

As we have noted, for the Navy—which always had been an expeditionary force—the change was that the principal potential adversary for both its surface forces and the underwater units disappeared. A blue-water fight against the adversary "boomers" (missile-equipped nuclear submarines) was no longer a possibility; one against the Soviet threat to our sea line of communications with our NATO allies also disappeared. Thus, the USN submarine force especially needed a new rationale for its existence. The problem for the aircraft carriers was perceived as less serious because they could be more easily swung from the blue-water fight to power projection ashore. The new concept was to swing the entire Navy and Marine Corps from the great sea battle on the high seas to a brown-water function in the littoral areas of the world. In the future, the controlling idea was that the maritime forces would prepare for forced entry against a variety of littoral states to establish enclaves into which the heavier forces of the Army and Air Force could be deployed, if they were needed. That was bad for the submarine parts of the Navy; it was a shot in the arm for the Marines, amphibious, and mine sweeping or laying forces.[55]

The Development of Airpower and the Sea Services

The Jeffersonian Era

Through much of American history, the United States has not been a major sea power. In the beginning, we had no hope of competing with Great Britain's Royal Navy; in any case, we had other fish to fry with our continental expansion and development. Our overseas commerce was important but the threats to it were usually limited. In any event, it benefited from the Pax Britannica, under which the Royal Navy made the seas somewhat safe for American commerce. So the vision that prevailed for most of the nineteenth century was Thomas Jefferson's preference for a small-ship navy whose main purpose was to defend the coasts and offer minimal protection to commerce. The main exception occurred during the American Civil War, in which the Union built up one of the world's great navies and used it to good effect in blockading the Confederacy and assisting the Army with riverine operations and a few amphibious attacks.

The New Imperialists and Mahan

At the first centennial's end, a sea change occurred. Because the frontier closed in 1890, any expansion would have to be overseas. A vast maritime technological revolution took place during and after the Civil War: the Navy converted to steam propulsion and metal ships; submarines arrived even before World War I, along with practical torpedoes; the effectiveness of naval gunnery made a quantum jump; and coaling stations for both commercial and naval vessels became essential en route to overseas markets. As Alfred Thayer Mahan saw it, the function of the Navy was no longer merely coastal defense, commerce protection, and raiding. Rather, the service should now gain command of the sea through a great naval battle between capital ships, as in Trafalgar, where Admiral Horatio Nelson defeated the Napoleonic naval threat. This new function would require a great fleet of huge, heavily gunned ships of the line.

The Test of the Great War

The United States did not get into the war in time for the great battle of Jutland and, in any event, that fight little resembled Trafalgar. The German U-boats demonstrated that a Jeffersonian-era assault on maritime commerce had more potential than Mahan thought, and that conventional command of the sea could do little to stop it. So no clear "lessons" of the naval war existed, and the US Naval Institute's *Proceedings* in the 1920s published many articles about Jutland and an equal number about the utility of naval aviation. Destruction of the German fleet deprived the US Navy of its main—almost only—threat.

Naval Aviation as an Auxiliary

The Navy of the 1920s was not nearly as Neanderthal as many Americans seem to believe. True, most officers valued aviation as an enormous enhancement of the effectiveness of gunfire, and it was that. But even then some admirals had visions of aircraft ultimately becoming the main striking force. British carriers of the early 1920s were clearly ahead of their U.S. counterparts, but by the end of the decade America had the best naval aviation in the world, and the *USS Lexington* and *Saratoga* were the leading carriers. The end of that decade saw Pacific Fleet exercises in which air forces practiced attacks on both Pearl Harbor and the Panama Canal. Still, for most people the main function of aviation was to win air superiority over the battle, and the best way of doing that was sinking the enemy carriers.

Hesitant Development of Naval Aviation as the Main Striking Force

Some doctrinal and organizational change followed the technical revolution that produced aircraft and carriers. The task force gradually replaced organization by ship type, and on the day of Pearl Harbor the United States had eight battleships and seven aircraft carriers under construction. The flattops included the 27,000-ton *Essex* class that would win the naval air war in the Pacific. Arguably, only on the eve of war did carrier decks feature Dauntless dive-bombers with the capability of lifting a bomb big enough, carrying it far enough, and aiming it accurately enough to threaten the horizontal armor of most of the world's battleships.

Pearl Harbor and the Test of War

Pearl Harbor was defective as a test of Mitchell's theories for the same reason the 1921 tests proved inconclusive: the American battleships were immobile and undefended. However, the Japanese quickly sent the Royal Navy's *Repulse* and *Prince of Wales* to their watery graves even though they were moving, but without any air cover. During the war, battleships transitioned from the main striking arm to support roles as anti-aircraft platforms and amphibious gunfire-support ships. The carriers quickly became the capital ships for both winning the sea battle and then projecting power ashore. Again, in 1945 the Japanese Navy was in its watery grave, and the US Navy lost its principal—and only—threat.

Revolt of the Admirals

The Navy for a time seemed to be a service without a mission. Nuclear attacks evidently said that air attack would decide the next war in a matter of hours; therefore, there would be no time for seapower to have an effect. Because the USSR was so heavily a land power, no other possible mission existed. In part, that explains the viciousness of the interservice rivalry surrounding the Unification Act and acquisition of the B-36. However, the Korean War not only opened the gates to the treasury but also showed that in the absence of jet fields, carriers could perform a very useful function in power projection ashore, notwithstanding the absence of any discernable naval threat.

The Blue-Water Navy and the Soviets

About the time the Navy began to make its case for power projection ashore in places like Korea, the Soviets provided that service with yet another reason for being: the building of a great submarine fleet, first to threaten the lines of communications to NATO's member states and then to threaten the American homeland itself with nuclear missiles. This mission remained viable for many decades afterwards, providing the rationale for sustaining great carrier and submarine fleets.

From the Sea

The collapse of the Soviet Union again deprived the US Navy of a threat upon which to build its house. The submarine fleet lost both its nuclear-attack role and its anti-submarine function. The carrier part of the Navy was somewhat better off because it could function in a conventional-attack role in many other areas of the world. But now an increasing focus on power projection ashore enhanced the brown-water parts of the Navy—the minesweeping and amphibious forces. Lately, one perceives the function as establishing an enclave ashore to prepare for the follow-on heavy forces of the Army and Air Force.

For the Army, the First Gulf War demonstrated that deployment from either the continental United States or from the European theater to the Gulf was a tedious and time-consuming task. It required huge amounts of sealift and airlift. The air battle went on for several weeks before the ground operation began, and then the latter lasted only four days. Not only did this set off much writing to the effect that airpower had not really won the war, but that ground power was the real determinant. It also stimulated a good deal of doctrinal angst for the Army. Clearly, the notions of ALB and FOFA were things of the past. The battle on the northern European plain among huge armored forces was not to occur. The new concept of basing in the

United States with deployment on demand portended large changes in the way that soldiers were to do business and the way they were to be equipped. Well before Allied Force (NATO war against Serbia), they were seeking ways to become lighter and faster and yet lethal, so as to remain relevant to quickly developing conflicts in unexpected and far-away places.[56] That was probably good for the infantry and aviation branches and not so good for the armor and artillery branches.

For the Air Force, the changed environment also portended the need for a major revision in its theory and doctrine. For many decades, it was basically a forward-deployed force. Its strategic bomber arm had been diminishing in influence for some time. The numbers of bombers declined from close to 2,000 in 1960 to hardly 300 thirty years later. The numbers of bomber pilots in the force diminished greatly as the mission migrated to the ICBM force and to the Navy's submarines. Yet the influence of SAC's missile officers did not rise in a commensurate way. Rather, that of the fighter pilots associated with Tactical Air Command and the overseas tactical fighter forces increased, perhaps disproportionately.[57]

The air refueling forces were created in the first instance to support the bombers, and as the latter disappeared the aerial tankers did not diminish proportionately. Rather, their mission in support of fighters on deployment and in combat grew. Also, the large C-141 fleet was retrofitted with an air refueling capability, and the tankers also gained a requirement to support Navy fighters. Thus, the transition from forward-deployed concepts to homeland-based notions, although it implied a need for long ranges, nonetheless did not have as an immediate impact on the (short-range) fighter commands as might have been expected. The huge residual tanker force was available to give them the range they needed for both deployment and employment. However, the large numbers of tanker officers remaining did not have an influence proportionate to their numerical strength. Tankers continued to be seen as mere supporting forces, and consequently of limited influence on strategy or acquisition decisions. However, by 2007 the KC-135 force was becoming so aged that a new tanker became the Air Force's highest acquisition priority.[58]

The reorientation had similar effects for the airlift forces. They were merged with the tankers into Air Mobility Command in 1992, and they too were usually perceived as support forces and thus of limited influence. However, perhaps their impact was not quite as limited as that of their brethren in the tanker part of the command. They were clearly necessary for the rapid deployment of the fighter forces to distant areas from the United States, and thus garnered some support from Air Combat Command as did the tankers. But the Army was also highly dependent upon the airlift part of the command. It had been so ever since the cargo hauling command transitioned from an air transport force resembling a government airline to an airlift force, much more associated with combat and optimized for hauling combat units as units (circa 1960). Thus, the airlifters could expect political support not only from Air Combat Command but also from the US Army. Perhaps that does something to explain why the United States has brought the C-141, C-5, and C-17 on the line since the KC-135 fleet was acquired.[59] Yet only the KC-10s have been added in recent times, and then only in very limited numbers and with a dual role as airlifters. In fact, a significant fraction of the KC-10 fleet was employed in airlift instead of refueling in the First Gulf War.[60] As the C-17s have come on the line, disproportionate numbers of C-141s have been retired. Even where the ton-miles capacity has remained the same, the fewer airplanes now on line to replace the Starlifters means some loss in flexibility because any one of them cannot be in more places than one at any given time. Moreover, the recent decisions to increase the size of both the Army and Marine Corps entails a need for increased airlift capability.[61]

An Air Mobility Timeline

1915	Aerial re-supply attempt during siege of Kut, Iraq
1918	Billy Mitchell's plans for infantry drop
1919	First transatlantic flight, NC-4, US Navy
1923	First aerial refueling
1926	Founding of Air Corps
1929	Seven-day refueling flight of *Question Mark*
1934	Airmail fiasco
1935	First flight of DC-3 (C-47)
1940	German airborne operations in Low Countries
1942	Establishment of Air Transport Command (ATC)
1942–45	Hump operations supplying China
1943	Allied airborne drops in Sicily
1944	Airborne drops at Normandy, France
1944	Airborne drops at Arnhem, Netherlands
1945	Operation Varsity drops across Rhine River
1947	Founding of US Air Force
1948	Establishment of Military Air Transport Service (MATS)
1948–49	Berlin Airlift
1952	Founding of Civil Reserve Air Fleet (CRAF)
1956	First production model of C-130
1964	First operational C-141
1966	Army/Air Force agreement on theater airlift
1966	Renaming of MATS to Military Airlift Command (MAC)
1968	Aerial re-supply at siege of Khe Sanh, South Vietnam

1973	Aerial re-supply of Israel during Yom Kippur War
1974	Transfer of all C-130s to MAC
1990–91	First Gulf War
1992	Disestablishment of SAC
1992	Establishment of Air Combat Command (ACC)
1992	Renaming of MAC to Air Mobility Command (AMC)
1992	Transfer of C-130s from AMC to ACC
1997	Transfer of US C-130s back to AMC
1999	Air war over Serbia
2001	War on Terror
2003	Second Gulf War

All of this did not do much to restore the fortunes of the residual long-range bomber part of the USAF. The fall of the USSR radically reduced the importance of its remaining nuclear deterrent mission, and the possibility of projecting conventional power to distant theaters by the use of air refueling for fighters, generally accessible in-theater bases, and surviving aircraft carriers reduced any need for new long-range bombers. The B-52 played a conventional role against the Republican Guard in the Gulf War, but its achievements were overshadowed by those of the fighters, and especially by the stealthy F-117. The B-1 had been developed by then but it had a checkered developmental history, and remaining technical difficulties kept it out of the combat in the Gulf. That program was terminated at only a little over 100 units. The stealthy B-2 was in development then but its very high unit price, among other things, led to limiting the acquisition to 21 airplanes.[62] There were periodic moves in Congress to add to that number but without the support of the Air Staff, so far none has succeeded. At the time of this writing, planning calls for the fielding of a new long-range bomber by 2018.[63]

Much of this was reflected in the publication of a new Air Force basic doctrine manual, Air Force Doctrine Document-1, in September 1997, only a year and a half before the onset of Allied Force, the NATO combat against Milosevic's Serbia.[64]

ORGANIZATIONAL CHANGE FOR AN EXPEDITIONARY DOCTRINE

We have seen that the USAF did reorganize in the immediate aftermath of the collapse of the Soviet Union by merging SAC and TAC into ACC. We also noted that it merged the Air Force Systems Command and the Air Force Logistics Command into the Air Force Materiel Command[65] and combined the tankers and airlifters into the Air Mobility Command. Most of that was done in the name of consolidation and economy.

The reorganization associated with the withdrawal from a forward-deployed concept was undertaken a little later. The combination of the drawdown, the increased requirement for temporary duty arising from United States basing without diminished overseas commitments, and the exodus of pilots to the airlines greatly stressed the remaining crew force. One reaction to this was to reorganize the entire operational part of the service into ten Air Expeditionary Forces (AEF). These forces would go through workup periods of training and then be liable for overseas temporary deployments on a regular schedule. The scheme was very similar to the way that the aircraft carrier wings had long been cycled through various phases and then sent on deployments on a scheduled basis. Two of the ten AEFs would be vulnerable for routine deployments at any given time. However, in emergencies the United States could call upon those not in the vulnerable period for unscheduled deployments to meet crises. The AEFs were composed of a variety of air units including air-to-air fighters, air-to-ground attack airplanes, some of the AMC tankers, and even tactical airlifters. However, some of the less numerous, high-demand aircraft remained outside of the scheme. These included strategic airlifters, many tankers, Airborne Warning and Control System (AWACS) aircraft, Joint Surveillance and Target Attack Radar System (JSTARS) planes, and others.[66]

Thus, there were fairly substantial technological, doctrinal, and organizational changes after the collapse of the Soviet Union and the First Gulf War before the commencement of the air campaign against Serbia. One of the most impressive changes was the maturation of information technologies and new ideas about information warfare. One of the inhibitors of all that had long been the cultural mindset of the Air Force and all the other services toward the intelligence career field.

10

Intelligence, Technology, and Information Warfare

As noted throughout this study, information has always been a key factor in successful military campaigns. Both aviation and space assets also first demonstrated their unique capabilities in the area of information—reconnaissance and spotting. Intelligence and information are not clearly distinct. A recent scholar on the newly fashionable subject of information warfare makes a distinction between it and information in warfare, the distinction being largely that the former proposes to use information as a weapon in its own right whereas the latter is the rough equivalent of what has traditionally been seen as intelligence or information supporting the combat elements that do the damage.[1] As it is often described, information warfare would include collection of information, the denial of information to the enemy, the disruption of their capability to observe or understand information, the destruction or modification of their communication systems, and the disabling or spoofing of their computer systems. It would also include preventing the enemy from doing the same to our capabilities. The measures used could include intelligence, counterintelligence, physical attack on communications systems or command centers, electronic jamming, propaganda, psychological warfare, decryption, and deception.[2]

Even more recently, the special field of cyberspace has been separated out, and is said to mean the use of the electromagnetic spectrum to further one's own interests and deny the same sort of utilities to one's enemies. David T. Fahrenkrug likens his view of cyberspace to Albert Thayer Mahan's concepts on command of the sea, and that of Giulio Douhet on command of the air. There are two principal functions involved. First, is to command the domain, and second it is to exploit it to achieve one's own ends and denying the enemy theirs. The biggest difference is that the sea, air, and space domains are there—givens—whereas cyberspace is completely man-made. At this writing, the USAF is in the process of setting up a specialized command to achieve dominance of cyberspace to be prepared to supply trained and equipped forces to the COCOMs to fulfill those functions.[3]

INTELLIGENCE, TECHNOLOGY, AND AIRPOWER: INFORMATION WARFARE

A part of the reason that the Union won the Civil War was that it had an information advantage: superior resources for developing telegraph lines.[4] It had always been so. Napoleon went to great lengths earlier in that century to develop semaphore systems for the rapid transmission of information.[5] We have seen previously that a large part of the reason for the U.S. victory in the Battle of Midway was the ability to break the Japanese codes.[6] Perhaps the case could be made that if only because of its faster pace, information is even more important in air warfare than it is in all other forms of combat. Many have argued that a large part of the reason for the British victory in the Battle of Britain was their early development of radar for the rapid, almost instantaneous gathering of the facts of battle. But there is more to intelligence than the mere gathering of facts.

THE INTELLIGENCE PROCESS

In naval warfare, the gathering of facts had long been done by lighter ships called frigates in Nelson's day, and cruisers later in the nineteenth century. In land warfare, that had been a function of the cavalry. Both retained that function for a short while after the dawn of aviation because there is more to intelligence than gathering data. First, the collection agencies must have direction as to what data is needed. The gathered information must be transmitted to analysts, processed and transformed into usable intelligence, and then distributed to those who need to know among the combat forces. All this must be done in time to be useful to the combatant commanders, and they must be able to trust the sources of information.[7] At first, it was readily apparent that aircraft could range widely, see more, and travel much faster than either cruisers or cavalry. However, in the case of the cruisers at least, they were capable of carrying heavier payloads—radios that in the early days were large, heavy, and not very reliable. By the time of the Second World War, radios were made much more reliable and small enough to carry aboard much more robust aircraft and that was one of the reasons for the demise of the horse cavalry and the reduction of the utility of cruisers. To the rapid flight had been added practically instantaneous communication (now called real-time information) and atop that, airborne radar .. frared systems were developed to assist in overcoming the limitations of darkness and weather. Much later, space satellites and UAVs were added to the mix to again reduce the gathering and transmission problems. But still, a complete knowledge is never available, and the final act in making decisions is a guess because of that. The next step is to then collate the scraps of information one does have into a meaningful pattern and fill in the blanks with assumptions.

INTELLIGENCE PERSONNEL

How can we identify or develop people who are good at gathering and interpreting the facts? I believe that there has long been something in our military culture, and perhaps even our national culture, that operated against easily getting really suitable candidates into the intelligence field—and perhaps even later into information operations or space.[8] Promotions therein were deemed poor. Many know that Admiral Raymond Spruance was the leader at the Battle of Midway. The name of the pilot who was shot down and was the only survivor of Torpedo Squadron 8, Ensign George Gay, is well remembered;[9] but who can recollect the name of the man who broke the Japanese code? Most military cultures have identified only those whose specialty carried them directly into combat—preferably in an offensive role—as worthy of admiration, command, and advancement. Further, many have looked upon physical labor or activity as more manly than intellectual pursuits. According to Alexander Orlov, in the Soviet context, "it takes a man to do the creative and highly dangerous work of underground intelligence on foreign soil; as to the digging up of research data in the safety of the home office or library, this can be left to women or young lieutenants who have just begun their intelligence careers . . . " A slightly different perspective from a different culture and a different age, but his attitude would resonate with many American military people of the day.[10]

By now, that is changing, and has been changing since World War II. We recognized then that the British were far ahead of us in that regard, and perhaps even that the USN had a leg up on the US Army and US Army Air Forces there.[11] General Carl Spaatz in Europe wrote back to General Arnold toward the end of the World War II that special efforts should be made to develop a cadre of regular officers who would devote their careers to intelligence. Much has been made of our intelligence failures during the war and, since 1974 of the great success of ULTRA, and that has done much to increase the respectability of the intelligence career fields.

Of course, there should be a variety of educations involved. But I think that many should be folks educated in the humanities and the social sciences with aspirations toward generalist knowledge rather than specialization. Essentially, the process of interpretation is one of first analysis and then synthesis to produce a usable product; that requires both specialists and generalists. Some of the latter would be history, political science, international relations, and public policy majors. Certainly, the intelligence structure should contain specialist folks who understand science, technology, and quantification. Whenever junior people can be seasoned in operational outfits or at least in units with numerous other intelligence people, that would be desirable. Also, were it possible to establish criteria that would help identify young people with especially inquisitive minds, that would also be handy. Necessarily, the outstanding intelligence officer ought not be a careerist nor one who has difficulty standing up against the conventional wisdom, especially that of senior officers.

INTELLIGENCE AND CULTURE

Often one reads that authoritarian societies have a built-in advantage over democracies in the intelligence field. I suppose that authoritarian regimes would indeed have some edge in directing the collection of intelligence early and of a wider nature because of a built-in paranoia; in the collection process because of a greater ruthlessness and secrecy being possible in such contexts; in interpretation because of an ability to devote greater resources to the art without public accountability; and in dissemination again because of a greater ability to transmit information in secret.[12] In the case of pluralist societies, there might be advantages in direction because of more numerous inputs from a wider variety of people being less likely to overlook an important requirement; in the collection process because of greater freedom of travel, a more numerous media personnel, a lesser tendency to kill the bearer of bad tidings, and more initiative among potential collectors (perhaps also the pluralist societies might find it more feasible to find traitors within the societies of their authoritarian opponents); in the greater variety of viewpoints, a lesser requirement to adhere to the company line, a generally more questioning attitude, and a greater access to a variety of sources to found the passive collection and interpretation of information; and in the dissemination because of a lesser requirement for security, a lesser need to hoard information as a source of domestic power and, perhaps, greater trust among participants.[13]

Alternatively, one encounters notions that it is a cultural question: in societies where the male or the father is dominant, thought is so controlled as to inhibit imagination and the flow of information. Among them might be the Arab and Asian cultures. One needs to be wary of a cultural or national conceit here.[14] The Russian experience with democracy is very shallow, and perhaps the feeling here that the Russian family or society has traditionally been more dominated by the fathers and the males than ours is not altogether sound. Yet those are widely held perceptions, and maybe there is some fire in that smoke. Insofar as it is valid, dissent would then be less tolerable than it is in the West, and thus adherence to the party line more important in Russia than it is among the older democracies. Also, the violent history of Russia and the many times she has been invaded may have increased those tendencies at the same time more attention was being paid to domestic and foreign intelligence.[15] Of course, it has been said often that paranoia is not altogether irrational in that type of society, and that may actually help with keeping an eye on things.

As for the Asian cultures, a common perception among nonspecialists is that they, too, tend to be dominated by the fathers and the males, and ancestor worship is common there. Supposedly, this leads to a highly conservative approach to life, to conformity, and to a lack of inquiry. Also, the history of the Middle Kingdom in China was a long time wearing out, and that attitude of superiority over other cultures might have been an inhibitor of good intelligence direction and collection, as well as interpretation.[16] The West has not had it all its own way in science, technology, and the industrial revolution. Many of our scientific advances were suggested to us long ago by the Chinese, and the learning of the ancients in Greece and Rome was preserved in the Arab cultures during the Dark Ages and then reborn by importing the knowledge—much of it scientific—from them.

But by now, one of the major effects of the growth of Islam since the time of Mohammed has been the founding of an exceedingly conservative and authoritarian culture.[17] At the same time, the Medieval culture of the West waned and the Renaissance and Enlightenment followed, leading to what we have thought is a more rational approach to life. Thus, it may not be too much of a stretch to assert that the West, on the average, does have an advantage in the long-term, although others can beat us frequently in certain instances—such as the Russian acquisition of the knowledge they needed for the development of a nuclear capability in record time through espionage.[18] Perhaps it would not be too much to speculate that the stark results of the Second Gulf War constitute evidence of this point. Compared to the fight in the Vietnamese culture, the performance of the Islamic/Arab culture in Iraq has been dismal. At least in part, this was probably a result of the authoritarian culture in which the virtual worship of the dictator was permitted.

INTELLIGENCE AND POLITICS

The field of intelligence has changed greatly since the onset of modern times. It has become more important and better organized because of the appearance of the nation-state in the three centuries before Napoleon. The end of the old regime as a result of the French Revolution and others further expanded the role of intelligence to cover all elements of society and all parts of Europe. The combination of the political and military leadership in one person under Frederick the Great and then Napoleon in their respective countries led to further sophistication and better coordination among political, diplomatic, and military intelligence. As we noted, there was a relatively minor speeding up of collection and dissemination of intelligence through the semaphore system developed by the French, and also by the beginnings of the rise of literacy because of the French Revolution and the concept of citizenship.

INTELLIGENCE AND ECONOMICS

The Industrial Revolution added a major element to that which had already been achieved in the political realm with the French Revolution. Not only was everybody in France supposedly deemed a citizen with a real stake in the health of the nation-state, but also the Industrial Revolution added an enormous economic capability to the countries in the West. This ultimately enabled the use of the will of the citizens to create huge and more efficient military and government structures capable of waging conflict on a much grander scale than theretofore—a phenomenon that continued through the whole century. All that increased the importance and the attention paid to intelligence.

Also during the course of the century, the populations of the Western countries increased enormously, and the means of travel also increased greatly. There were huge migrations during the nineteenth century induced by the need of those populations to find more room to make a living and enabled by these new means of travel. All that movement increased the possibility of gathering information and even planted potential traitors in many different places. By the end of the century, the invention of the telegraph and the laying of transatlantic and transpacific cables, as well as transcontinental telegraph wires everywhere, greatly increased the speed of transmission and the importance of timeliness in intelligence gathering. Horatio Nelson almost missed his chance for glory because of the difficulty and slow pace of gathering information on the movements of the French fleet. All through the century, nationalism was increasing and the railroads came along to further facilitate the capabilities of governments to get truly massive forces into battle in a shorter period of time than ever before. The existence of the multinational, multilingual empires in Austria-Hungary and Russia further enhanced the potential for intelligence collection. Many of the military formations of the former were officered by folks who could not speak the same language as their troops.

A precursor of what was to come was seen in the Crimean and American Civil Wars. The telegraph first had its major influence in speeding up things on the strategic level—and signals intelligence (SIGINT) first became prominent. Aerial reconnaissance and spotting was also tried (Napoleon made a stab at it in Egypt in the previous century) although its impact, even at the tactical level, was limited. When the heavier-than-air-craft came on a century later, it was first used in the same function as balloons, albeit with greater success. In one way, aircraft were a step backward because the transmission of information from balloons was possible by telephone lines. But as we have seen, aircraft were not equipped with practical radios for some years after the first flight. (Ira Eaker remarked that there was no radio aboard the Question Mark flight in 1929 because they deemed it too heavy; rather the messages were received by writing in chalk on the sides of the tanker aircraft.)[19] Through most of World War I, the tactical intelligence was disseminated by dropping messages attached to streamers or by landing at the headquarters or the battery site to deliver the messages orally.

By 1914, literacy in the West was nearly universal and printing was far advanced, as was the manufacture or cheap paper. Thus, the media expanded exponentially from where it had been when Robert E. Lee was reading the *Philadelphia Inquirer* during the Civil War. This greatly enhanced the role of overt or passive collection, and much was gained by that. But there was a downside because that also expanded the possibilities of the role of propaganda and misinformation. During World War I, the sinking of the *Lusitania* and the famous Zimmerman telegram sent to the Mexicans by the Germans suggesting an alliance that might recover the Alamo for the latter were spread all over the papers and had important effects on public opinion. The *Lusitania* was indeed carrying arms and was a British, not an American, ship. The telegram was intercepted by the British, and they made sure that it was revealed to the Americans and made public.[20]

INTELLIGENCE, PROBABILITIES, AND PRECONCEPTIONS

It is trite to say that surprise was still common at the time of World War II—one case in point being Stalin and Barbarossa. As always, it is impossible to be sure about what goes on in another person's head, never mind a communist from another age and another culture, and one with good reason to be paranoid and secretive. But the presumption here would be that they, like all of us, were prone to accept intelligence that fit their preconceptions. They were brought up on a steady diet of Marxism/Leninism that preached a stout theme that all capitalists are evil and must be eliminated. That had to be done before one could reach the socialist utopia, and it had to be done throughout the world. And the archetype of evil capitalist was, by far, Great Britain, with the United States being a distant second. So when the warning of Barbarossa came to them from Great Britain and the United States, the suspicion is that they decided it was misinformation generated by the evil capitalist. They had plenty of previous experience to suggest that and, to be frank, many in the United Kingdom and the United States would have been perfectly happy to stand aside and allow the two totalitarian dictatorships kill off each other.[21]

Possibly, Stalin was also thinking in terms of probabilities. Hitler made a very large point that the Kaiser had failed because he permitted the First World War to be a two-front war that Germany could not win. Hitler was explicit about that in his book, *Mein Kampf*, and asserted therein that mistake must not be repeated. As we have seen, the Germans did not win the Battle of Britain, and maybe Stalin was thinking that Hitler would indeed probably adhere to his own prescription and avoid battle with the USSR until the British were beaten, or at least had made peace.

Perhaps it would not be too much to fashion an axiom out of that. The aggressor can think in terms of a special time and place and contemplate improbable acts of attack. However, the defender must think of all the possibilities, and generally will choose to prepare for the most probable attack—and thus surprise is not surprising.

That axiom cannot have been that esoteric in 1941, after Barbarossa. How could we have been so surprised by the attack on Pearl Harbor when Billy Mitchell predicted it in writing in the 1920s, even predicting that it would happen on a Sunday morning? There is more writing on this subject than any of us will ever be able to read.[22] One of the problems is that you can find an equal or greater number of predictions of many other potential disasters. It was difficult to tell from the diplomatic traffic which was which but afterwards, in the knowledge of what actually happened, it was much easier. There were countless assertions that the US Navy would be crippled by a surprise attack on the Panama Canal. Perhaps more of the Pacific Fleet's interwar exercises included an attack by the Red Fleet on the Canal than on Pearl Harbor—although both were practiced in maneuvers. Attacks on the Philippines were seen as much more likely than either of those. But maybe even more doubted that the Japanese would take on the United States when they could just as easily stay away from all of those and make huge gains against Thailand, and especially the East Indies, that had the oil that we were denying them. Alternatively, there were huge resources on the Asian mainland that would have greatly helped the Japanese (although not with the oil problem) but Russia was standing in the way—as she had for 50 years, at least. Now with the *Wehrmacht* rattling the gates of Moscow, what better chance would ever come for evening the score with the Russians?[23] In any case, the Japanese already made a pact with the Germans and were formally a part of the Rome-Berlin-Tokyo Axis. Why not be a loyal member of the pact and join in the assault on the Soviets, especially when there seemed to be little danger in doing so? (The Soviets simply did not have much of a battle fleet even if they had been free to use it.)

Besides, why would you take on the two greatest fleets in existence backed by populations many times greater than your own? As we have seen, even Yamamoto himself was against taking on the United States, and he spent a good deal of time in this country and knew us well. He argued that Japan could not win against those odds, but Japanese nationalism was running wild and they made such huge profits from joining the correct side in World War I that they wanted to repeat that pleasant experience, so he was shoveling sand against the tide. He planned the Pearl Harbor attack but from the outset he saw it as a forlorn hope—that they would probably lose, but given that he was forced to go to war, an attack on the American fleet in its home base was deemed the least bad choice.

The point is that it is easy to suppose that the American strategists (who were up to their waists in alligators in any event) were thinking in the terms of probabilities, and that Yamamoto was right—the Pearl Harbor attack did not have high probabilities of long-term success (or arguably of short-term success, either). Being involved in a complex war in the Atlantic, plus serious political problems at home (the draft was renewed in August in the Senate by only one vote), Americans may have felt compelled to anticipate the probable rather than the improbable. Similarly, the notion that one could find 19 people sufficiently intelligent to evade detection, pilot four jets into major buildings in the United States, and willing to commit suicide is highly improbable to folks in the Western culture. It is no surprise that the September 11th attacks came as a complete surprise all the way around—notwithstanding that the World Trade Center had been attacked by more conventional means previously. One must plan for the probable; there are seldom if ever enough resources and time to plan for every improbable contingency.

For all of that, and in spite of Pearl Harbor and Barbarossa, General Dwight Eisenhower was surprised by the Ardennes Offensive of December 1944. Also, he knew about ULTRA and was getting information directly from German message traffic. How could such a surprise happen? He had intelligence about the relocation of German formations in front of the Ardennes. He made the assumption that these movements were of a defensive nature, as they had been almost constantly since the thrust towards Mortain just after the Saint-Lô Breakout six months earlier. The feeling was very strong that fall that no nation, not even Germany, could long stand up under that type of pounding from all directions.[24] Its cities were being burned down and its troops were being killed by the tens of thousands. Folks were going hungry everywhere. The submarine campaign was long in the past and had been a dismal failure. They were running out of gasoline and coal and we knew it (rather, they had the coal but they could not move it to where it was needed). We had been consistently reading their mail through ULTRA.

But it probably was easy to forget that driving them back on their own lines of communications meant less use of radio and the increasing use of land lines (which were not vulnerable to ULTRA). Also, we might have become complacent about the careless operations security of the German forces and were counting too heavily on it. Thus, the psychology of the thing might well have made Eisenhower think that the chances of the *Wehrmacht* undertaking a major offensive were highly improbable. Why would the Germans put the last viable formations into a huge salient, vulnerable to being pinched off and destroyed? Why would they not retire behind the

Rhine, where they could fight a defensive battle for a much longer time than would be possible in the west on the offensive in an exposed position, running out of gasoline? Is surprise surprising? No.

INTELLIGENCE AND AIR FORCES?

Are there differences in intelligence for war in the air as compared with surface conflict? I suppose that there is a shorter fuse on it, and maybe in general it is more concerned with a wider variety of factors than is land war. For example, economic factors are generally of much more immediate concern to airmen than they are to soldiers.[25] Also, their field of regard tends to be wider than that of the Army and Marines, at least in the immediate sense. Can we say that the airmen are more concerned with the macro view of strategy and intelligence, whereas the soldiers are more into the micro view? Terrain and topography are even more important to soldiers than airmen.

It is clear then that information has been vital in warfare since the beginning of time, and we shall return to the subject in our last chapter. In the next chapter, information will be one of many subjects touched upon in an examination of the Second Gulf War and air combat at the dawn of a new century.

11

The Second Gulf War: Air and Space Combat at the Dawn of a New Century

ALLIED FORCE/WAR IN AFGHANISTAN/SECOND GULF WAR

Allied Force was the code name for NATO's operation against Slobodan Milosevic's Serbia that commenced in late March 1999, and was completed in early June that same year. The initial reaction to the terrorist attack on the United States in September 2001 was an immediate invasion of Afghanistan (Operation Enduring Freedom) that quickly brought down the Taliban government there and diminished the support for Al Qaeda. The Second Gulf War, known as Operation Iraqi Freedom, began in March 2003.

THE GENESIS OF THE CONFLICT WITH SERBIA

The Balkan Peninsula is a crossroads where many religions and civilizations meet and have often clashed. Among these are the long conflicts among Orthodox Catholicism, Roman Catholicism, and Islam. Also, Western Europeans, Slavic peoples, Greek civilization, and the Ottoman Turks have bounced off one another for time immemorial. Serbia itself was the scene of the opening act of World War I, one of the worst in human history. The iron hand of Josip Broz Tito imposed a modicum of peace and order from the end of World War II to his death in 1980. That, and the disappearance of the stabilizing effect of the Cold War, led to a reemergence of the tribal conflicts of the region. Europe seemed impotent to do much for itself in restoring order, and the killing and mayhem seemed likely to go on forever, and perhaps even to spread southward toward the NATO Allies of Greece and Turkey. Also, the ethnic cleansing of the Albanians in Serbia's Kosovo province was perceived as so inhumane that it demanded intervention within her sovereign territory—quite in violation of traditional international law and at variance with the NATO Treaty.[1]

THE DEPLOYMENT

Serbia is just across the Adriatic from one of the major NATO Allies, Italy. The United States and the rest of NATO were involved in adjacent areas for many months, even to the point of conducting combat and airlift operations in Bosnia and bringing about the Dayton Accords for that problem.[2] Thus, NATO already had some bases and a command structure in the region that could be used. Some air forces were already present, including about 300 aircraft. Others were nearby in the other NATO countries, and the prospective battle area was accessible to aircraft carriers and Tomahawk cruise missile-carrying vessels. Serbia had a standing army and a substantial air defense system that was well-trained, although its equipment was somewhat dated. The leaders of that system received some instruction from the Iraqis, who had recently suffered under a Western air onslaught.

There has been much criticism in the media about the strategy for the campaign against Serbia. At the beginning, the NATO political leaders—including President Bill Clinton—proclaimed that there would be no ground campaign,[3] perhaps because of an overestimate of what airpower had done to bring about the Dayton Peace accords. Much of the criticism has had to do with that announcement because it relieved the planners in Serbia of one concern and enabled them to concentrate on their defenses against the air attack. Some of the criticism has asserted that it represented a hesitant approach and a resurrection of the infamous gradualist strategy of Rolling Thunder, this after the vigorous attack on Iraq seemed to be the opposite and to portend better things to come.[4] Compared to Iraq, the initial attacks were tepid, a minor fraction of the attack sorties used in Desert Storm. Both campaigns started with an assault on the air defenses and the command and control system of the enemy, but that of Allied Force was much lighter. In the Iraqi case, the abundance of aircraft and the vigor of the campaign permitted a practically simultaneous air superiority operation, a strategic air attack in Iraq, and a tactical attack for the "preparation of the battlefield."

The hesitant attack on Serbia did not resemble that at all. After the initial attacks on the air defense system, General Wesley Clark directed the onslaught against the deployed Serbian ground forces in Kosovo. That went on for a time with little visible result. After the NATO Fiftieth Anniversary meeting in Washington in April, Clark was able to win the clearance to attack an increasing number and variety of targets in Belgrade and Serbia proper as well as authorization for the deployment of additional air forces.

General Clark and many pundits and scholars have defended this approach.[5] They have often argued that Milosevic's one best hope was to divide the Alliance, bringing about its paralysis. Thus, the only way to overcome Milosevic was to persuade him that bringing about Alliance disunity was a forlorn hope. To do this, Clark and others have argued that it was essential to allow all 19 allies to have a voice in target selection—all the way down to the point of recalling aircraft already launched against targets. This line of reasoning holds that it was the appearance of Alliance unity and resolve, above all other factors, that would have the greatest impact on the Serbian President's decision to give way.

THE COURSE OF THE BATTLE

The assault on the Serbian IADS did not destroy it to the degree that had been the case in Iraq. In part, that was due to a different strategy on the part of the Serbs. They held their fire in large degree. They only launched enough SAMs and fired enough AAA to demonstrate that they had an air defense system-in-being, one that could still threaten NATO aircraft throughout the campaign. That was one of the reasons that the attacking fighters were often limited to a minimum altitude of about 15,000 feet. That reduced the accuracy of the NATO attack to some degree but the effect was not as serious as it might have been before the age of precision-guided munitions. It did make the visual identification of targets more difficult. The enemy defense system shot down only two aircraft out of tens of thousands of opportunities (both pilots were rescued) but even keeping them at higher altitudes was a beneficial effect from the Serbian point of view.[6]

The air attack on the fielded forces in Kosovo certainly did not result in the rapid collapse of Serbia. The NATO figures released on the destruction of enemy vehicles were apparently inflated, but no one had much doubt that Milosevic's army was withdrawn in fairly good order and with the greater part of its combat capability intact.[7] The results were certainly not as good as they had been against Iraq, and some of the reasons for this include the different environment, wherein targets are more easily hidden, a better Serbian deception operation with camouflage and decoys, and the higher altitude. All of these impeded target acquisition, and some caused the waste of guided bombs. Little noted among the critics was the fact that in dispersing their combat vehicles and hiding them in haystacks and barns, the Serbians gave up their mass and mobility—and an immobile tank is no longer a tank. In effect, the Alliance at least got the half loaf of achieving a number of mobility kills by merely posing a real threat. Of course, the Serbian Army did not really need tanks to complete its ethnic cleansing mission. Small light infantry and police were enough to do that, and at the same time they did not provide much of a target for air attack.[8]

After the April 1999 NATO Anniversary meeting, General Clark was enabled to escalate the tempo of the campaign and increasingly to attack targets inside Serbia itself. Great damage was done to "strategic" targets like electrical power systems, petroleum refineries, bridges, armament factories, and even the homes and business facilities of Milosevic, his family, and his cronies. Much ink has been spilled as to whether this part of the campaign caused the Serbian President to throw in the towel, but the debate has been sterile because it is impossible to penetrate his mind.[9] Nor do we have access to the Serbian archives or to interviews with enemy leaders, as was the case after World War II.

THE OUTCOME

As noted previously, there have been various interpretations of the outcome and the factors causing Milosevic's capitulation, even those asserting that it really was not a capitulation. But even the unconditional surrender of Germany and Japan in World War II did not bring agreement on the outcome or its causes down to this day. Thus, one's own conclusions almost inevitably must be based on an intuitive judgment. When faced with this type of a decision, most people will opt for straddling the fence—it was a partial victory or a partial defeat, and it was caused by some combination of many factors.[10] Thus, the arguments still are heard on why the Union appears to have won the Civil War, and true believers on all sides are not much persuaded to change their minds as a result of either the Gulf War or Kosovo. But the Serbians did withdraw from Kosovo, albeit in good shape. No NATO personnel were killed in combat. Tens of thousands of Kosovar Albanians have indeed returned to their homes. Single causes are almost never a complete explanation of complex outcomes like this, but the fact remains that there was no naval battle and there was no land battle—not a single shot was fired from a US Army weapon. Only naval air, surface vessels, submarines with their cruise missile weapons, and land-based airpower were engaged. Even if we cannot assert that the fear that there would be NATO boots on Serbian turf or the power of Russian diplomacy did not affect Milosevic's thought, perhaps we can be a little more confident in trying to identify some doctrinal implications for airpower.[11] Though the U.S. forces were much smaller than they had been a decade earlier, there was to be precious little rest for them. The weapons had hardly cooled when the World Trade Center towers came tumbling down, as did one wall of the Pentagon.

THE WAR IN AFGHANISTAN: OPERATION ENDURING FREEDOM

No American will forget September 11, 2001—the first real attack on the American homeland since the War of 1812.

ORIGINS OF THE WAR

Al Qaeda had committed acts of war against Americans long before September 2001. Two U.S. embassies in Africa suffered explosions, and the *USS Cole* was severely wounded in port in the Middle East. The response in the 1990s was limited cruise missile attacks against training camps in Afghanistan and against a target in the Sudan, with no real results. The 2001 attacks at New York and on the Pentagon caused about the same number of American deaths as did the Japanese assault on Pearl Harbor, 60 years earlier. This time, the result was the global War on Terror.

This provoked an immediate American reaction in the assault on Afghanistan to tumble the Taliban government and damage Al Qaeda. The combination of indigenous ground forces, American special forces, and naval and land-based airpower brought quick and dramatic results.[12] Notwithstanding the quick victory, the conflict had its bad hours. Operation Anaconda in March 2002 was in the end successful, but was more costly than seemed necessary. The Army had not deployed artillery, and the intelligence on the enemy was scanty. The battlefield command structure was an ad hoc organization. There was much recrimination in the aftermath with the Army folks raising the traditional complaint about close air support—insufficient and not on time. The Air Force rebuttal was that it had not been made privy to the planning for the battle on time and that the Army did not understand the doctrine for close air support.[13] Indeed, the Tenth Mountain Division deployed to Afghanistan without its organic tactical air control personnel.[14] Unhappily, the operation got off to a shaky start when an AC-130 caused some fratricide on friendly Afghanistan troops, and it was quickly found that there were far more enemies present than had been anticipated. In the end, the valley was cleared but there were more casualties than expected, and the bag of enemy casualties was disappointing. The controversy did contribute to some improvement in joint training and doctrine on the subject and was soon overshadowed by events.[15] Shortly after, in 2002 and early 2003 momentum built up for a resumed attack on the forces of Saddam Hussein.

THE SECOND GULF WAR, 2003

The rationale was that Saddam Hussein had not complied with the disarmament settlements after the First Gulf War and the associated U.N. resolutions. Further, it included a fear of suspected continuation of Iraqi efforts to acquire WMD. Finally, some argued that there was a hidden connection between Saddam Hussein and the Islamist terrorist movement, and that warring on him would be another part of the War on Terror. Thus, Operation Iraqi Freedom was launched in March 2003 with the objective of regime change.[16]

DEPLOYMENT

To some extent, a part of the force needed for the Second Gulf War was already in place. For years, air units had been conducting Operations Northern Watch and Southern Watch. Their object was to enforce no-fly zones over the northern and southern ends of Iraq in defense of the Kurds and the Shiites being persecuted by Saddam. The rules of engagement prohibited offensive action but did permit reaction to threats from the Iraqi IADS—to return fire if fired upon or if painted[17] by air defense radar. In the process, the Iraqi air defense system was seriously degraded over the years—in effect, command of the air was won before the war commenced.[18]

The Coalition for the Second Gulf War was not nearly as broadly based as the first. It did not have the support of the United Nations Security Council and there was little direct support from other Arab states. The principal ally was Great Britain. Major ground forces had to be brought back to the theater, although there were fewer than in the earlier case. Some grumbling was heard from retired Army folks that the forces were insufficient,[19] but in the event they proved more than adequate for the formal combat part of the struggle. General Tommy Franks was at the head of Central Command (CENTCOM) and was the overall leader of the campaign. The principal ground forces came from the US Army, the US Marine Corps, and the United Kingdom. The former were formed up on the left flank, the Marines on the right flank, and the British took charge of the assault on Basra in the south.

CONDUCT OF THE CAMPAIGN

During Desert Storm, the air campaign preceded the ground assault by many weeks. As we have seen throughout this study, the establishment of air superiority is almost always the first mission of air forces—and at Normandy and elsewhere, it has often been deemed a prerequisite for invasion. This time, in the formal sense the air and ground campaigns commenced practically simultaneously.[20] In reality, over the years Northern and Southern Watch had already established air superiority, and the Coalition ground forces never saw a single enemy aircraft overhead.[21]

The air forces did not conduct any "battlefield preparation" phase as they had before the ground combat in Desert Storm. Nonetheless, the march north on both flanks and on Basra proceeded with impressive speed and minimal casualties. Practically all of the sorties expending ordnance in support used their firepower on ground targets, sometimes ahead of the ground forces and sometimes in their direct support. By this time, the command and control system had been further improved over that of Desert Storm to the point where targets could be changed in the air with minimum notice. One famous case was an attempt to bomb Saddam himself in Baghdad with a

B-1. About 20 minutes after notification of the target, the airborne bomber released its weapons on the target, achieving direct hits. Unhappily, Saddam had just left the location but the new capability was impressive.

As the troops moved northwards, the advance was so rapid that it tended to outrun its supplies. Thus, a short halt was called midway into the campaign to give the logistics tail a chance to catch up. Also, the Tallil Airfield was captured, permitting the moving of close air support airplanes forward and enabling them to reduce the response time to ground requests for attacks. It also gave the C-130s and helicopters a place to land with supplies to help replenish the forces. Similarly, the Baghdad Airport was captured early on, and that made it possible to bring in C-130s with replenishment for the forces for the final charge into the capital.[22]

Along the way, a sandstorm rose up that lasted three days. The Iraqi ground forces seem to have taken that as an opportunity to move, as had the *Wehrmacht* in the Ardennes Offensive, free from the airpower threat. However, things had changed since the First Gulf War. By then, air supremacy was achieved allowing the forward flights of the JSTARS aircraft,[23] with its capability to see moving vehicles on the ground. A couple of JSTARS were available during the First Gulf War but the GPS/INS bombs had not. Now the JSTARS could locate the targets and give their coordinates to a wide variety of attacking aircraft that could then use their GPS weapons or their infrared sensors to strike at them through clouds or sandstorms. Using those assets, it appears that the Coalition achieved technological surprise upon the Iraqis moving under the cover of the storm and disabused them of any notion of offensive action.[24]

In three weeks time, US Army Abrams tanks were able to charge down the streets of Baghdad and the Iraqi regime collapsed. Saddam was not immediately captured but went into hiding. Unhappily, the aftermath was disappointing because of the disorganization, the loss of law and order in the capital, and the looting that followed. Airpower could not be much help in that.

UAVs AND PRECISION WEAPONS

As we have seen, in this conflict we were finally able to close the enemy's "last sanctuary" in bad weather—or so it seems. The JDAM and JSOW[25] and the like are wonderful additions to the arsenal, but enemies are innovative and often find new ways to hide. The use of churches, cultural monuments, or hostages comes to mind. Still, in this conflict about two thirds of the weapons employed were precision guided, and that made a more radical difference than in Desert Storm. The operational and logistical economies in that are enormous—and it is conducive to parallel attack operations as opposed to the traditional sequential, undertaking all parts of the air campaign at once rather than starting with an air superiority effort first and dealing with the rest later. In turn, this tends to bring about greater shock and confusion among the enemies. UAVs were present in greater numbers and used in a wider variety of ways with great effect, including lethal effect. By then, even the Predator could be controlled from a station in Nevada—the ultimate in standoff. However, UAVs in general were getting more expensive and thus less expendable than theretofore, and that diminished their advantage over manned aircraft somewhat. So far, their accident rates were higher than those of manned aircraft.[26] But along with space and the destruction visited upon Saddam's command and control system, the UAVs yielded a huge information advantage over the enemy.

OUTCOMES

The victory of the formal military campaign was an impressive one, but it was only a sample of one. Also, Iraq earlier was seriously weakened by her war with Iran and the First Gulf War, not to mention the international sanctions and the no-fly zones imposed on her afterwards. Still, the technological virtuosity of the Coalition was clearly a large step beyond that of Desert Storm. The command and control system was a huge advantage. As noted, the Coalition had a dramatic information edge over Saddam from the outset, and the ability to place weapons precisely on a target upon a notice of a few minutes at any time of day or night added to it. By the time of Iraqi Freedom, the cruise missiles were further improved with GPS mid-course guidance that radically eased the mission planning process.[27] During the Second Gulf War, the Iraqis made some crude attempts to jam GPS that were quickly put down. That gave some fodder for the advocates of space weaponization, albeit that in that instance the jamming was eliminated from within the atmosphere. The United States and the commercial world were becoming so dependent upon GPS in many ways that its unhindered operation became a vital interest. Thus, the argument in favor of a lethal space control capability was apparently strengthened.[28] The UAVs were much more numerous and capable, some even having an on-board lethal capability in their Hellfire missiles. The Second Gulf War was yet another demonstration that the United States and her Western allies were difficult to beat on the conventional battlefield, and that has led to much concern about asymmetric warfare.[29]

THE DOCTRINAL IMPLICATIONS FOR AIR AND SPACE POWER

The Kosovo experience yields no reason to doubt that air superiority and air supremacy are highly desirable for all operations. It also suggests that the conduct of such a campaign, even against a third-rate power, can be rather complex. Although the air-to-air portions of the Serbian integrated air defense system were dispensed with in short order, the ground-based defenses were not. In part, this was because they simply hid and refused battle. Although those ground defenses achieved only two aircraft kills (and no aircrew kills), it was clear enough that their mere continuing existence achieved some good for the Serbian side. Occasional fire while keeping the bulk of the system in hiding had the effect of keeping NATO airpower at medium altitudes rather than permitting it to roam at will at lower levels where it might have been even more effective. Perhaps that will lead to a doctrinal shift that will look upon the achievement of air superiority as more of a process of indefinite duration rather than an event that will occur near the beginning of the campaign. In this instance and many others, no evidence seems to emerge that would contradict the notion that air superiority campaigns are best waged under centralized control at the theater level.

If Kosovo demonstrated the continuing value of command of the air, the effect was even greater in the Afghanistan and Second Gulf War experiences. In both cases, the United States was able to use large, slow-moving offensive aircraft like AC-130s and B-52s with relative impunity—which allowed even more care in identifying and hitting targets with minimal collateral damage. Neither case involved any air-to-air threat, and the few losses incurred went down to surface fire. The F-15s and F-16s, with support from AWACS[30] and the elaborate command and control systems plus huge information advantages, seemed entirely adequate. Yet if the Israeli experience after 1967 is any guide, the United States probably should be on guard against any complacency with respect to either the air battle or the SEAD functions. Obviously, there are other areas of the world (like North Korea) where the air threat would be much greater than it has been in the last three experiences.

It seems pretty clear that the Serbian army withdrew from Kosovo in good order and without nearly the damage that was claimed by NATO in the heat of battle. That seemed to fit well with some of the preconceptions of the "boots on the turf" partisans, but in another way it created a dilemma for them. If the attack on the ground army did not have a role in Milosevic's decision, then what did? One alternative might be the strategic air attack on Serbia. That would not be comfortable for non-airmen, but the other alternative explanations are also worrisome. The threat of a possible invasion is often cited, but it is possible to make that kind of assertion about any human conflict—it is impossible to either prove it or disprove it, and it is likely to be taken as "whistling in the dark" by partisans who cannot stand another answer. Similarly, the Russian diplomacy explanation is too easy to see as "grasping at straws" to avoid an answer that is unpalatable.

One possible way around the dilemma is to conclude that neither tactical nor strategic bombing should get the credit. The decisive thing was that NATO was bombing at all, irrespective of the targets being aimed at or hit. That notion depends upon the assumption that Milosevic's great hope was to achieve dissension among the NATO allies. After the April NATO

Anniversary meeting in Washington, the escalation of the bombing was clear evidence that the unity of the Alliance could not be broken. Thus, the explanation goes, the Serbs got out before things could get even worse. Be that as it may, proponents and opponents of strategic bombing could find explanations either way, and that is the experience typical since 1917, at the latest.

Interdiction has always had an abstract appeal to airmen. The idea is that enemy formations can be found more concentrated, less well defended, and less capable of imposing disproportionate losses on air units behind the battlefield than on it. There can be more enemy kills per aircraft loss beyond the battle zone than on it. However, because there was no significant ground battle during the Kosovo campaign, it does not yield any evidence one way or another on tactical interdiction. The dropping of the bridges* across the Danube might have been described as strategic interdiction in other days, but because the campaign did not go on long enough for economic warfare to be much of a factor the experience yields little instruction. It has aroused a good deal of pain and complaint since the war.[31]

Likewise, neither the First Gulf War nor Kosovo yielded much instruction in the area of close air support. Notwithstanding the very low casualties in Desert Storm, plus the abundant "Push" support provided as well as the long preparation of the battlefield, the corps commanders in the First Gulf War complained long and loud about what they perceived as inadequate air support from the air forces. Close air support has long involved both a political and a emotional dimension and the rub still has not been eliminated, notwithstanding that both the Army and the Marine Corps have substantial air forces of their own—in the Marines' case including fixed-wing aircraft. The argument has traditionally been (and remains) between the airmen's preference for centralized control for the sake of massing at critical spots and the soldiers' desire for decentralization for the sake of immediate responsiveness. Lately, the trouble has increased because of technology. The new reach of new Army weapons has caused the corps commanders to extend the fire support coordination line forward to the point where it infringes greatly on what used to be Air Force turf.[32] In the case of the Second Gulf War, a good deal of close air support was supplied the ground forces. The campaign only lasted three weeks, and it appeared to be such a smashing victory that there was less cause for recrimination than in earlier cases. The new capability of JDAMs in bad weather was pleasing all the way around. Some of the fratricide came from the ground Patriot batteries against the air. Close air support from some of the helicopter forces was a dangerous business for the flyers, although it may be a different story in terrain with

* This would be so more because of the water traffic beneath them than the ground traffic across them. The Danube waterway has long been a vital link to the economy of the whole region, and good results were had by mining it in World War II.

more opportunities for concealment. The Army came away with continuing fondness for the USAF A-10 and its close air support weapons, as witnessed by the post-conflict furor when it was thought that the USAF was on the point of removing it from the inventory.[33]

SPACE

The maturation of space operations has complicated airpower doctrine in significant ways, and not just in the area of information warfare and intelligence. The conceptual framework for air superiority has relatively recently been expanded from just the air battle to one that has increasingly involved anti-aircraft fire, surface-to-air missiles, and radar both for surveillance and fire control. Huge investments have been made in airborne early warning and control systems, and now the potential exists to move that function to space platforms in part or perhaps whole. Also, if the airborne laser systems prove capable of destroying missiles instantly and from on high, why not aircraft—and why not move that function to space as well? There has been much speculation about the need to command space as well as the air.[34] Would that be a part of the same battle as the one for air superiority, or might it even supersede it in the way that air superiority seems to entail command of the sea as well?

The power of the history of airpower seems almost determinant here. The air platforms were first used as reconnaissance and spotting assets, but the demand soon came from below to add lethal aircraft to assure one's access to those things—and to deny the same advantages to the enemy. Many emerging space theorists assert that history repeats itself and space is beginning in the same way.[35] First it was used for weather and strategic reconnaissance; now the demand is rising to expand into a space warfare capability to assure our access to its advantages and to deny the same to potential enemies. Beyond that, some are arguing that sooner or later the United States will have to go beyond the mere controlling of space with lethal means but also develop a capability to strike from space at targets on the surface—force application.[36]

Perhaps the inhibitions to that are stronger than those working in the early days of airpower. President Dwight Eisenhower's Open Skies notion plus some of the arms control treaties are held to be reasons of law and policy that would prohibit the expansion of warfighting capability to space. Space has been militarized for many years, but so far lethal instruments have been little applied except for hesitant U.S., Soviet, and Chinese programs developing anti-satellite capabilities so far not deployed.[37] Some argue that weaponizing space will undermine the arms control regime that is said to have done so much in stabilizing the nuclear arms race and avoiding a bloody outcome to the Cold War. Other arguments hold that the United States holds an enormous advantage in conventional war power and also has an enormous lead in the nonlethal use of space. They continue that to deliberately change the game into lethal space warfare would move conflict into an arena where we do not have those enormous advantages—to deliberately level the playing field so that many actors would be much better able to compete than is the case now. Be that as it may, the experience of the 1990s does nothing to diminish the importance of intelligence, and the utility of space in that part of the work has only increased.[38] The experiences in Afghanistan and the Second Gulf War both seem only to confirm that. Air reconnaissance continues to have a role with the larger platforms like AWACS and JSTARS. But the role of manned tactical air reconnaissance seems destined to continue its decline in favor of the unmanned aerial vehicles like the Predator and the Global Hawk, which have accomplished so much of that work in Afghanistan and the second war against Iraq.

As we have noted previously, the complexity of the gathering of information and preventing the enemy from doing so has caused the Air Force to assert that a new domain has come into being on a par with land, sea, air, and space. The new arena is described as "cyberspace" and covers the entire electromagnetic spectrum. The aim is to achieve cyberspace superiority to enable the free use of the domain to the United States and to deny it to the enemy. That includes both defensive and offensive operations as well as measures to mislead enemies as well as to deny them access. The analog of cyberspace with the air and space domains is not perfect. In the air, the American tradition has certainly favored the offensive over the defensive forms of war. The ubiquity of cyberspace is so great that it might be conducive to defensive attitudes. In 2006, there were about 15 million personal computers in the Department of Defense inventory, many of which were connected to an Internet where billions of users around the world had access. In that domain, it may be difficult to identify potential attackers, and in any case the means for counterattacks against their infrastructure and information centers of gravity may not be available.[39]

AIR MOBILITY

The years since Iraq invaded Kuwait also did nothing to diminish the importance of one of the traditional backwaters of the USAF: air mobility.[40] On the contrary, the shift to an expeditionary posture for the Air Force and the Army's determined move to make itself light enough for movement to the battle zone by air both worked to increase the demand for lift and for air refueling. The result has been to increase somewhat the purchase of C-17s and increased pressure to further expand the fleet. Similarly, the continued relevance of tankers to both deployment and employment has led to Navy efforts to build up its organic air refueling capability, and to increased pressure to develop a new tanker to add to the aging KC-135/KC-10 fleet. All this seems to sustain the present organization with all the mobility forces within the USAF's Air Mobility Command and, in turn, that organization reports to the joint U.S. Transportation Command, which controls land, sea, and air transportation. Usually, one individual serves as the dual-hatted commander of both, and there seems to be little incentive to change that. The combat in Afghanistan and the Second Gulf War seem to suggest that the U.S. forces will retain their expeditionary character in the future, and consequently the role of the mobility airlift and tanker forces will only increase.

COUNTERINSURGENCY

The impressive victories in the various combats since Desert Storm lead to speculations that few would challenge the United States in conventional battle. Rather, they would be clever enough to revert to "asymmetric" means, usually in the form of insurgencies and guerrilla warfare. That revived some of the thinking about air war that had arisen in the Vietnam era, including the Nixon Doctrine that places like Vietnam would have to rely on their own ground forces with economic, technological, and training assistance from the United States. There was little planning for the postwar period in connection with Operation Iraqi Freedom, and the ground forces proved to be inadequate to maintain security. A result was an insurgency and a revival of counterinsurgency thinking in America. The conventional wisdom was that lethal airpower had severe limitations in a contest for the "hearts and minds" of the populations, in part because it was insufficiently discriminate. That thought was mitigated somewhat by the deployment of forward air controllers in Afghanistan with the indigenous forces to help reduce fratricide and collateral damage through a more positive control of targeting.

But still, as in Vietnam nonlethal airpower (including airlift) reduced the guerrilla potential for attacks on the lines of communication, especially in places like Afghanistan where the highway infrastructure was primitive in any case.[41] We have seen that during the Vietnam War, an agreement was made between the Army and the Air Force where the former would get out of the fixed-wing business and the role of the latter in helicopters would be drastically limited. As a consequence, the Air Force received all of the Army two-engine Caribous (C-7 in Air Force nomenclature) to go along with the many twin-engine C-123s it already had. The C-7s soldiered on in the Air Force Reserve Components for a time after the war, but neither they nor the C-123s were replaced when they reached the end of their service lives.

The surviving tactical airlifter is the C-130, continuously in production since 1956. The latest version is the "J-Model," and all are highly capable at the retail end of the line of communications to the battle area. But their short field capabilities are not as good as those of the C-7s and C-123s, and their cargo capacities or often much more than is really needed for small-unit operations in primitive areas. Moreover, few counterinsurgent nations have training, maintenance, and financial resources to support C-130 operations, so a replacement for the two-engine airlifters has long been needed. Helicopters are a help at the retail level but they are thought more vulnerable to the ground defenses because of their speed limitations, among other things, and their range is generally much shorter than that of fixed-wing transports. As always, the budget has been limited and the strategic airlift C-141 was wearing out at a rate that made the funding of the C-17 program (much bigger and more expensive than the C-130) an urgent priority.[42] Similarly, few counterinsurgent nations can afford sophisticated ground-attack aircraft and their supporting structures, so a simpler, cheaper aircraft is often thought necessary there as well. In the case of Southeast Asia in the 1960s, many T-28 trainers were modified into fighter-bombers and sent across the Pacific. Counterinsurgent states can seldom be persuaded to acquire an airplane that is not also in the U.S. inventory, so a suggestion here has been that the USAF T-6 trainer be modified to serve in an attack role and be provided through the Foreign Internal Defense Program to those countries in need.[43]

TECHNOLOGY

Nothing since the end of the First Gulf War seems to have deflected the technology vector. Information improvements have grown to the point where some are arguing that the "Fog of War" has been or is about to be lifted.[44] The coming of JDAMs and JSOW with their adverse weather capabilities have aroused great enthusiasm. Some have argued that this closes the enemy's last sanctuary—that of weather. The dust storms in Iraq seem to have halted practically all other lethal measures except JDAMs. Others have even suggested that they help diminish yet another sanctuary discovered by Saddam Hussein and Slobodan Milosevic, the humanitarian sanctuary. The huge weapons caches that were found in Iraqi schools demonstrate that is a continuing concern. Some help might come from the new, small INS/GPS weapons able to pick out military-relevant targets from among cultural and civilian surroundings with a minimum of collateral damage. The JDAMs have already been scaled down to the 500-pound bomb, and the design of a precision small-diameter bomb of about 250 pounds is complete and it is being deployed. Not only will that reduce collateral damage to cultural and humanitarian buildings but it will also increase the pace of the offensive to fulfill the goals of parallel attack. In turn, that may shorten future conflicts and reduce the killing and expense. And finally, space technology has grown so rapidly that all sorts of lesser powers, corporations, and even criminal elements may have access to it to use against us.

In Afghanistan and the Second Gulf War, the UAVs and the UCAVs appear to have had a substantial and growing role. Like many of the precision-guided munitions, they were becoming increasingly dependent upon space in several ways. The role of the UAVs has been a great supplement to the information coming from space and manned reconnaissance, and perhaps will remain necessary at the retail end of things for a long time to come. The damage done to the helicopter forces by the ground defenses in 2003 suggests a greater reliance on UAVs not only for information but also for the lethal application of force in high-threat environments. Since the beginning of airpower, one of its limitations has been in the realm of persistence. Its limited endurance has tended to focus its application on offensive functions. This has been diminished some by the coming of space surveillance, and the ability of uninhabited air vehicles to dwell over the battlefield at both low and high levels for long periods enhances the effect. Increasingly, the ability to do so with a lethal capability further helps. Insofar as this can be done in substitution for manned systems, there are potentially huge cost savings involved not only in the reduction in the cost of the airframes but also in terms of reduced training and maintenance expenses. Also, because of space communications and huge increases in bandwidth, the control of even the small Predator from the homeland has become practical, and thus the "footprint" in the overseas theater made smaller with huge benefits in logistical terms.

Implied in much of the writing on the space aspect of this is that a major reorganization could be just around the bend. Senator Bob Smith of New Hampshire has been in the vanguard of the movement that was unhappy with the Air Force stewardship of space. It threatened that if the airmen do not do better with it, and especially develop a space warfighting capability, then Congress must move to create a fourth service: the US Space Force. Official Air Force policy denies that, and holds that air and space are part of the same continuum, the vertical dimension of warfare. Air Force Space Command had been founded in 1982,[45] and a joint US Space Command in 1985.[46] The latter did not last long before many its functions were transferred to US Strategic Command and it was deactivated. However, the continuing debate is far from settled.[47]

A major message of this book has been that uncertainty is a certainty. That makes any prediction of the future a hazardous occupation. Nonetheless, our last chapter will deal with some possible futures while fully recognizing that nothing in it can be a firm prediction.

12

The Future of Air and Space War: Speculations

In this last chapter, we will try to synthesize some of the ideas that have been explored in the long search for precision attack and standoff. We will begin with speculations on the future of defense organization, continue with remarks on the various roles and missions of air and space power, deal with some ideas about the future of naval aviation, and try to estimate how the further development of UAVs and smart weapons may affect all of that. At the end, I will include a short list of recommended further readings on the topics covered in this book.

ORGANIZATION: THE FUTURE OF JOINTNESS

There were some successful joint operations of Union forces during the American Civil War along the rivers and the East Coast, but they were relatively minor. Substantial work was attempted in the Spanish-American War, but the landings in Cuba were a fiasco. Some attempts were made to work out technology and tactics in the next five decades, but those relating to command arrangements for joint operations were largely fruitless until after Pearl Harbor.[1]

According to Kevin Holzimmer, the operations under MacArthur in the southwest Pacific from 1943 on worked much better than they had in the Spanish-American War, but it was done by cooperation among the leaders of the various services rather than by formal command arrangements. He argues that the improvement was a result of a change in leadership styles in the Army and Navy that arose in turn from the education received at the Army and Navy War Colleges. The old style was based on the individual thinking of the various service commanders, whereas the new style promoted by the war colleges was more of a managerial method of decision making by conference. James Winnefeld and Dana Johnson made a somewhat similar argument about the command process with the "Cactus Air Force" in the South Pacific early in the war. In that campaign, there were flying units from the Army, Marines, and Navy commanded at different times by officers of all those services. Winnefeld and Johnson account for the good cooperation as due to the desperate circumstances of the time—either cooperate or die.[2]

The southwest Pacific and South Pacific campaigns might be special cases. At the theater level in the Pacific, it was more difficult. Admiral Chester Nimitz was in command at Pearl Harbor and ran the campaign across the central Pacific; General Douglas MacArthur was in Australia and planned and conducted the operations through New Guinea and up to the Philippines. Neither had any authority over the other, and the Joint Chiefs of Staff never did impose a unified plan over them.[3]

Things were different in the European theater, to be sure. There the coalition partner, Great Britain, was much more nearly equal to the United States than was Australia. Thus, not only were the problems among the services a major concern but also those among allies. A measure of cooperation was achieved through the work of the Combined Chiefs of Staff, and the personality of General Dwight Eisenhower was an important factor in getting the various sides to work together as well as they did. Both national concerns and egos complicated the work, and perhaps the worst part of the problem there was the unified control of airpower. It was a major issue between the soldiers and the airmen in the North African and Mediterranean Campaigns, and for a time between the Army Air Forces and the US Navy in the Battle of the Atlantic. Again, in the months before the invasion of France, the control of airpower issue was a major concern. This time, the soldiers and some airmen were on the side of making all airpower subordinate to battlefield commanders, whereas the British and American airmen advocating strategic bombing of Germany wanted to continue that campaign in addition to supporting the ground battle. Eisenhower made the decision in favor of the former group but did allow some deviation to the long-range bomber men during the summer of 1944, and then in September of that year control of the strategic air forces was returned to the Combined Chiefs of Staff.[4]

Attempts were made just after World War II to build in more unity of command through the foundation of the office of the Secretary of Defense in 1947, but at first that authority was very limited (coordination, not command), and the Secretary was permitted only a limited staff.[5] That was gradually modified at irregular intervals until, as we have seen, the Goldwater-Nichols Act of 1986 greatly increased the Secretary's authority and that of the regional unified commanders. Meanwhile, a third service was added to the mix when the US Air Force was created in 1947.

Things were no better in Korea. Again, the major bone of contention was the unified control of airpower. The "unification" legislation of 1947 left several air forces in existence: the USAF, naval air, Marine air, and even the Coast Guard. The Air Force was only months old when the Korean War started, and many of its most experienced people from World War II had left the service. Strategic bombing was the main justification for its creation, but the heavyweights of the Air Force were always for a balanced air force to include tactical airpower as well as transport and aerial delivery forces. However, the huge national debt run up during World War II was the major concern for the political leadership. Therefore, it decided that there must be a major drawdown among the services, especially those dedicated to conventional warfare, because many thought that the nuclear forces would be able to maintain security at a much lower cost. Thus, it happened that when the cuts were imposed, the fighters, light bombers, tactical airlift, and reconnaissance forces took the most severe punishment. They were just the forces that would be most needed in Korea.

Attempts were made to unify the command and control of airpower in Korea but without much result. In theory, MacArthur's headquarters was a joint organization but the soldiers dominated the decision process. The traditional rub, that between the Army preference of close air support and the airmen's usual desire to put a major effort into interdiction campaigns, again raised its head. The admirals argued that the carrier task forces had to retain their independence because their strongest suit was their mobility to reach trouble spots elsewhere. The Strategic Air Command had the mission of deterring the USSR, and thus would not send its best units to Korea and was reluctant to yield even temporary control over any of them.[6] The same set of problems persisted throughout the Vietnam War. The Strategic Air Command bombers were temporarily put under the control of General Westmoreland, the tactical air campaign was also controlled by him through the Seventh Air Force Commander, and the bombing campaign up in North Vietnam was controlled by Pacific Command Headquarters.[7]

As we have seen, all this led to the Goldwater-Nichols Act of 1986. In general, many have claimed that the command and control problem was overcome by the time of the First Gulf War of 1991.[8] But what of the future? The great successes of the military campaigns since Goldwater-Nichols probably means that there is not a huge pressure to go further rapidly, at least so far as organization is concerned. For the most part, the services have settled into their train and equip roles, and the regional commanders into the work of planning and conducting campaigns. Some argue that the recent conflicts suggest that the Department of Defense is working in a sufficiently unified way but that the interagency process is not. On the surface, the addition of a fourth military service for space might look like a retrogressive step, but the Secretary of Defense and the Chairman of the Joint Chiefs are both much more powerful than they were in 1947. They might be able to impose a measure of unity even with a fourth service, but they cannot control the interagency process. The case in point is the efficiency with which the combat campaign in Operation Iraqi Freedom was conducted and the disappointments in building a stable peace in the aftermath. There are some media people who wonder if the regional commanders have not become too powerful and, in effect, taken over a part of the function of the Department of State and its ambassadors. Other commentators are more concerned with the problems in interagency cooperation arising in part from the fact that the geographical commanders have a much wider jurisdiction, whereas ambassadors, Agency for International Development people, and CIA agents are usually accredited to only one country.[9]

AIR, SPACE, AND CYBERSPACE SUPERIORITY

The one idea most constant in air theory and doctrine since the days of the First World War is that air superiority is essential. Giulio Douhet thought that would be best achieved by attack of the enemy air forces on their ground—at their airfields and in their aircraft factories. Billy Mitchell thought it would best achieved by air combat between competing pursuit (fighter) forces, or by some combination of air battle and ground attack. In World War II, perhaps because of the original impracticality of escort fighters, the hope was that it could be achieved by bombers attacking in the style of Douhet. In the end, the judgment was that air superiority was achieved over the Germans through a combination of air battle, attack on the *Luftwaffe* on the ground, and the attack on its fuel sources at the synthetic oil plants. During the last year or so of the war, the heaviest Allied losses went down to German surface-based air defenses.

During the Korean War, although the air battle between the F-86s and the MiG-15s got all the publicity, air superiority over by far the greater part of the Peninsula was achieved in part by the B-29 attack on enemy airfields being built close to the front. In part, it was also possible because of the Soviet policy of restricting its air forces to the immediate region of the Yalu River, perhaps because of the nuclear threat resident in the stateside B-50s and B-36s. The USSR also declined to assist the North Koreans in building airfields close enough to the ground fighting to contest air superiority there. Still, the general picture we came away with was that the loss ratio was very much in our favor, and that air superiority depended mostly on air combat.

In Vietnam, the loss ratios were not nearly so favorable as they had been in Korea. They were only a little in our favor, but again most of the publicity and subsequent research and reform were given to the air combat. Less noticed was that the vast majority of our losses even in the north were to the ground-based defenses. One result of all that is that the Bomber Barons have largely disappeared now, and the fighter pilots now own the air force. Another is that the latter are absolutely determined to spend a huge chunk of the national substance in developing and fielding a huge number of the greatest fighters of all time: the F-22 Raptors. Yet there is an undercurrent in political circles, and even in the Air Force itself, that wonders whether the days of the manned fighter are numbered. The USAF has been consistent in asserting that it has needed close to 400 of the new fighters, but it was denied by the Department of Defense under Secretary Rumsfeld that has limited the buy to 183. Now that he has left office, it nonetheless appears that the airmen's goal will never be reached.[10] In December 2007, Admiral Michael Mullen, Chairman of the Joint Chiefs of Staff, publicly expressed concern about recent crashes of the Air Force's primary air-to-air fighter, the F-15C, which have been attributed to system fatigue. He supported the Air Force need not only for new air superiority fighters but additional airlifters and tankers as well.[11]

The reasons the requiem for the manned fighter is predicted are many. One is the notion that the function of air-to-air combat may in the future be assumed by UAVs. Another is that the new double-digit missiles[12] developed in Russia will make the world too unsafe for manned aircraft. Yet another is that the passive defenses may become so effective that air attack itself will become unproductive. Still another is that enemies will move the battle to other arenas, such as biological attack on the North American homeland. Still another might be the development of a lethal capability in the space forces, or the coming of directed energy weapons that will yield a kill for every shot and will do it at the speed of light. Finally, the manned fighter might just price itself out of the market and the U.S. taxpayers will revolt against it. Richard Szfranski is not alone in these horrifying thoughts, and he concludes that the bringing of a manned fighter into battle might be tantamount to going to the gunfight armed with a knife.[13]

Are the critics right? I know that the air-to-air gun received a premature requiem in the 1950s, and many a F-4 fighter pilot wished that they had one in the skies over North Vietnam. That became a *cause célèbre* in the years that followed, and all of our fighters (except the F-117, which really is not a fighter) since then have been equipped for gunfighting—including the new F-22 and the F-35. Yet that "reform" was accompanied by less-noticed improvements in air-to-air missiles to the point where nearly all of the U.S. air-to-air kills since then have been done with missiles. The only exceptions have been a couple of kills of helicopters by the A-10's GAU-8, a weapon designed to kill tanks. Thus, it is possible to wonder if the skeptics might be right again, and that the F-22 will indeed be the last manned fighter—and that it will achieve few kills that could not also be handled by the F-15 equipped with the advanced missiles now in the inventory. Perhaps command of the battlespace will indeed be achieved from the ground and from far space? Or maybe unmanned combat air vehicles will be able to perform the air combat mission as well as the others?

The notion of expanding Giulio Douhet's concept of Command of the Air into the domains of space and even cyberspace is difficult to resist. The United States and the rest of the West have become so dependent upon space and cyberspace that the disruption of either would by now be an assault on our vital interests. The GPS system alone has a vital role in both military and commercial navigation systems, and space communications and electronic networks have become essential to the everyday conduct of business in both government and private enterprise. For a long time, space has been honored as an armament-free area, a sanctuary, but the Chinese launch of a successful anti-satellite weapon and the recent disruption of the Estonian banking systems are seen as fire bells. Both have given new impetus to the arguments of those who have deemed the weaponization of space inevitable, and the consequence would be the necessity to develop methods to guarantee our access to both space and cyberspace—and to deny that access to enemies as well.[14] Thus, as Air Force Space Command and the Air Force itself see it, the space forces have two functions: first, control of the domain (space control) and then exploitation of the advantage (force enhancement). Essential to both is space situational awareness—knowing what is going on in space is ever more difficult. There are around 10,000 space vehicles and pieces of debris in orbit, and satellites are becoming much smaller and more difficult to characterize. Atop that, Congressman Terry Everett points out that our space surveillance systems have been diminished since the end of the Cold War.[15] Both the control and enhancement functions can involve combat operations in either space or on the ground. For example, an ASAT firing from the ground would be a space control weapon, whereas a ground-based radar might be attacked by an airplane for the same purpose. The GPS enhancement of the JDAMs and other weapons is an obvious application of the latter, and possible directed-energy weapons from space platforms might one day be lethal weapons for battle on the ground.[16]

The values of the integration of air and space power are obvious, to be sure, but it is not as easy as it appears. Not the least obstacle is a gap between the cultures of the space forces and the flying elements, albeit that both are trying to control and exploit the vertical domains. The USAF has established Air Force Space Command in Colorado Springs to help bring this about, and squadrons have been founded for both control and enhancement operations. An undergraduate space training program has long been in place, and there are billets for Space Warfare Officers in all the Air Force's Air Operations Centers. Also, there is a space squadron, established in the 1990s, at the elite Fighter Weapons School, where such officers are completely integrated with their flying counterparts in all the courses at the institution. They are also fully integrated with their classmates from other fields at all of the Air Force professional military education courses, and assigned to many places outside

Air Force Space Command to help integrate space and air operations in an effective way. Still, the limited number of Space Warfare Officers available and the cultural differences between the rest of the space officers and those of the flying air units makes full integration a tedious process. Yet neither the space people nor the flying forces can be fully effective in the absence of a rather full understanding of their opposite numbers, and both funding and unit parochialism can retard the learning process.[17]

STRATEGIC ATTACK/GLOBAL STRIKE

In 1947, the main justification used for the foundation of an autonomous air force was strategic bombing. From the very beginning, aviation seemed to promise the long dreamed-of capability of being able to reach out from afar with precision to smite the enemy without putting one's self within range of their bayonets. However, it turned out to be much more complicated than imagined. Both the Germans and the British attempted to reach far beyond the battlefield to strike targets that were not immediately involved with the fight on the ground. One of the problems in World War I was that the bombers were vulnerable to the defenses in the daytime and could neither hit nor even find the targets at night.

A much more elaborate theory and technology was developed in both Great Britain and the United States in the interwar period regarding strategic bombing—the reaching out to strike vital targets far beyond the front lines. As we have seen, in the American case the early preference was for daylight bombing so as to use bombsight technology to achieve surgical precision along with the long reach that would make strategic bombing decisive (and justify the separation of the Air Corps from the Army). In the British case, the separate air force was already in being, and not as much work was done on the technology to accompany the theory as was the case in America.

In World War II, that use of airpower turned out to be a disappointment, or at best a limited success. The original theory was based on the notion that "The Bomber Will Always Get Through!" The sky was and is a very big place, and to find a penetrating bomber in the "footless halls of space" using only one's eyeballs is a daunting proposition. Little did they dream that in such a short time, electronic means would come along to undermine that "stealth" or invisibility—radar. The result was that the British were early driven over to nighttime bombing with a consequent loss of precision and thus the necessity of choosing area, rather than precision, targets. In general, there was a pretty powerful case that the heroic British effort was a failure.

The Americans refused to leave their daylight preference and although for a time they were better at hitting their targets, German radar and some other things made the bomber losses so horrific that the attacks could not be sustained. The standoff yielded by high altitude was not enough. In the end, neither the German economy nor morale collapsed before the Allied armies were across their border, albeit the USSBS did assert that the strategic bombing was one of the factors deciding the outcome. It also declared that advanced industrial societies could not live after losing air superiority over their homelands. In any event, the atomic bomb came in just at the end, seeming to overcome all the problems that had been experienced in the strategic bombing of both Germany and Japan. Few in the Army and Navy were ready to concede that it was a decisive factor in the war, and further (because of its alleged inhumanity)[18] that the atomic bomb would ever be used in future conflicts.

The opponents of strategic bombing argued that the Korean and Vietnamese Wars proved that it was impotent. The proponents said that whatever was practiced in those wars was not strategic bombing because the vital industrial and military targets were across the borders in the People's Republic of China or the USSR—and consequently off limits. In any event, the latter group also argued that it was the strategic bombers that kept the limited wars limited. By the end of the Vietnamese War, the long search for surgical precision had been consummated in the development of the LGB. The long reach was also developed not only in bombers but even in fighters with aerial refueling. That reach was beyond the dreams of Billy Mitchell and Giulio Douhet. Long before that, starting with the Doolittle Raid from the *USS Hornet* (1942), the Navy proved that aircraft carriers could fill gaps that were beyond the range of big bombers, as had Admiral Yamamoto with his expedition against Pearl Harbor over a range of thousands of miles. Arguments were heard that land-based airpower could soon reach any point in the world, and thus the carriers were becoming obsolescent because of their low sortie rates, limited sustainability, and high expense and vulnerability.

The First Gulf War of 1991 did not do much to improve the prospects of long reach through aircraft carriers; it took those that were not on the scene some time to steam that far from the homeland. Even when in the area, the distance of their stations in the Red Sea and the Persian Gulf limited the time that their aircraft could fly into enemy territory. Also, at that moment their air units still had only a limited capability to deliver precision weapons. The air campaign that was mounted was one of the more intense in history, and the Coalition enjoyed an abundance of airpower and had access to some excellent airfields close to the battle zone. Both the British and USAF units were equipped with some very good precision weapons, and were amply supplied with air refueling to get them to the Middle East and to extend their reach into the battle zone.

The argument continues over strategic bombing. The vast majority of weapons were used on what are called tactical targets, but those used on what was somewhat loosely defined as strategic got the publicity. The television media was heavily deployed to the vicinity of the strategic targets, and videotapes were supplied to it that yielded a public impression of extreme surgical precision along with the long reach to deliver bombs and missiles anywhere in Iraq. Yet only ten percent or so of the weapons were guided. Also, the battlefield preparation with airpower seemed highly decisive when the ground war started and was completed with a four-day march with what seemed a complete victory. Even the proponents of strategic bombing argue that it takes more time to have its effect than does tactical attack, and even that interdiction takes more time than close air support. The war was so short that some argued that the effect must have come from the tactical attack more than those delivered at a distance from the battlefield.

In the case of the air war over Serbia (1999), strictly speaking there was no tactical bombing—there was no battle on the ground for it to support. However, in the beginning General Wesley Clark, the NATO commander for the operation, insisted the bulk of the effort be made against targets among the Serbian-fielded forces deployed in Kosovo. Postwar analysis suggested that the effect was very limited. Later in that war, Clark permitted the targeting of objectives in Serbia proper, and soon afterwards the enemy threw in the towel. That seemed to suggest that airpower won the war, and the attacks on the targets in and around Belgrade, not those against the fielded forces, were the decisive ones. The opponents of strategic bombing were quick on the field with notions that what had really decided the issue was Soviet diplomacy or the implied threat that a ground campaign was about to be sent in, notwithstanding President Bill Clinton's assertion at the outset that there would not be one. Neither naval nor land-based airpower was at a serious disadvantage in the campaign because the carriers were able to operate in the nearby Adriatic Sea and it was just a short hop from the NATO bases in Italy to the targets in Serbia. In this war, the proportion of precision munitions used was greater than in the First Gulf War, but still many unguided weapons were also employed. However, the worst embarrassments arose from two incidents using precision bombs, all of which hit the targets they were sent against—the Chinese Embassy in Belgrade (an intelligence failure) and a bridge being crossed by civilians just as the bomb impacted (an inadvertent operational error).

The campaign against Al Qaeda and the Taliban in the wake of the attack on the World Trade Towers and the Pentagon was different. This time we did not have access to land bases just across a narrow sea. That put the burden, at least for a while, on long-range systems: aircraft carriers and bombers. There are but few bombers in the U.S. inventory any more, and the distance to Afghanistan from the closest bases is so huge that it stressed our limited (albeit practically unique) air refueling force. As with the early weeks of the Korean War, the aircraft carriers carried the burden while land bases were sought and developed. Even at that, a substantial proportion of the U.S. air refueling capability was necessary to sustain the naval aircraft in the long flight across Pakistan to the target area and return. The long-range bombers, some flying out of Diego Garcia in the Indian Ocean, were able to contribute early on, and their large payloads and precision weapon capabilities helped.

Gradually, it was possible to find and develop some bases in the area, and that relieved some of the stress. It enabled the insertion of some shorter-range combat aircraft. Also, the employment of some UAVs in that theater increased over those used in Desert Storm, and their development promised some important economies in the future. By now, most of the weapons were precision guided in both naval aircraft and those of the Air Force, and the economy of that compensated some for the distance and the expense of getting there. Again, there were no strategic targets in Afghanistan in the classical sense, so what was happening was a tactical operation, albeit at very long distances. The airpower employed assisted the indigenous military forces and our own special operations forces in important ways. It helped bring down the Taliban in very short order, and put Al Qaeda on the run, even though Osama bin Laden remained at large.

In 2003, the United States and some of her partners launched another campaign at great distance, this time again against their Desert Storm foe, Saddam Hussein. There was no sustained air campaign to prepare for the ground war, and the fighting was launched on the ground and in the air practically simultaneously. (It is to be noted that Northern Watch and Southern Watch over Iraq over the past decade had already severely damaged the Iraqi air defense system before the war.) It only lasted three weeks, so there was not really time enough for either interdiction or strategic attacks to work their effects. A B-1 attack was launched in record time and using precision weapons, and came very close to killing Saddam himself—who was saved only by having departed the site a little earlier. That might be deemed a strategic target, but it is only a sample of one. Practically all of the air-to-ground weapons used by the Navy and the Air Force were guided munitions, and by now the JDAM was demonstrating a new capability that has effectively closed what was hoped to be the enemy's last sanctuary—the weather. At a time when practically all other operations ground to a halt by one of the famous sandstorms of the region, U.S. aircraft succeeded in a precision strike against Iraqi Army units right through the weather—much to the amazement of the enemy. The dream seemed to have come true. Airpower apparently was now able to make a long-sought surgical strike right into the last sanctuary, and to do it from a distance far beyond the reach of the enemy—likely without his knowledge of our presence: surgical precision with healthy standoff.

The old definitions of "strategic" and "tactical" indeed seemed to have lost some of their explanatory power. However, the recent campaigns did stimulate concern over the scarcity of truly long-range striking resources. We were down to a very few aircraft carriers (just 12) and they cannot be everywhere at all times. Our long-range bomber force was diminished to fewer than 200 aircraft. The most ancient of these, the B-52s, are more than 40 years old, and the B-1s are limited in number and beginning to show their age as well. There are but 21 of the new stealthy B-2s, and only 16 of those are combat coded. They are so expensive that the loss of any of them would be a stiff price to pay. Also, most of the tanker force that supports them (as well as supporting airlifters, naval aircraft, and even AC-130 gunships) are just as old as the B-52s. A replacement program for bomber aircraft would be very expensive and take several decades. Yet the demonstrated utility of all three of the bombers, along with that of the carrier force, has stimulated recent concern for our ability to maintain a truly long reach with surgical precision to any spot on the globe.[19]

For a while, there was some talk of turning out some econo-B-2s now that the Soviet Union had disappeared. The original was designed for nuclear war against a superpower enemy. The requirements now do not seem as stringent. Other suggestions were to radically increase the number of targets that could be hit by a single B-2 sortie. That could be achieved by reducing the size of the 2,000-pound JDAM to 500 pounds and then develop a new small smart bomb at 250 pounds using the same sort of guidance (GPS/INS).[20] The consequence is thought to be just as much effectiveness with an accurately delivered small bomb and less collateral damage than is the case with the standard 2,000-pound weapon. But one can stuff many more 250 pounders into a B-2 bomb bay than is possible with the bigger bombs.

By 2007, there was increasing concern in America that the long search for precision in delivery would not be enough. Since the First Gulf War, there had been a revival of the idea that mere destruction could not be a complete goal—that the effects of that on strategy and political outcomes had to be a targeting design goal. In some ways, that was reminiscent of the industrial web theory of the 1930s, whereby the destruction of a single or a few nodes in an industrial system would yield disproportionate political effects because of second- and third-order outcomes. The attack on German rail systems in the fall of 1944 was an example that caused multiple effects throughout the Nazi economy. But that was a total world war where collateral damage was usually seen as a beneficial byproduct. In 2007, the threat of global, total war had much diminished, and the unintended collateral damage could and often did more harm than was the benefit of the destruction of the intended target. As Major Jack Sine viewed it, that demanded an expansion of the definition of precision. He holds that precise delivery of lethal weapons, even very small ones, could sometimes do more harm than good. Sine felt that the new definition of "precision" should include all the effects—intended destruction as well as unintended—that in some circumstances a nonlethal weapon, such as a shorting of an electrical grid or an inserted computer virus, could shut down a functioning system without physical damage or death. Such a weapon, even if not as accurate as a precision-guided munition, might well deliver more precise effects than putting explosive directly on target even in minimal amounts.[21]

Other ideas include the updating of the B-1, the building of an FB-22 derivative of the new and stealthy F/A-22, the development of a cruise missile-carrying aircraft built on a large cargo airframe, or the creation of various new UCAV. Finally, some have thought about reviving an old technology that has not worked out in a couple of earlier instances. The Navy's airships had a hangar deck that could carry four small scout aircraft (a beautiful sample of one is on the balcony of the National Museum of Naval Aviation in Pensacola, Florida). Because of the naval limitation treaties, the United States was handicapped in the area of scouting because she had fewer cruisers than the British and Japanese navies. For a time, the airships seemed to offer a way around that. They were not so limited and could cruise much faster over much longer distances than the seaborne cruiser. Adding airplanes to their capability greatly extended their field of vision and further added to their potential advantages over conventional cruisers. However, after Admiral William Moffet died aboard the crash of one of the airships (1933) the idea lost its appeal, and in any event the naval arms limitation treaties soon expired and were not renewed. The other example arose from the bad World War II experience with the effort to develop a long-range escort fighter for the strategic bombers. The postwar bombers were given a much longer range, and again exceeded anything that could be hoped for from a fighter. So the idea was developed and tested for a parasite fighter, to be carried by the bomber to the danger zone and then launched and recovered by a trapeze device not dissimilar to those that had been aboard the Navy airships. That was also dropped when the Air Force went over to air-refueled jet bombers and counted on high speeds rather than fighter escort to protect the bombers.[22]

Lately, the idea has come forth to buy some Boeing 747 freight liners and equip them in a way similar to that used to transport the space shuttle from Edwards AFB to Florida. The new 747s would be equipped with a elevator mechanism atop to lower F/A-22s to a cradle. There would be a shield in front of the mechanism to allow the fighter pilot to rest aboard the airborne aircraft carrier and yet climb up through a hatch to the aircraft when the mission time came up. This stealth fighter would be launched outside the range of the new Russian SAMs and strike its targets in non-permissive air defense environments. With its mission complete, it would fly back to the 747 and be captured with the elevator mechanism to be lowered back into place to be refueled and re-armed for another strike. Meanwhile, a smaller UCAV would be carried below the 747. It would be launched and recovered in a way similar to the scout aircraft on the airships of the 1930s but would be dedicated to escort the F/A-22 in electronic warfare defense suppression missions and also surveillance operations. It could also be recovered for recycling or return to the home station.[23] The idea is nothing if it is not imaginative, and the skeptic will wonder if it is too expensive to contemplate or too complicated to work. Clearly, the idea is no substitute for aircraft carriers, if only because of sortie rate and sustainability limitations, nor is it a substitute for the development for a new long-range strike system, manned or unmanned. However, it is proposed only as an interim solution to a perceived shortfall in our long-range striking capability.

More recently, the Air Force proposed moving up its program for a new long-range strike vehicle by many years. It is an unmanned vehicle capable of large bomb loads and long loitering times over enemy territory. Doubtlessly, that would be very expensive, and the proposal is that a part of the cost be covered by the earlier retirement of some of the inventory systems. That would include a part of the B-52 fleet and all of the U-2 and F-117 inventory. The mission of the U-2 could be increasingly covered by the Global Hawk unmanned system, and that of the F-117 by more modern stealthy aircraft like the B-2 and the F-22 and the unmanned JASSM. As of the spring of 2006, it remained to be seen whether Congress will favor such a scheme.[24]

CLOSE AIR SUPPORT

As we have repeatedly seen, one of the most troublesome dimensions of evolving air theory and doctrine since the First World War has been close air support. The rub has been between the responsiveness demanded by soldiers and the ability to mass airpower anywhere in the combat theatre desired by the airmen. Further, the problems of fratricide and that of the greater effectiveness per aircraft loss in interdiction have further fueled the arguments. A result has been that the airmen have generally favored centralized control and the soldiers and marines have wanted decentralized direction.

Technical and operational difficulties have further complicated the issues. Finding and targeting dispersed and hidden targets on the battlefield has always been tough from the air. Hitting such small and protected targets has been equally difficult. Traditionally, this has resulted in a high waste of lives, munitions, and airplanes. Moreover, the airmen argue that artillery can deliver explosives on targets within its range more cheaply than aircraft, and do so in all weather and darkness.

Advances in both technology and procedures have already diminished these problems some, and the future promises additional improvement. One great inhibitor has always been unreliable communications. The great advances in miniaturization, solid-state technology, and space communications have greatly improved things there—although problems still exist. Continued doctrinal development and training are also helping. One measure has been the specialization of the career field of ground control producing Joint Tactical Air Controllers, with training common to all services. The Global Positioning System (GPS) is making a huge difference, and promises to make more. It has resulted in precise location of prospective targets by both ground and air units and is greatly reducing the potential for errors that cause fratricide, collateral damage, and needless waste of expensive sorties and munitions. Technologies including portable laser rangefinders are helping ground units establish the location of desired targets from afar with a precision only dreamed of heretofore. Ranging equipment is now becoming available that can transmit the coordinates of such targets directly to the aircraft and its munitions, and that greatly reduces errors arising from human causes or faulty communication.

But there is more to it than that. The adaptation of GPS to use with inertial measuring systems in munitions has produced weapons that are much cheaper (and therefore more numerous) than those with radar, infrared, or even laser sensors. Also, weather can inhibit the delivery of some of those systems, and in the past both the ground controller and the aircrews were required to "put eyeballs on target" before they could be cleared to release such bombs and missiles. But as the GPS/INS weapons enter the inventory and the crews and controllers are trained to use them, those requirements are less than they used to be. Now the airmen can release the weapons from above the clouds without ever seeing the target—thus the weather will no longer be the inhibitor it once was, fratricide will be reduced, and aircraft losses per target destroyed even on the battlefield will be much reduced. All that will be done from much higher altitudes than were typical prior to the coming of precision weapons. Conceivably, the use of precision weapons from unmanned aerial vehicles will gain our confidence sufficiently to enable their use close to friendly troops, and multiply the advantages of the new technology without the more expensive aircraft that put crews at risk.[25]

The final result of the advance in close air support promises to be a much safer and more effective and economical execution of the function. It also suggests that the pace of operations against enemy fielded forces will be much enhanced, and battles and perhaps wars will be thus shortened and made less costly. And dare we repeat a favorite argument of both Giulio Douhet and Billy Mitchell that thus they will at the same time be more humane or less inhumane.

THE FUTURE OF NAVAL AIRPOWER

The requiem of naval airpower has repeatedly been made prematurely, and its death is not upon us yet. Billy Mitchell himself predicted this, and one still sees arguments that ICBMs or huge stealth bombers with intercontinental ranges will make expensive carrier aviation obsolete. However, the end is not yet in sight. There was much hand-wringing over the subject in the days of the B-36 and Admirals Revolt controversies, and Korea came along to provide a not-so-new mission for the aviators of the sea services. More recently, when the War on Terror was carried to Afghanistan, there again insufficient airfields available for land-based airpower and the B-2s were simply too few and too expensive themselves to handle that fight without assistance. So again the carriers filled a gap that would otherwise not have been covered. What of the future? Is the requiem so long predicted now really around the corner?

Maybe not. One of the things that may again put it off is the coming of "net centric warfare," not only to the navy but also to all the services. Another is the great benefit of inexpensive, small, and precise munitions that will mitigate the limits of storage space and sortie rates from carriers. Further, the use of stealthy UAVs from carrier decks will reduce the penalties of lost attackers and reduce the need for supporting aircraft for strike forces. In turn, that will allow a greater portion of the deck loads to be devoted to the shooters themselves. As the attack aircraft become more stealthy with the acquisition of the F-35, those effects will be further enhanced. All that will be combined with the traditional advantage of seapower: the free use of all the seas of the world without violating any state's sovereignty and persistent presence close to troubled areas yet over the horizon.[26] Roger Barnett has argued that the notions that large ships can easily be located, and therefore sunk, are faulty. He says it may be technically possible but prohibitively complicated and expensive to do so,[27] but technology is moving rapidly.

The Defense Science Board in 2002 agreed with Barnett that the nuclear carriers are not yet that vulnerable.[28] In fact, it asserted that they are less at risk because of their maneuverability as opposed to the fixed locations of major air bases ashore. However, the Board did worry that the carrier force is saddled with a huge investment in "legacy" aircraft (the F/A-18) that limited the degree of change that could be made in new carriers. Also, it lamented that the nuclear carriers are built according to a design derived 40 years earlier, and that requires much heavier personnel costs than are now feasible. The Board complained that the Navy really had not pressed carrier design to its technological limits, but in the end it agreed that there were built-in constraints that limited the amount of change that could be utilized. Thus, it recommended that the design of the upcoming CVNX-1 be developed along the lines already laid down, which are more or less conventional. It also thought that more change could be incorporated in the next carrier, CVNX-2, and that a standing organization should pursue carrier design on a continuous basis. Yet it also recommended the possibility of a future mix of large-deck carriers with a number of smaller, faster ships be considered.[29] As we noted previously, there is an interdependence between ship and aircraft design. The United States has a huge investment in the relatively new F/A-18 fighter-bomber that must be accommodated in new ship designs.

Network-centric warfare may be a fundamental improvement. The nuclear carriers are huge and hugely expensive, but they have been built to contain all the functions essential to defensive and offensive airpower in a relatively independent package. We have already noted some of the ways in which that load might be limited or reduced by other technologies, and it might further be reduced by putting most of the other functions ashore, leaving all the room aboard for the lethal portion of the carrier's equipment. In this way, it is argued, the ships will ultimately become smaller, less heavily manned, and much cheaper—and it will be possible to build many more of them. Among those functions moved ashore and carried out from afar would include sensor, computing, and command and control technologies with their accompanying personnel. Perhaps the future will reduce the need for manned air-to-air capabilities for the defense of the ships, leaving more space for air-to-ground shooters or allowing further reduction in the size of carriers. Fortuitously, the *Coral Sea* was 700 miles away from the scene of the action in the *Mayagüez* affair.[30] Before her air group was able to drop its first bomb on the Cambodian mainland, the *Mayagüez* crew was already released. The point is that if ship size can be reduced through the use of UAVs or VTOL aircraft or the absence of support aircraft, then it will be possible to build many more of them. The effect of that would be many more deployed on station and the reduction of the average time necessary to steam to the locus of action. Also, the willingness to put such ships in harm's way would be greater if there were more of them—thus their utility would be greater.[31] Moreover, in most crises the sooner action can be taken, the less force is required to settle things.

Increasing globalization has led to a revival of another old mission of the naval forces—piracy suppression. There has been a huge increase in maritime traffic all over the world, and piracy that was practically exterminated by the middle of the nineteenth century has reappeared in places like the waters off Somalia, the Gulf of Siam, and the Straits of Malacca. Elsewhere there has also been a huge increase in other illicit activities at sea such as terrorism, human trafficking, and drug smuggling.[32] Piracy suppression was achieved to a large degree by international cooperation among the seafaring nations, and now the global interdependence has given practically all states an interest in reducing the threat. For example, in 2007 the US Navy equipped with helicopters has been doing important work off Somalia in combating the threat.[33]

INFORMATION OPERATIONS

As always, there are skeptics on network-centric warfare. Albeit the idea has been promoted most prominently by the Navy, the old tradition of that service has been that independent command at sea is paramount. The Defense Department has recognized that the network has become one of our centers of gravity, and it requires a defense in depth.[34] Also, there are those who worry about micromanagement in all the services. A main point of John Guilmartin's *A Very Short War* was that the directions coming all the way from Washington's highest levels did get in the way of effective operations at the scene of operations at Koh Tang Island.[35] The on-scene leaders during the last hours of the fall of Saigon were also burdened by the excess of direction from afar from a whole crowd of commanders communicating from places all the way up the chain to Washington.[36] More recently, F. J. Bing West reported from Iraqi Freedom that network-centric warfare still has not been perfected down to the unit level in the Marine Corps. There the operation was conducted by on-scene unit commanders, who still did not have complete "connectivity" with the net. He says the Blue Force tracking in the Army was better, but initiative at the lower levels still was required.[37] All that is a sign that the network and information operations are still maturing. A major point from the beginning has been that the whole thing will not only enable us to make better decisions but also make them much faster than the adversary can. In part, this is because the span of control of the leaders will be greater and the organizations flatter. The anticipation is that there will be fewer layers of command and that will speed up decision making. However, basic to it all is the notion that many, perhaps most, decisions will be pushed down to lower levels, often to the junior officer or noncommissioned officer in the field. As of the time of the Iraq War in 2003, that process had not yet been completed, and it is important that it be done.[38]

Still, it cannot be denied that the U.S. advantages in information warfare at least from Desert Storm onward have been very great. At the end, the Iraqi leadership did not have the foggiest notion as to what their own losses were. Although Saddam's communications were never completely shut down they were severely limited, and those that did survive were greatly slowed. Not only was the Coalition able to make decisions based on much better information, it was able to do so in a much more timely manner. Still, at that stage there were still delays in getting feedback, termed bomb damage assessment (BDA).[39]

As great as the information edge was in 1991, it has grown even greater and more vital. As usual, the development of the technology and techniques took different patterns in the different services, and that among other things inhibited smooth operations and ultimately required some improvement. Lately, the Department of Defense has moved to coordinate information operations better than it had been. It made the four-star commander of U.S. Strategic Command the centralized authority over the field of information operations, given the function an explicit definition, and improved the organization. Most importantly has been the identification of information operations as a core competency in the Department, theoretically on a par with seapower, landpower, and airpower. The Joint Forces College at Norfolk, Virginia, was designated as the lead in educating the force in that core competency, and the Naval Post-Graduate School in California has been identified as the Department of Defense Center of Excellence for information operations. Fundamentally, information operations are designed to undermine the enemy's decision making process and protect our own. Among other things, it includes the following capabilities: psychological operations, computer network operations, operations security work, electronic warfare, and military deception.[40]

The Joint Forces Command at Norfolk is active in the effort to improve and better coordinate the work of gathering information and putting it into usable form for the various regional commanders. The Department of Defense has made the capability to achieve information superiority on a par with air and space superiority and command of the sea. A part of this was the installation of standing joint force operational headquarters in the various regions. A continuing effort is being made to supply the joint commanders with a head start in understanding their situation in any crisis through the creation of a database known as the Operational Net Assessment (ONA). It includes data from multiple sources both within and outside the government, along with an evaluation and collation of that information into meaningful knowledge readily accessible to joint commanders and their staffs by electronic means. It also gives suggestions as to possible courses of action in the event of an array of possible crises, and an analysis of the expected effects of those actions along with some notions as to what some of the unintended effects might be, both first order and secondary effects. The uncertainties involved are readily admitted, but the availability of this huge database so facilitates the acquisition of an understanding of new situations that it improves the odds that the regional commanders will be able to achieve decision superiority over adversaries. The ONA is not at all restricted to military concerns but includes data and analysis in the realms of economics, politics, social concerns, and more. Nor does it limit its analyses to possible military actions, but includes ideas on the use of all the instruments of foreign policy, both friendly and adversarial. The resulting comprehensive and integrated database is immediately available to the new Standing Joint Force Headquarters Core Elements in each of the regions. It will thus be able to study the possible problems facing the joint commands long in advance, and enter any conflicts in a more timely way with more comprehensive and accurate information than that available to the adversary.[41]

Certainly, the Coalition had huge information advantages over Iraq during the First Gulf War. However, it was deemed necessary at the time for the personnel of the Air Operations Center to reach back to Washington through informal channels to get information that they could not get from the formal intelligence structure, or could not get in time via that route. The paramount importance of information superiority has been recognized, and dramatic improvements have been made to improve the chances that the advantage will continue and grow.

But President Dwight Eisenhower early on recognized that the American monopoly and later its hegemony in nuclear technology could not last indefinitely. Although it is clear that the United States remains without a peer in space or in information operations, the blazing speed with which the Soviets acquired their own nuclear capability serves as a warning. It does not require a Manhattan Project to acquire some information operations technology and technique, and perhaps the requirements for a space capability are not quite as demanding as were those for nuclear weapons. Thus, the U.S. advantages in information warfare are so great and so obvious that they seem highly likely to be diminished, if not overtaken in the future. There are important advantages in being second in a new field, as were the Soviets in the late 1940s. One is that just proving something is possible is a difficult part of research and development. The first one in the field does that, and therefore eases that step for those who follow. For all the crying needs America has for improvements in other domestic and foreign policy programs, it would be foolhardy to reduce the pressure for further progress in information warfare. At all levels of warfare, from the cockpit to the national capital, superior situational awareness has always been and doubtless will always be a huge advantage. Although uncertainties will always exist, the network-centric system and information operations must always strive to improve our own situational awareness at all levels and degrade that of our enemies. David D. DiCenso warns that information operations can be variously interpreted. Some claim that computers are not weapons because they do not directly cause physical damage; others liken interference with the flow of information to the blocking of the flow of goods through traditional blockades—sometimes interpreted as acts of war.[42]

BLOCKADE IN THE WAR ON TERROR

Conventional blockade by interdiction on the high seas has always been a troublesome problem. As in the American Civil War, it has seemed impossible to completely cut the flow of material into an enemy's ports.[43] Yet the modern age seems to dictate the capability to do so, what with the proliferation of non-state actors and with their potential capabilities to acquire and wield WMDs. However, the task seems more challenging than ever before. There has been a huge growth in seaborne traffic since the end of World War II, and globalization suggests that it is to continue indefinitely. The need to monitor this traffic increasingly by airborne and spaceborne means is apparent, yet the containerization of cargo makes the identification of contraband cargo more difficult than ever.

The difficulties with blockade complicate life for the Coast Guard and Navy, and they are assisted by their own air units with electronic means of reconnaissance and surveillance, as well as by other air organizations. At first look, it would seem that observation from space would be the answer to this, but as things stand it would have to be done from geostationary orbit or by a huge constellation of lower satellites—and even at that, those systems would be lacking in flexibility and responsiveness. Also, they would be inordinately expensive and have even greater difficulties in identifying contraband cargo.[44]

UAVs could be an important aid in blockades in some situations. They are cheaper than aircraft, can be stealthy, and offer observation from much lower altitudes, yielding better resolution. Yet they cannot help without transmitting data, and that act reduces their stealth. They do have the virtue of being cheaper and more flexible and responsive than space satellites. However, their endurance, though greater than aircraft, is not unlimited.[45]

Still less expensive than UAVs would be the employment of lighter-than-air vehicles in near space, either free-floating or guided. At altitudes between about 65,000 and 100,000 feet, they would be above air traffic yet below orbital heights. They would also be above all bad weather phenomena and in a realm of relatively low winds. Yet their station-keeping qualities would be superior to that of satellites, and their responsiveness to the theater commander's needs could be better. Conceivably, their endurance could be made to last for years, and located at lower altitudes they could deliver better resolutions than satellites or employ less expensive sensing equipment. Lighter-than-air craft would be useful not only for blockade but also for land warfare as observation platforms or communications relay stations. It would be difficult for the enemy to reach them at that altitude, and their loss would be less damaging than the loss of a satellite. Not only are they cheaper than satellites but also they could be replaced on station more quickly.[46]

At the end of the day, Roger Barnett argues that the best place to interdict WMD traffic is at the terminals—and it is better done at the origin than the destination. The pre-certification that the container traffic is free of WMDs is a major dimension of this, and that is in part a diplomatic problem that being addressed now.

THE FUTURE OF SPACE AND AIRPOWER: INTEGRATION OR SEPARATION?

We have seen that so far, space has played a supporting role to land, sea, and air power. However, there has long been a debate underway as to its future. At present, all the services have a role in space, but the USAF has been dominant in the development and management of military space assets. The Air Force policy has been that space and air are parts of the same domain: the third dimension. Thus, it should be in charge. However, the Billy Mitchell precedents seem to be very powerful, and many argue that a US Space Force is inevitable—and perhaps in the not-too-distant future.[47] They argue that the air and space domains are radically different and therefore require two different bureaucracies for the maximum development of each.[48] A part of that argument is that as long as space remains a USAF responsibility, the air arm cannot fully develop the unique capabilities of airpower, as well as those peculiar to spacepower. Airpower can do many things better than spacepower, and the reverse is true. In many applications, aerial forces are more flexible than space assets, and as sensor resolution usually depends on distance from the target they can often be more precise than space-borne devices. Also, airpower has the great benefits of being inside the atmosphere, and that allows it to develop both lift and maneuverability much more easily than is the case in the vacuum of space. For example, in the vacuum of space it not only requires energy to start a movement but also to stop it; this translates into economy of force application for airpower. The expense of maintenance and re-supply in the airpower realm is much less than it is for space because of the relative costs of lift in the two realms, plus the ease of return for airpower to its base support. Also, it seems inevitable that spacepower must be controlled and executed in a centralized way, whereas air units can execute operations in a decentralized manner, yielding flexibility in some circumstances.[49]

Evolving Spacepower

1942	October. Although rockets had been known for centuries, a modern starting point for the exploration of space might have been the first launch of a German V-2 ballistic missile.
1954	USAF Western Development Division headed by General Bernard Schriever was founded for the purpose of developing an ICBM for the United States.
1955	USAF acquires the site of the future Vandenberg AFB for ballistic missile testing.
1955	First nuclear powered submarine, *USS Nautilus*, underway.
1955	May. President Dwight Eisenhower makes Open Skies proposal to the USSR, which rejects the idea.
1955	October. Western Development Division acquires responsibility for the development of USAF space systems in addition to the ICBM mission.
1956	First successful launch of Atlas ballistic missile.
1957	October. Soviets launch *Sputnik*, causing an acceleration of U.S. space and missile effort.
1959	Atlas ICBM achieved operational status at Vandenberg AFB.
1960	May. Gary Powers flying a CIA U-2 over the USSR is shot down.
1960	August. Discoverer Satellite returns reconnaissance images of the USSR to the United States.
1960	Submarine launched ballistic missiles (SLBM) operational.

1962	First SAC Titan ballistic missile squadron declared operational and goes on alert.
1963	October. First SAC Minuteman solid-fueled ICBM put on alert at Malmstrom AFB, Montana.
1965–75	Extensive use of weather and communications satellites in the Vietnam War.
1964	TRANSIT satellites for submarine navigation within 25 meters put on orbit.
1967	Outer Space Treaty, prohibiting the placement of WMD in orbit or on the moon.
1969	July. Neil Armstrong first human to step on to the moon.
1970	First Minuteman III missiles put on alert at Minot AFB, North Dakota, with multiple independently targetable reentry vehicles (MIRV) in their warhead.
1971	First launch of Defense Support Program (DSP) infrared satellite for missile launch warning put into geostationary orbit.
1972	United States and USSR sign the Anti-Ballistic Missile Treaty, severely limiting the deployment of defenses against ICBMs because they were thought to be destabilizing to the nuclear balance.
1982	September. Foundation of Air Force Space Command in Colorado Springs, Colorado.
1983	March. President Ronald Reagan makes a speech recommending the development of a Strategic Defense System of multiple layers aimed at protecting the United States from a massive ICBM attack. Such a system was never developed, but it did produce some useful technological spin-offs.
1986	First Peacekeeper ICBMs with ten MIRV warheads placed on alert at Francis E. Warren AFB, Wyoming.
1991	First Gulf War labeled the first space war—intense usage of missile warning, intelligence, communications, weather, and navigation satellites, down to the level of individual vehicles.
1993	U.S. ICBM forces transferred from the Strategic Air Command, then being deactivated, to USAF Space Command for training and equipping. Now managed by Twentieth Air Force, they are under the operational control of U.S. Strategic Command for combat operations.
1993	Space Warfare Center founded in Colorado Springs, Colorado.
1994	First launch of jam-resistant MILSTAR communications satellite.
1995	April. GPS navigation satellite constellation achieved full operational status.

1998	Control of U.S. weather satellites transferred to National Oceanic and Atmospheric Administration (NOAA).
2002	October. U.S. Space Command disestablished, and U.S. Strategic Command founded at Offut AFB, Nebraska. The Air Force Space Command, along with the corresponding commands of the other services, then supplied the equipped and trained space forces for the unified U.S. Strategic Command. Space and Missile Center transferred from Air Materiel Command to Air Force Space Command.
2004	National Space Security Institute for the professional development of career space personnel in place in Colorado Springs, Colorado. The educational program of three levels is intended to start with the company grade years and progress to the lieutenant colonel/commander level with the appropriate courses and certifications.

On the space side of the equation, reconnaissance and surveillance can be done with greater standoff and less risk to American personnel than can air operations. Space platforms have enormous durability on station, whereas those in the atmosphere are limited in endurance by fuel supplies and crew endurance. One of the greatest assets of space power is that of freedom of the realm—in peacetime, one cannot transit through the airspace above any state without its consent, but the same is not true for space platforms. Sea-based airpower has always had a great advantage in the freedom of the seas, and in space the benefit is even greater. If airpower has the benefit of operating within the atmosphere for lift and maneuverability, spacepower works in a realm that is infinitely larger than the atmosphere and that yields it a measure of security—and the potential for surprise. In some circumstances, if directed-energy weapons are used in space, the response time from that realm can become instantaneous.

Yet it appears that jointness has been very successful in the combat we have been in the last couple of decades, and apparently the creation of a separate space force would fly in the face of that. Also, there is a powerful political sentiment in the United States and elsewhere that advocates the space sanctuary, one that is free of lethal weapons of all sorts. There is a moral dimension and a legal one to that. The Outer Space Treaty prohibits the orbiting of weapons of mass destruction, for example.[50] Finally, there are those who worry about the precedent set by Admiral "Jackie" Fisher in the development of the *Dreadnought* a century ago. In so doing, it is said he made obsolete every capital ship on the planet, and thus threw away what had been an enormous advantage enjoyed by Great Britain. She had a huge numerical advantage in those obsolescent ships, and the consequence of the *Dreadnought* was taking the battle onto new fields where her advantage in the beginning was only in the ratio of 1:0. Similarly, the United States now has a huge advantage in conventional war on the surface and in airpower, but as there currently are no lethal forces in space, were she to put one there, the advantage would deteriorate to a ratio of merely 1:0, making it far easier for potential adversaries to catch up.[51]

At the end of the day, the ideas that are the current foundation of air and space power theory and doctrine have a long history. Almost all of them have precedents in the First World War. The luster of some has diminished; that of others still is bright. As I see it, the main elements as they stand right now are:

- Air and space superiority remains the main mission, although it is far more complex now than ever before. It remains an enabler for all other operations. In the future, the concept will have to be expanded to vertical dimension superiority to include the control of space. This is the one best reason for the integration of air and space, for the evidence demonstrates that the decentralization of airpower in defensive efforts in Africa and Japan in World War II was disastrous. The lack of serious opposition in space or in the air during the last three conflicts is particularly worrisome for it could lead to complacency in this, the most vital part of the air and space mission. Lately ideas of a third domain, cyberspace, have emerged. It is described as the electro-magnetic environment and held to have so much in common with the air and space domains as to make it an essential partner to them. Loss of a capability to operate in cyberspace could be as deadly to national security as in all the other domains.
- Strategic attack has not turned out to be as wonderful as the theorists of the 1920s supposed, but neither is it as futile as some of the old and current critics made it out to be. It clearly had an important impact on World War II as it was the major pillar of deterrence, and that may have prevented war for a long time—and I believe it was a significant factor in Kosovo. It is too early to estimate the degree to which the rapidity of the march on Baghdad arose from the attack on the vital targets at the center of the enemy structure. But beyond active combat, it may be that the passive role of deterrence did work during the Cold War, and the maintenance of an ICBM force still could act to retard nuclear proliferation and deter new nuclear powers from actually using their weapons.
- Interdiction was a disappointment in both Korea and Vietnam, and it has not lived up to its promise of the 1920s. However, it had important effects in World War II in Africa and Normandy, and it may have prevented defeat in Korea and delayed our loss in Vietnam. It was a factor in the success in the First Gulf War. Its effects, although tending to be earlier than those of strategic attack, nevertheless take time so that neither the Kosovo conflict nor the Second Gulf War really went on long enough for

the full result to appear. The sea interdiction across the Mediterranean and in the Pacific in World War II was so successful that perhaps it could serve as an analog for the development of like methods in space.

- Close air support was a success in World War II, helped greatly at the Pusan Perimeter in Korea, was applauded by the great majority of Army leaders in Vietnam, and was not much needed in the First Gulf War. I believe the Israelis have it right: it is an expensive substitute for artillery but in an emergency it must be used on the battlefield, notwithstanding the costs. As our land units were not engaged in Kosovo, it was not a factor there. The battle in the Second Gulf War was probably not extensive enough to draw any firm conclusions on close air support. Perhaps the damage suffered by the helicopters suggests that fixed-wing close air support is still vital, and the day may come when we will wish the new F-35 had two engines like the current A-10. It seems quite clear to me that UAVs can be a big help in this function. Also, the advent of GPS may turn out to be a quantum jump in the capability of close air support in finding targets and avoiding fratricide.
- Reconnaissance has achieved wonderful things from World War I onward, but space and information warfare notwithstanding, I do not believe the "fog of war" will ever be eliminated. There is a chance that information overload will sometimes make it worse—it may enable us to do something stupid with blinding speed. I suppose that the combination of space, UAVs, and reconnaissance pods for jets will make it difficult for manned specialized aerial reconnaissance units to rise from the ashes. Is information warfare a new medium of conflict or merely an improved version of what has always been done? To create a separate realm of cyberspace might be seen by some as going against the jointness tide. Information is vital to all forms of military power, and should be a part of an integrated study of warfare, not a separate discipline.
- Air mobility is a universal good; everybody realizes this and that is why the debates surrounding its use are so fierce. Maybe some suggestion will arise from the Second Gulf War that the C-17 is too big and expensive to get into the combat area early enough so that a supplement to replace the C-130 is in the future. There are already rumblings to that effect in the Army, and maybe it will get back into the fixed-wing business if the Air Force does not meet the challenge in a timely way. There already have been moves in that direction in the Joint Combat Aircraft program looking to a fixed-wing airplane smaller than the C-130. Conceivably, as argued by Chad Manske, UAVs in the company of mother ships may prove helpful in the delivery of cargo. There can hardly be any doubt that there is a desperate need for more updated air refueling capability, albeit it is expensive and certainly generates much political controversy.
- Carrier airpower is a good thing for places where you do not have airfields and in emergencies; Afghanistan demonstrates that. But it is very

expensive, its sustainability is cumbersome, and its ability to mass firepower on a target is limited. Maybe the Air Force will save the aircraft carrier by reducing these handicaps through developing low-cost JDAM-like guidance and applying it to tiny bombs. That would enable more effective lethal payloads on aircraft, greater storage on carriers, and a longer time on station before the need for replenishment arises.

- Space is a good thing, but it is a part of the third dimension, as is airpower. Thus, I believe that it should be integrated with airpower and that the United States should not be the first to weaponize space, although it should make sure that it has the technology on the shelf to do so more rapidly than can any competitor if the need arises. Hopefully, this essential unity will not be overlooked merely because our command of the vertical dimension of battle has not been much challenged in the last several wars. "Jointness" has been increasingly successful in combat since the Cold War, and it seems to me that creating a fourth service would tend to move in the opposite direction.
- The technologies of UAVs and precision-guided munitions are also a good thing, notwithstanding the standard charge that Americans—and especially their air and space people—are obsessed with technology. Both of these technologies have already swung the pendulum back in the direction of the offensive use of air and space power and promise further economies. As with information warfare, the United States must understand that it cannot enjoy its hegemony in these fields indefinitely—others will learn to use the technologies, or employ forms of conflict where their advantages are nonexistent or irrelevant. Also, in our age there is a danger of getting carried away with precision-guided munitions and UAVs. One large problem is that in the era of total war, stray bombs causing collateral damage were often considered bonuses. In the age of limited war, that is no longer the case. Even if we can hit any target with precision, there still are pitfalls. The relatively new sensor fused weapon offers a case in point. It consists of a dispenser containing 40 submunitions. Each of those swirls about looking at the surface with an infrared detector that can identify hot tank engines and cue a shaped explosive charge to fire at it precisely.[52] Unhappily, it cannot be relied upon to tell the difference between a tank engine and the motor of a school bus. There have also been multiple efforts to develop automatic target recognition—a formidable task. Therefore, it seems likely that it will be a long time before Americans are generally willing to completely divorce the process from human decisions, notwithstanding great technological advances—in all probability, we shall insist on keeping a human "in the loop" to limit the chances for collateral damage or fratricide.
- In the long term, one worry on the airpower horizon might wind up trumping all the others: the limitations on the supply of liquid fuels. We have seen that it was a major reason driving the Japanese decision

> for war in 1941. It was also a major concern of the United States, at least from the Carter administration onward—and airpower, both civil and military, is a major consumer of liquid fuels in the United States. A substitute is a crying need. Neither wind, nuclear, nor solar power can help. The USAF is involved in a substantial effort to make economically feasible the production of synthetic liquid fuels from coal. There are huge supplies in North America, and the process has been technologically feasible for a long time, as the Germans proved in World War II. The prices of crude have recently risen above the level to make synthetic production attractive, but the plants are so expensive that there must be greater assurance that the price will remain above the breakeven point for a long time to make the building of them reasonable. However, it is the attractiveness of energy independence, so attractive not only to the aviation community but to all Americans, that it is demanding major efforts.[53]

We do not really know whether air and space power can win alone. However, I do believe that the possibility may sometimes exist, and political and military leaders have a sacred moral obligation to the mothers and fathers of America not to waste their sons and daughters. Thus, I agree with Admiral James Winnefeld and Dr. Dana Johnson that the leadership must not commit our children to ground battle before they have thoroughly and honestly considered whether the object can be gained with air and space alone[54] and, if not, if it is really important enough to be bringing back body bags. Anyone who would waste them merely to achieve prestige, a domestic political gain, or an advantage for their organization betrays that sacred obligation.

A Dozen-Book Sampler for Your Reading on Air and Space Theory and Doctrine

Two for the Overview

Phillip S. Meilinger (ed.), *The Paths of Heaven: The Evolution of Airpower Theory* (Maxwell AFB, AL: Air University, 1997). This book was written by the faculty and some of the graduates of the School of Advanced Airpower Studies. This work is the most comprehensive in the field, and its reviews have been good. It is certainly a prime candidate for your personal professional library.

Peter Paret, *Makers of Modern Strategy* (Princeton, NJ: Princeton University Press, 1986). The editor is one of the deans of military history. The book is a little dated now, and it covers military theory and strategy in addition to its chapters on airpower. You should have some foundation in the military theorists like Carl von Clausewitz, Antoine Henri Jomini, Alfred Thayer Mahan, and others as your foundation for the study of air theory and doctrine. You can get a good start on that from this book.

Ten for Depth and Mastery

I. B. Holley, *Ideas and Weapons* (Washington, DC: Government Printing Office, 1953, 1983). Holley is a long-time professor at Duke University, World War II aerial gunner, retired MGEN in the USAFR, and frequent lecturer at Air University. He is a member of the Aerospace Power Journal Advisory Board, and this book is clearly one of the pillars of the study of air theory and doctrine. It demonstrates the interrelationship between theory, doctrine, and weapons technology, and spoke of their connections with organization long before the revolution in military affairs became a prominent concept in security studies.

Giulio Douhet, *The Command of the Air* (Washington, DC: Office of Air Force History, 1921, 1983). Whether you are a fan of strategic bombing or not, you should be quite familiar with this work. There are many experts who use Douhet's name with abandon, and you should be able to discern whether they really are an expert on the subject.

William Mitchell, *Winged Defense* (New York: Putnam's Sons, 1925). This is the primary source on a principal actor in the development of American air theory and doctrine. Some have said that he was not an original thinker but rather a spokesman for many others who contributed to the mindset of the Air Service and Air Corps. This is only one of his books, but it is an expression of this thinking about the time of his court-martial. His mindset did change as the years passed. As with Douhet, there are many who use Mitchell's name recklessly, and you therefore need a first-hand knowledge of this work.

James S. Corum and Richard R. Muller (eds. and trans.), *The Luftwaffe's Way of War: German Air Force Doctrine 1911–1945* (Baltimore, MD: Nautical & Aviation Publishing, 1998). There is so much myth on Douhet, Mitchell, and the *Luftwaffe* based on third-hand knowledge that a special effort has been made with this list to include as much primary source material as possible. Corum and Muller are Air University's *Luftwaffe* experts, and here provide translations of previously unpublished original documents.

John C. Slessor, *Air Power and Armies* (Oxford: Oxford University, 1936). The author was an instructor at the British Army Staff College when he developed this work, at first as a set of lectures. It is a clear statement of ideas regarding the tactical use of air forces in cooperation with armies, and suggests that the RAF was not then completely "obsessed" with strategic bombing. Slessor rose to become Chief of Staff during the heyday of strategic bombing.

John Warden, *The Air Campaign: Planning for Combat* (Washington, DC: Pergamon, 1989). This author was a 1965 graduate of the Air Force Academy, a forward air controller, and then a fighter pilot in Vietnam. He wrote this work first as a thesis at the National War College, and later wrote the strategic part of the air campaign plan for the First Gulf War. He completed his service as Commandant of the Air Command and Staff College.

Robert A. Pape, *Bombing to Win: Air Power and Coercion in War* (Ithaca, NY: Cornell University, 1995). The author first wrote this as a political science dissertation at the University of Chicago, and edited it while a professor at the Air Force's School of Advanced Airpower Studies. It has stimulated more debate among airpower scholars than perhaps any other book published since the end of the Cold War.

Benjamin S. Lambeth, *The Transformation of American Airpower* (Ithaca, NY: Cornell University, 2000). The author is one of the leading contemporary airpower thinkers and a long-time RAND scholar. He is widely published, an expert on Soviet and Russian airpower, and the current work has been well scrubbed and represents the latest American thought on the subject.

David Spires, *Beyond Horizons: A Half Century of Air Force Space Leadership* (Peterson AFB, CO: Air Force Space Command, 1997). This work is an authoritative study on the development of U.S. spacepower.

Peter L. Hays et al. (eds.), *Spacepower for a New Millennium: Space and U.S. National Security* (New York: McGraw-Hill, 2000). There is a huge literature growing on space theory and doctrine, but the field is not yet mature enough to make for easy identification of a set of authoritative works on the subject. This editor is widely published on the subject, and his Tufts dissertation is on spacepower. The current work is made up of a number of chapters by leaders in the field and it will provide the air warrior/scholar with a good starting summary.

One For Good Measure

Stephen B. Randolph, *Powerful and Brutal Weapons: Nixon, Kissinger, and the Easter Offensive* (Cambridge, MA: Harvard, 2007). This book is a great case study of the interrelationship between politics and war.

Notes

CHAPTER 1

1. Michael Howard, "Military Science in an Age of Peace," Chesney Memorial Gold Medal lecture, October 3, 1973, reprinted in *Journal of the Royal United Services Institute*, Vol. 119 (March 1974): 3–11.

2. Howard, 3–11.

3. United States Air Force, *Air Force Doctrine Document 1*, September 1997, v.

4. Lee Kennett, "Strategic Bombardment: A Retrospective," in R. Cargill Hall (ed.), *Case Studies in Strategic Bombardment* (Washington, DC: Air Force History and Museums Program, 1998), 627.

CHAPTER 2

1. Lee Kennett, *The First Air War* (New York: Free Press, 1991), 23–40, this work being one of the best short treatments of airpower in World War I; Daniel Yergin, *The Prize: The Epic Quest for Oil, Money, and Power* (New York: Free Press, 1991), 168.

2. Kennett, 32; Correlli Barnett, "The Fallibility of Air Power," *Journal of the Royal United Services Institute*, Vol. 145, (October 2000): 59.

3. John H. Morrow, Jr., *The Great War in the Air: Military Aviation from 1909 to 1921* (Washington, DC: Smithsonian, 1993), 363.

4. Kennett, 211–212.

5. A leading authority on air fighting in general is Mike Spick, *The Ace Factor: Air Combat and the Role of Situational Awareness* (Annapolis, MD: Naval Institute, 1988), 30–34; Yergin, 171–172.

6. George H. Quester, *Deterrence Before Hiroshima* (New Brunswick, NJ: Transaction, 1966, 1986), 16.

7. Quester, 6–49; Raymond H. Fredette, *The Sky on Fire: The First Battle of Britain, 1917–1918* (New York: Holt, Rinehart & Winston, 1966); Michael S. Sherry, *The Rise of American Air Power: The Creation of Armageddon* (New Haven, CT: Yale, 1987), 12–21; George K. Williams, *Biplanes and Bombsights: British Bombing in World War I* (Maxwell AFB, AL: Air University Press, 1999), for an authoritative treatment of the RAF side of the story.

8. Russell Braddon, *The Siege* (New York: Viking, 1970), 242.

9. Kennett, 87.

10. Two particularly valuable books have recently been published on these subjects: Robert P. White, *Mason Patrick and the Fight for Air Service Independence* (Washington, DC: Smithsonian, 2001) and James J. Cooke, *Billy Mitchell* (Boulder, CO: Lynne Rienner, 2002).

11. The ideas of Douhet may be received directly from Giulio Douhet, *The Command of the Air*, trans. by Dino Ferrari (Washington, DC: Office of Air Force History, 1983), or indirectly from Bernard Brodie, *Strategy in the Missile Age* (Princeton, NJ: Princeton University, 1959, 1965), 71–144.

12. William F. Trimble, *Admiral William A. Moffett: Architect of Naval Aviation* (Washington, DC: Smithsonian, 1993), 58.

13. Robert Frank Futrell, *Ideas, Concepts, Doctrine: Basic Thinking in the United States Air Force*, Vol I, 1907–1960, 2nd ed. (Maxwell AFB, AL: Air University Press, December, 1989), 29.

14. Futrell, 36.

15. Futrell, 24.

16. The authority on Mitchell is Alfred F. Hurley, *Billy Mitchell: Crusader for Air Power* (Bloomington, IN: Indiana University, 1964, 1975), or Mitchell himself in William Mitchell, *Winged Defense: The Development and Possibilities of Modern Airpower Economic and Military* (New York: Dover Publications, 1925, 1988). A new and worthy work that gives a fuller picture of Mitchell and his personality is James J. Cooke, *Billy Mitchell* (Boulder, CO: Lynne Rienner, 2002). A very useful complement to those studies on Mitchell is the biography of his boss by Robert White, *Patrick Mason and the Fight for Air Service Independence* (Washington, DC: Smithsonian, 2002). A new and highly readable work on the subject is Douglas Waller, *A Question of Loyalty: General Billy Mitchell and the Court Martial that Gripped the Nation* (New York: HarperCollins, 2004).

17. Maurer Maurer, *Aviation in the U.S. Army, 1919–1939* (Washington, DC: Office of Air Force History, 1987), 69–84.

18. Mark R. Peattie, *Sunburst: The Rise of Japanese Naval Air Power, 1909–1941* (Annapolis, MD: Naval Institute, 2001), 80–81.

19. John B. Hattendorf, B. Mitchell Simpson III, and John R. Wadleigh, *Sailors and Scholars: The Centennial History of the U.S. Naval War College* (Newport, RI: Naval War College Press, 1984), 4.

20. Edward L. Beach, *The United States Navy: 200 Years* (New York: Holt, 1986), xvii.

21. Actually, the Navy had deployed some aircraft with its forces to Vera Cruz, Mexico, during the fighting there in 1914. John Towers was among the people sent, and one of the aircraft actually received battle damage from small arms fire. Leo

F. Murphy, *Flying Machines Over Pensacola* (Gulf Breeze, FL: Pensacola Flying Machines, 2003), 51–53.

22. Clark G. Reynolds, "William A. Moffett: Steward of the Air Revolution," in James C. Bradford (ed.), *Admirals of the New Steel Navy* (Annapolis, MD: Naval Institute Press, 1990), 378.

23. A leading authority on the early days of naval aviation is Charles M. Melhorn, *Two-Block Fox: The Rise of the Aircraft Carrier, 1911–1929* (Annapolis, MD: Naval Institute, 1974).

24. CDR C. W. Nimitz, "Thesis on Tactics," unpublished Naval War College thesis, Naval War College Archives, Newport, RI, April 28, 1923, RG 13. Nimitz devoted this whole thesis to the subject but gave considerable attention to the impact of aircraft and submarines.

25. William F. Trimble, *Jerome Hunsaker and the Rise of American Aeronautics* (Washington, DC: Smithsonian, 2002), 62; Peattie, 85. In Japan, the idea of a separate air force was also debated within the services but it was strongly rejected by the navy, in part because it feared that the army would dominate such an air force.

26. Thomas C. Hone, "Navy Air Leadership: Rear Admiral William A. Moffett as Chief of the Bureau of Aeronautics," in Wayne Thompson (ed.), *Air Leadership: Proceedings of a Conference at Bolling Air Force Base, April 13–14, 1984* (Washington, DC: Office of Air Force History, 1986), 94.

27. Hone, 90–94.

28. In an August 5, 1919, lecture at the Naval War College, Captain TT Craven, USN, Naval History Collection, RG 15, said: "In the future, is it not safe to predict, in light of recent events, that while slow battleships will be retained in navies, for the present, no one will wish to invest heavily in them in the future? Possibly they may soon become obsolescent."

29. Letter, Rear Admiral William S. Sims in Newport, RI, to Chief of Naval Operations, Washington, DC, February 1, 1921, "United Air Service," in Archives, Naval War College, Newport, RI.

30. Rear Admiral W. A. Moffett, Lecture (read by LCDR B. L. Leighton), "Aircraft in the Navy—Their Use and Limitations," April 6, 1923, at Naval History Collection, Naval War College, Newport, RI, RG 4, 11, the artificial conditions being noted in naval circles at the time.

31. Hone, 97.

32. Thomas B. Buell, *Master of Seapower: A Biography of Fleet Admiral Ernest J. King* (Boston: Little, Brown, 1980), 365.

33. William F. Trimble, *Admiral William A. Moffett: Architect of Naval Aviation* (Washington, DC: Smithsonian, 1994), 91–97.

34. Trimble, 62–63. The *Langley* had been converted to an aircraft transport well before World War II and the Japanese sank her with a load of USAAF P-40s off Java early in 1942.

35. Moffett Lecture, 1923, 8; E. B. Potter, *Bull Halsey* (Annapolis, MD: Naval Institute Press, 1985), 136; Peattie, 21–22; Captain J. H. Towers, "The Influence of Aircraft on Naval Strategy and Tactics," unpublished thesis, May 7, 1934, Naval War College, Newport, RI, RG 13; copy also in Library of Congress, Manuscripts Division, Towers Papers, Box 4, 17, in which he also says that surface sailor and aviator alike understand the importance of air superiority over the Fleet; just as American sailors got many of their early ideas about carriers and aviation from the

British, so too did the Japanese. The evolution of airpower thought in all three navies had much in common, including the imperative requirement for air superiority over the battle fleet.

36. Clark G. Reynolds, *Admiral John H. Towers: The Struggle for Naval Air Supremacy* (Annapolis, MD: US Naval Institute, 1991), 171. Towers, one of the very first naval aviators, told the General Board of the Navy in 1919 that if it did not control the air above the Fleet, then it would not have the Fleet long.

37. Towers thesis, 1934; copy also in Library of Congress, Manuscripts Division, Towers Papers, Box 4, 17–20; US Navy, Naval War College, Staff Lecture, "Fast Carrier Task Force," July 26, 1945, Archives, Naval War College, Newport, RI, RG 4, 1.

38. Peattie, 79. He argues that in the Japanese navy, too, the capital ship sailors had some logic on their side until very late in the game.

39. James J. Cooke, *Billy Mitchell* (Boulder, CO: Lynne Reinner, 2002), 125–130.

40. Peattie, 22. The argument took a similar form in the Japanese navy, where the aviators tended to overestimate the deadliness of their weapon but the battleship advocates were convinced that their weapons were not heavy enough to penetrate the horizontal armor of capital ships until the late 1930s. In both navies, the vulnerability of thin-skinned carriers was well understood and led to the conclusion that the carriers would therefore be inherently offensive in nature—an assumption shared by their land-based aviation brethren everywhere.

41. Hattendorf, 120.

42. Reynolds, 254–257.

43. Eric Larrabee, *Commander in Chief: Franklin Delano Roosevelt, His Lieutenants, and Their War* (New York: Simon & Schuster, 1987), 170, with Admiral King himself having run the mock attack in 1932; Richard B. Frank, *MacArthur* (New York: Palgrave MacMillan, 2007), 45.

44. RADM John D. Hayes, USN (Ret.), "Admiral Joseph Mason Reeves, USN," *Naval War College Review*, XXIII (November 1970), 48–57; Hayes, "Admiral Joseph Mason Reeves, USN, Part II," *Naval War College Review*, XXIV (January 1972), 50–64.

45. Peattie, 52.

46. *Veinticinco de Mayo* = "Twenty-Fifth of May," an ex-British aircraft carrier.

47. Hone, 100; William F. Trimble, *Admiral William A. Moffett: Architect of Naval Aviation* (Washington, DC: Smithsonian, 1993), 205; Peattie, 60. The Japanese navy came to similar conclusions on the size of carriers at that time.

48. Trimble, 15; Peattie, 17. The *Ranger* was the first American ship designed as an aircraft carrier from the keel up. The British *Hermes* and the Japanese *Hosho* had both been so designed more than a decade earlier. The *USS Langley* was converted from a collier hull in the early 1920s, and both the *Lexington* and the *Saratoga* were converted from battle cruiser hulls later in that decade. The *Lexington* was sunk during the Battle of the Coral Sea in May 1942, but the *Saratoga* survived the war only to be sunk shortly afterwards in one of the atom bomb tests. The *Ranger* also survived the war.

49. Peattie, 90–93.

50. Peattie, 46.

51. She was decommissioned in 1991 and is now on display at Corpus Christi, Texas.

52. Hattendorf, 78; Yergin, 306. In 1910–1911, the War College prepared a contingency plan for war against Japan.

53. Larrabee, 191; Edward S. Miller, *War Plan Orange: The U.S. Strategy to Defeat Japan, 1897–1945* (Annapolis, MD: Naval Institute Press, 1991).

54. Henry G. Cole, *The Road to Rainbow: Army Planning for Global War, 1934–1940* (Annapolis, MD: Naval Institute, 2003), 119.

55. Reynolds, 410.

56. Peattie, 198, 201.

CHAPTER 3

1. The school was established as the Air Service Field Officers School, became the Air Service Tactical School, and then in 1926 the Air Corps Tactical School. It was based at Langley Field, Virginia, until 1931 and then at Maxwell Field, Alabama. The current authority on the subject is Robert T. Finney, "History of the Air Corps Tactical School, 1920–1940," *USAF Historical Study 100*, Maxwell AFB, AL, 1955; copy in the Air University Library.

2. Williamson Murray, "Retrospect," in John F. Kreis, *Piercing the Fog* (Washington, DC: Air Force History & Museums Program, 1996), 404–405.

3. Mark R. Peattie, *Sunburst: The Rise of Japanese Naval Air Power, 1909–1941* (Annapolis, MD: Naval Institute, 2001), 87. In Japan, long-range bombing was owned by the navy, and good bombers with exceptionally long ranges were developed (Mitsubishi Kate and Betty bombers). However, when they got into combat over China after 1937, they suffered heavily even to Curtiss Hawk biplane defenders and found that escort was necessary, but not much of that was appreciated in the United States.

4. David MacIsaac, "Voices from the Central Blue: The Airpower Theorists," in Peter Paret (ed.), *Makers of Modern Strategy: From Machiavelli to the Nuclear Age* (Princeton, NJ: Princeton University, 1986), 624–630; Bernard Brodie, *Strategy in the Missile Age* (Princeton, NJ: Princeton University, 1959, 1965), 98; Lee Kennett, "Strategic Bombardment: A Retrospective," in R. Cargill Hall (ed.), *Case Studies in Strategic Bombardment* (Washington, DC: Air Force History & Museums Program, 1998), 623; Williamson Murray and Allan R. Millett, *A War to be Won: Fighting the Second World War* (Cambridge, MA: Belknap, 2000), 304. The idea that bombing could reduce human suffering by shortening wars antedates both Mitchell and Douhet, for it was voiced by Captain William Crozier, US Army, at the Hague Conference of 1899.

5. The most famous of the faculty skeptics was Claire Chennault. His argument was that interceptors served by a competent ground observer corps could inflict unacceptable losses on daylight bombing forces. It is noteworthy that he, along with most of the bomber folks, thought that fighter escorts were probably impractical. The authority on Chennault is Martha Byrd, *Chennault: Giving Wings to the Tiger* (Tuscaloosa, AL: University of Alabama, 1987), 51, on the impracticality of escort. One example among many of the student skeptics was Otto P. Weyland, who attended in 1938; James C. Hasdorff and BGEN Noel Parrish, *General O. P. Weyland, USAF, Oral History*, November, 19, 1974, San Antonio, TX; copy at Air Force Historical Research Agency (AFHRA), Maxwell AFB, K239.0512-813, 33, where he says, "The students, including me, didn't always agree with the instructor staff

on the school solutions." Another student skeptic was Thomas A. Sturm, *MGEN Gordon P. Saville, USAF Oral History*, March 26–29, 1973, Sun City, AZ; copy at AFHRA, K239.0512-1322, 18–20.

6. John W. R. Taylor (ed.), *Combat Aircraft of the World: From 1919 to the Present* (New York: Paragon, 1966), 476, 453, 527. The Boeing B-9 appeared the year before the Martin B-10, and it was a monoplane with retractable landing gear but it was not procured in numbers, fewer than 20 having been produced.

7. Maurer Maurer, *Aviation in the U.S. Army, 1919–1939* (Washington, DC: Office of Air Force History, 1987), 283–343; James P. Tate, *The Army and Its Air Corps: Army Policy Toward Aviation, 1919–1941* (Maxwell AFB, AL: Air University, 1998), 143–151.

8. Wesley Frank Craven and James Lea Cate, *The Army Air Forces in World War II, Vol. 6: Men and Planes* (Washington, DC: Office of Air Force History, 1983), 39.

9. Jeffry S. Underwood, *The Wings of Democracy: The Influence of Air Power on the Roosevelt Administration, 1933–1941* (College Station, TX: Texas A&M, 1991), 168–171; Wesley Frank Craven and James Lea Cate, *The Army Air Forces in World War II, Vol. 1: Plans and Early Operations* (Washington, DC: Office of Air Force History, 1983), 600–605.

10. Alan J. Levine, *The Strategic Bombing of Germany, 1940–1945* (Westport, CT: Praeger, 1992), 31–32; Williamson Murray and Allan R. Millett, *A War to Be Won: Fighting the Second World War* (Cambridge, MA: Belknap, 2000), 305.

11. Rebecca Brooks Gruver, *An American History, Vol II: From 1865 to the Present* (Reading, MA: Addison-Wesley, 1976), 798–803; Maurer, xix–xxxiii; Paul Kennedy, *Rise and Fall of the Great Powers* (New York: Random House, 1987), 267, on the impact of the war on the British economy.

12. The authority on the subject is Irving B. Holley, Jr., *United States Army in World War II, Special Studies, Buying Aircraft: Materiel Procurement for the Army Air Forces* (Washington: Center of Military History United States Army, 1989), 6–33.

13. One of the most important samples of scientific migrants was Theodore von Karman as described in Michael H. Gorn, *The Universal Man: Theodore von Karman's Life in Aeronautics* (Washington, DC: Smithsonian, 1992); Richard A. Preston and Sydney F. Wise, *Men in Arms: A History of Warfare and Its Interrelationships with Western Society*, 4th ed. (New York: Holt, Rinehart & Winston, 1979), 325–326.

14. Preston and Wise, 278–294; William E. Leuchtenburg, *Franklin D. Roosevelt and the New Deal, 1932–40* (New York: Harper, 1963), 30–31, 296; John D. Hicks, *Republican Ascendancy, 1921–1933* (New York: Harper, 1960), 233.

15. The German plan for the beginning of World War I was based on the assumption that she had to have a short war against superior numbers. It also assumed that the Russians would be much slower in their mobilization than would be the French. Thus, the notion was to smash around the northern end of the French defenses by going through Belgium, swing around Paris and cause the early capitulation of the French. This was to happen early enough to mount the German forces on their superior railroads to hustle far to the east to meet the oncoming Russians—the Schlieffen Plan. (Obviously, it did not work.)

16. Murray and Millett, 62.

17. Hew Strachan, *European Armies and the Conduct of War* (London: Allen & Unwin, 1983), 151–152; Jack English, "Lessons from the Great War," *Canadian Military Journal*, Vol. 4 (2003), available online at http://www.journal.dnd.ca/engraph/Vol4/no2/history_e.asp, accessed January 15, 2004.

18. Carl H. Builder, *The Masks of War: American Military Styles in Strategy and Analysis* (Baltimore, MD: Johns Hopkins, 1989), 74.

19. Stephen Peter Rosen, *Winning the Next War: Innovation and the Modern Military* (Ithaca, NY: Cornell, 1991); Rosen, "New Ways of War: Understanding Military Innovation," *International Security*, Vol. 13 (Summer 1988), 135.

20. Ryan Henry, "Defense Transformation and the 2005 Quadrennial Defense Review," *Parameters* (Winter 2005-06): 5–15.

21. Murray and Millett, 31–32; Hanson Baldwin, *Battles Lost and Won* (New York: Avon, 1966), 57.

22. LTC John Gordon, USA (Ret.) and LTC Walter L. Perry, USA (Ret.), "The Operational Challenges of Task Force Hawk," *Joint Forces Quarterly* (Autumn/Winter 2001-02): 52–56, available at http://w3ww.dtic.mil/doctrine/jel/jfq_pubs/1229.pdf, accessed January 16, 2004; Michael R. Gordon and Eric Schmitt, "Attack Copters Idle as Pentagon Blocks their Use in Kosovo," *New York Times* (May 16, 1999), available at http://aeronautics.ru/nytimesapaches.htm, accessed January 16, 2004; Andrew F. Krepinevich, *Operation Iraqi Freedom: A First-Blush Assessment* (Washington, DC: Center for Strategic & Budgetary Assessments, 2003), 30.

23. Rosen, "New Ways of War," 135.

24. Rumsfeld was a Navy pilot in his younger days; McNamara was an analyst in the Army during World War II.

25. Rosen, *Winning the Next War*, 255–257.

26. Carl von Clausewitz, who died in 1830, authored the monumental *On War*, often held to be the greatest book on military theory ever written.

27. Terrence J. Gough, "Origins of the Army Industrial College," *Armed Forces & Society*, Vol. 17 (Winter 1991): 259–275.

28. Eliot Cohen, *Supreme Command* (New York: Free Press, 2002), pursues the theme throughout the book that the highest political leaders have the duty to intervene in the military to as low a level as necessary. He uses the cases of Abraham Lincoln, Winston Churchill, Ben Gurion, and Georges Clemenceau. Lieutenant General Michael C. Short, USAF, argued the contrary in a Public Broadcasting System interview, available at http://www.pbs.org/wgbh/pages/frontline/shows/kosovo/interviews/short.html, accessed January 20, 2004.

29. John M. Blum, "United Against: American Culture and Society During World War II," in Harry R. Borowski (ed.), *The Harmon Memorial Lectures in Military History, 1959–1987* (Washington: Office of Air Force History, 1988), 579–581.

30. Thomas A. Fabyanic, "Professionalism in Transition: The Officer Corps in the Age of Deterrence," *Air University Review* (September-October 1978), available at http://www.airpower.Maxwell.af.mil/airchronicles/aureview/1978/sep-oct/fabyanic.html, accessed January 14, 2004.

31. Stephen B. Johnson, in *The United States Air Force and the Culture of Innovation* (Washington, DC: Air Force History & Museums Program, 2002), 221–228, argues that two of the factors that made the USAF competitive with the other services from the early days were contracting out much of the research and development

work to industry, academia, and non-profits instead of keeping it in arsenals led to greater imagination and diversity, and the early development of a systems approach and systems engineering also helped speed up the process and integrate its various parts. Personality also played a part in the fortunate combination of talents and opportunity in General Bernard Schriever; see also Thomas C. Hone, "Navy Air Leadership: Rear Admiral William A. Moffett as Chief of the Bureau of Aeronautics," in Wayne Thompson (ed.), *Air Leadership: Proceedings of a Conference at Bolling Air Force Base, April 13–14, 1984* (Washington, DC: Office of Air Force History, 1986), 83–117.

32. Johnson, 221; further, Alan L. Gropman, *The Air Force Integrates, 1945–1964* (Washington, DC: Smithsonian, 1998), presents a pretty persuasive case that the USAF was far ahead of the rest of society in the integration of blacks, and an equally persuasive case could be made for the movement toward gender equality.

33. If there ever was a true discontinuity in the evolution of military technology, it was the coming of nuclear weapons. For more on the subject, see "Technology, Thought, Troops: General Carl A. Spaatz and the Dawn of the Nuclear Age," in David R. Mets and William P. Head, *Plotting a True Course: Reflections on USAF Strategic Attack Theory and Doctrine—The Post-World War II Experience* (Westport, CT: Greenwood, 2003), 7–43.

34. On Japan, see Forrest E. Morgan, *Compellence and the Strategic Culture of Imperial Japan* (Westport, CT: Praeger, 2003), and Alvin D. Coox, "The Rise and Fall of the Imperial Japanese Air Forces," in Alfred F. Hurley and Robert C. Ehrhart, *Airpower and Warfare: The Proceedings of the Eighth Military History Symposium, October 18–20, 1978* (Washington, DC: Office of Air Force History, 1979), 84–93. There is a huge body of literature on the American and British cases. One of the best of the latter is Stephern Roskill, *Naval Policy Between the Wars* (New York: Walker, 1968), and for the former, James J. Cooke, *Billy Mitchell* (Boulder, CO: Lynne Rienner, 2002), and Robert P. White, *Mason Patrick and the Fight for Air Service Independence* (Washington, DC: Smithsonian, 2001). On the controversy of the late 1940s, a good work from the naval point of view is Jeffrey G. Barlow, *Revolt of the Admirals: The Fight for Naval Aviation, 1945–1950* (Washington, DC: Department of the Navy, 1994).

35. J. Douglas Beason and Mark Lewis, "The War Fighter's Need for Science and Technology," *Air and Space Power Journal* (Winter 2005): 71–81.

36. An authoritative work on the subject is Charles M. Melhorn, *Two-Block Fox: The Rise of the Aircraft Carrier, 1911–1929* (Annapolis, MD: Naval Institute, 1974).

37. "Concorde's Last Flight," BBC Bristol Website, November 26, 2003, available at http://www.bbc.co.uk/bristol/content/concorde, accessed January, 29, 2004.

38. Samuel P. Huntington, *The Clash of Civilizations and the Remaking of World Order* (New York: Simon & Schuster, 1996), 211–214, 218–225; Morgan, 57–66.

39. For a persuasive argument on the sources of American individualism, see Carl N. Degler, *Out of Our Past* (New York: Harper & Row, 1970). This may make surprises like Pearl Harbor and the attack on the World Trade Towers all the more surprising because of our cultural stereotypes.

40. Max Weber, *The Protestant Ethic and the Spirit of Capitalism*, 2nd ed. (New York: Routledge Classics, 2001).

41. Arnold J. Toynbee, *A Study of History* (London: Oxford, 1972).

42. Lon O. Nordeen, *Air Warfare in the Missile Age*, 2nd ed. (Washington, DC: Smithsonian, 2002), 123–148.

43. Triad = bombers + intercontinental missiles + submarine-launched ballistic missiles.

44. For the argument on elitism, see Builder, 17–30, 41–43; for the other side, see Richard M. Clark, *Uninhabited Combat Air Vehicles* (Maxwell AFB, AL: Air University Press, 2000).

45. Vannevar Bush, *Modern Arms and Free Men* (Westport, CT: Greenwood, 1949, 1985), 81, 85, 121.

46. Johnson, 29–30.

47. Some of the most useful works on the Battle of Britain include Paul Addison and Jeremy A. Crang (eds.), *The Burning Blue: A New History of the Battle of Britain* (London: Pimlico, 2000); Winston S. Churchill, *Their Finest Hour, Vol. II: The Second World War* (Boston: Houghton Mifflin, 1948–1953); Derek Dempster and Derek Wood, *The Narrow Margin* (Washington, DC: Smithsonian, 1960, 1990), a couple of British journalists who did their homework—if you want the details, including a good bit on technology, then this is a good work for the purpose; John Ferris, "Fighter Defense Before Fighter Command," *Journal of Military History* (October 1999): 845–85; Raymond H. Fredette, *The Sky on Fire: The First Battle of Britain* (New York: Holt, Rinehart, & Winston, 1966), a retired USAF major with a fine writing style, this book has been widely sold; Francis K. Mason, *Battle Over Britain* (New York: Aston, 1969); Robin Higham, "The RAF and the Battle of Britain," in Benjamin F. Cooling (ed.), *Case Studies in the Achievement of Air Superiority* (Washington, DC: Office of Air Force History, 1994), 115–178; David R. Mets, "The Battle of Britain," in Thomas E. Griess (ed.), *The Second World War, Vol. I: Europe and the Mediterranean* (Wayne, NJ: Avery, 1984), 55–86; R. J. Overy, *The Battle of Britain: The Myth and the Reality* (New York: Norton, 2001); Carl A. Spaatz, "Leaves from My Battle-of-Britain Diary," *Airpower Historian*, Vol. 4 (Spring 1957), 66–75; Telford Taylor, *The Breaking Wave* (New York: Simon & Schuster, 1967), a prominent United States lawyer who worked on World War II war crimes trials and who has written several authoritative books on World War II; John Terraine, *A Time for Courage: The Royal Air Force in the European War* (New York: Macmillan, 1985); Peter Townsend, *Duel of Eagles* (New York: Simon & Schuster, 1971), one of the participants in the battle.

CHAPTER 4

1. Neville Jones, *The Beginnings of Strategic Air Power: A History of the British Bomber Force, 1923–39* (London: Cass, 1987).

2. Jeffry S. Underwood, *The Wings of Democracy: The Influence of Air Power on the Roosevelt Administration, 1933–1941* (College Station, TX: Texas A&M, 1991), 17, 50–55.

3. Among the useful works on Great Britain between the wars are Jones; Tami Davis Biddle, *Rhetoric and Reality in Air Warfare* (Princeton, NJ: Princeton University, 2002), Chapter 2; and George K. Williams, *Biplanes and Bombsights* (Maxwell AFB, AL: Air University Press, 1999).

4. The air defense at Guadalcanal fought without the benefits of radar for several months until a set became operational at Henderson Field in November or December 1942—and even then, the coast watchers generally gave the defenders longer warning than did the radar. Lt. Col. Momyer's 33rd Pursuit Group fought in Tunisia during the opening months of Torch without benefit of radar coverage for their home field—and dependent upon Chennault-style ground observers and the telephones of the day, they generally had the Stukas overhead before they received warning (Momyer managed to shoot down four in one sortie immediately over the field at Thelepte). As noted in the Spaatz Diary cited previously, two years earlier the Stuka had proven a dismal failure in the Battle of Britain, where it was working in a radar environment.

5. Peter Calvocoressi and Guy Wint, *Total War: The Story of World War II* (New York: Random House, 1972), 132; Gerhard L. Weinberg, *A World at Arms: A Global History of World War II* (Cambridge, UK: Cambridge University Press, 1994), 148.

6. Basil Collier, *Defence of the United Kingdom* (London: His Majesty's Stationery Office, 1957), 92, 164.

7. B. H. Liddell Hart, *History of the Second World War* (New York: Putnam's, 1970), 89; Hanson Baldwin, *Battles Lost and Won* (New York: Avon, 1966), 60.

8. E. B. Addison, "The Radio War," *Journal of the Royal United Services Institute*, XVII (February 1947): 31–34.

9. Weinberg, 150.

10. Baldwin, 57–60; Dowding's achievement was all the more remarkable because airmen and air theorists generally looked upon ground defenses with disdain for a long time; William Mitchell, Lecture, Army War College, 24 November 1922, Army War College File No. 240-49, Archives, U.S. Army Military Institute, Carlisle Barracks, PA, in which he said, "Some improvement has been made in anti-aircraft artillery. However, as I said before, we care little for anti-aircraft artillery . . . "; Giulio Douhet, in *Command of the Air* (Washington, DC: Office of Air Force History, 1982), said it thusly: "The airplane has complete freedom of action and direction; it can fly to and from any point of the compass in the shortest time—in a straight line—by any route deemed expedient. Nothing man can do on the surface of the earth can interfere with a plane in flight, moving freely in the third dimension. All the influences which have conditioned and characterized warfare from the beginning are powerless to affect aerial action . . . " (p. 9).

11. Calvocoressi and Wint, 132; Liddell Hart, 93.

12. Calvocoressi and Wint, 127.

13. Richard Muller, *The German Air War in Russia* (Baltimore, MD: Nautical & Aviation Publishing, 1992), 3–5.

14. Baldwin, 65–69.

15. Calvocorssi and Wint, 130; Baldwin, 83; Carl A. Spaatz, "Diary of Brigadier General Carl Spaatz on Tour of Duty in England, 17 May 1940 to 19 September 1940," in Spaatz Papers, Manuscripts Division, Library of Congress, Box 7.

16. Baldwin, 79; Calvocoressi and Wint, 135.

17. Liddell Hart, 94.

18. Weinberg, 149; Liddell Hart, 104.

19. Liddell Hart, 92.

20. With many small projectiles in a high-rate-of-fire gun, you have a high probability of hitting a target; with a gun with a slower rate of fire but a heavier

projectile, you have a lesser probability of hitting the target but if you do hit it, a higher probability of destroying it.

21. Liddell Hart, 90.

22. Baldwin declares that Hitler was only "lukewarm" about the threatened invasion, and that he was expecting Great Britain to make peace without further fighting.

23. Daniel Yergin, *The Prize: The Epic Quest for Oil, Money, and Power* (New York: Free Press, 1991), 315.

24. For a discussion of the potential and difficulties of using historical precedent for the development of space policy, see Mark P. Jelonek, "Toward an Air and Space Force: Can We Get There from Here? Naval Aviation and the Implications for Space Power" (unpublished masters thesis, School of Advanced Airpower Studies, Maxwell AFB, AL, 1998).

25. One sample is the third issue of *High Frontier* (Winter 2005), the journal of the Air Force Space Command, which is replete with allusions to airpower development between the world wars, Billy Mitchell, and the separation of the Air Force from the Army.

26. For arguments about the possible negative results of building an offensive capability in space, see Brian R. Sullivan, "Spacepower and America's Future," in Peter L. Hays et al., *Spacepower for a New Millennium: Space and U.S. National Security* (New York: McGraw-Hill, 2000), 259–280,

27. JDAMS = Joint Direct Attack Munitions System, a GPS/inertial guided bomb.

28. For thought-provoking studies on United States' space policy, see Walter A. McDougall, *The Heavens and the Earth: A Political History of the Space Age* (Baltimore, MD: Johns Hopkins, 1985, 1997); David N. Spires, *Beyond Horizons: A Half Century of Air Force Space Leadership* (Peterson AFB, CO: Air Force Space Command, 1997); and Everett C. Dolman, *Astropolitik* (London: Cass, 2002).

CHAPTER 5

1. Daniel Yergin, *The Prize: The Epic Quest for Oil, Money, and Power* (New York: Free Press, 1991), 314–315.

2. Thomas Wildenberg, *Destined for Glory: Dive Bombing, Midway and the Evolution of Carrier Airpower* (Annapolis, MD: Naval Institute, 1998), 214–215.

3. Mark R. Peattie, *Sunburst: The Rise of Japanese Naval Air Power, 1909–1941* (Annapolis, MD: Naval Institute, 2001), 34.

4. Samuel Eliot Morison, *Two-Ocean War* (Boston: Little, Brown, 1963), 50–51.

5. Richard B. Frank, *MacArthur* (New York: Palgrave MacMillan, 2007), 43–45.

6. Thomas B. Buell, *Master of Seapower: A Biography of Fleet Admiral Ernest J. King* (Boston: Little, Brown, 1980), 196.

7. A. Russell Buchanan, *The United States and World War II* (New York: Harper, 1964), 221–223,

8. E. B. Potter, *Nimitz* (Annapolis, MD: Naval Institute, 1976), 63–77.

9. E. B. Potter, *Bull Halsey* (Annapolis, MD: Naval Institute Press, 1985), 271–272.

10. An incident occurred here that was long a factor irritating AAF-Navy relations in that a group of B-17s had gone to Midway and had bombed the Japanese ships before the Navy battle began. As usual in combat, the operators came back with much magnified claims (it was later proven they got no hits at all), and the media so inflated them further that it appeared that the B-17s led by Lieutenant Colonel Walter Sweeney had won the battle and turned the tide. That was the same Sweeney who later, as a four-star general, commanded the Tactical Air Command at the time of the Cuban Missile Crisis, and informed President Kennedy that the USAF could not guarantee a surgical strike that would take out all of the Soviet missiles. The Midway activity further suggested that getting a surface ship from altitude was tougher than Mitchell and Pearl Harbor seemed to suggest.

11. Frank, 77–78.

12. Thomas E. Griffith, Jr., *MacArthur's Airman: General George C. Kenney and His War in the Southwest Pacific* (Lawrence, KS: University Press of Kansas, 1998), 71–121, and Geoffrey Perret, *Old Soldiers Never Die: The Life of Douglas MacArthur* (New York: Random House, 1996), 308–343, on the war in the Southwest Pacific; Thomas B. Buell, *The Quiet Warrior: A Biography of Admiral Raymond A. Spruance* (Annapolis, MD: Naval Institute Press, 1987), 167–175, and Wesley Frank Craven and James Lea Cate, *The Army Air Forces in World War II, Vol. 4, The Pacific: Guadalcanal to Saipan* (Washington, DC: Office of Air Force History, 1983), 37–60, on Guadalcanal.

13. Frank, 74–75.

14. Buell, *Quiet Warrior*, 202.

15. Potter, *Nimitz*, 331–345; Wesley Frank Craven and James Lea Cate, *The Army Air Forces in World War II, Vol. 5, The Pacific: Matterhorn to Nagasaki* (Washington, DC: Office of Air Force History, 1983), 341–368.

16. Potter, *Nimitz*, 331–345; Craven and Cate, 341–368.

17. Potter, *Nimitz*, 331–345; Craven and Cate, 341–368.

18. Theodore Roscoe, *On the Seas and in the Skies* (New York: Hawthorne, 1970), 442–443.

19. Potter, *Nimitz*, 358–377.

20. Potter, *Nimitz*, 327.

21. Curtis E. LeMay with MacKinlay Kantor, *Mission with LeMay* (Garden City, NY: Doubleday, 1965), 388.

22. John A. Lynn, *Battle: A History of Combat and Culture* (Cambridge, MA: Perseus, 2003), 239–280, arguing that those who assert that the decision to drop the bombs on Japan was motivated by racism are wrong. Others have asserted that it was done not to defeat the Japanese but rather to impress the Soviets. Still others have argued that the total war momentum had built up to the point that everything with a even a remote chance of saving American lives was certain to be implemented, and still others that it not only saved American lives by making an invasion unnecessary but Japanese lives as well.

23. *The United States Strategic Bombing Survey, Pacific War* (Maxwell AFB, AL: Air University Press, 1987), 107.

24. Yergin, 373–375.

25. Thomas B. Buell, "The Battle of the Atlantic," in Thomas Griess (ed.), *The Second World War: Europe and the Mediterranean* (Wayne, NJ: Avery, 1989), 205–225.

26. Buell, "Battle of the Atlantic," 225.

27. Gerhard L. Weinberg, *A World at Arms: A Global History of World War II* (Cambridge, UK: Cambridge University Press, 1994), 365; Buell, "Battle of the Atlantic," 208; Peter Calvocoressi and Guy Wint, *Total War: The Story of World War II* (New York: Random House, 1972), 415, 418.

28. Wesley Frank Craven and James Lea Cate, *The Army Air Forces in World War II, Vol. 1: Plans and Early Operations* (Washington, DC: Office of Air Force History, 1983), 51, 514, 518, where we are informed that the Air Corps Tactical School thought that airpower could defeat invasions of the homeland and interdict enemy seaborne commerce but it could not alone protect U.S. commerce on the oceans.

29. It is worth noting that the United States wound up with submarines, the Fleet Boats, that accidentally were much better suited to war on commerce than were the German U-boats. The American submarines were designed primarily as adjuncts to the battle fleet for scouting and attack on Japanese naval units. However, the U.S. bases in the Pacific were so few and far apart that the boats had to be designed with great range and much more habitability than the Nazi U-boats—ideal characteristics for solo, long-range anti-commerce operations.

30. Dan Van der Vat, *Stealth at Sea: The History of Submarines* (Boston: Houghton-Mifflin, 1995), 157–158.

31. John Keegan, *The Price of Admiralty: The Evolution of Naval Warfare* (New York: Penguin, 1988), 252, 278.

32. Williamson Murray and Allan R. Millett, *A War to Be Won: Fighting the Second World War* (Cambridge, MA: Belknap, 2000), 236, 241, 260.

33. The Liberator did not have quite as high a ceiling under full load as did the Fortress, and thus the crews in the bomber offensive over Germany preferred the small margin of safety from anti-aircraft fire that the B-17 enjoyed. The bombing altitude was not as important in the Pacific because the Japanese ground-based air defenses were not nearly as formidable as were the German. In the Battle of the Atlantic, to some degree the visibility could be better at a lower altitude, the reciprocating engines could operate more economically than at higher levels, and the anti-aircraft threat was not nearly as bad as over Germany. Weinberg, 375, on the Liberators and covering the black hole.

34. Murray and Millett, 238. Medium- and high-frequency radio energy can travel either by ground waves or by bouncing off the ionosphere, but the very-high frequency and ultra-high frequency sets worked only by line of sight and were of much shorter range, though they do have advantages.

35. Anthony Cave Brown, *Bodyguard of Lies* (London: W. H. Allen, 1977), 251–253.

36. Keegan, 272.

37. Stephen Budiansky, *Air Power* (New York: Viking, 2004), 276; Weinberg, 369.

38. Murray and Millett, 240.

39. Craven and Cate, *Plans and Early Operations*, 514–535.

40. Dan van Der Vat, 284.
41. Keegan, 312.
42. Keegan, 313.
43. Keegan, 314. The Walter or Walther boats were powered by a closed system fueled with hydrogen peroxide. That allowed them to run beneath the surface with an engine not dependent upon either air or batteries. It enabled optimizing the hull design for high speed underwater rather than on the surface. The hydrogen peroxide scheme had bugs in it that had to be worked out, and was to be made obsolete by the coming of nuclear power for submarines. But the improved hull design was applicable to nuclear submarines and gave them an underwater speed superior to that of surface vessels.
44. Roscoe, 306–308. The submarine was ultimately hauled to Illinois and put on display in Chicago.
45. Brown, 251; Weinberg, 386–389.
46. Buell, *Europe and the Mediterranean*, 225.
47. A modern term meaning the command of the electromagnetic spectrum.
48. Levine, 31–32; Murray and Millett, 305.
49. James Parton, *Air Force Spoken Here: General Ira Eaker and the Command of the Air* (Bethesda, MD: Adler & Adler, 1986), 221–222.
50. Lee Kennett, "Strategic Bombardment: A Retrospective," in R. Cargill Hall (ed.), *Case Studies in Strategic Bombardment* (Washington, DC: Air Force History & Museums Program, 1998), 628.
51. Drop tanks are disposable tanks carried externally. The first part of the mission is flown with fuel from them and upon engagement with the enemy, they are dropped to improve maneuverability and lessen the danger of explosion. Actually, they had been used in World War I but had long been rejected for combat as too cumbersome and dangerous.
52. Levine, 91. Ultimately, the P-51 Mustang was the only escort that could reach as far as Berlin but that was about its outer limit, and Iwo Jima had to be captured in 1945 to enable it to reach Japan with the B-29s.
53. Daniel R. Mortensen, "The Legend of Laurence Kuter," in Daniel R. Mortensen (ed.), *Airpower and Ground Armies: Essays on the Evolution of Anglo-American Air Doctrine, 1940–1943* (Maxwell AFB, AL: Air University Press, 1998), 93–140; Griffith, 71–121.
54. Williamson Murray, "Retrospect," in John F. Kreis (ed.), *Piercing the Fog* (Washington, DC: Air Force History & Museums Program, 1996), 405.
55. Wesley Frank Craven and James Lea Cate, *The Army Air Forces in World War II, Vol. 2, Europe: Torch to Pointblank* (Washington, DC: Office of Air Force History, 1983), 41–106; Vincent Orange, "Getting Together," in Daniel Mortensen (ed.), *Airpower and Ground Armies* (Maxwell AFB, AL: Air University Press, 1998), 1–44.
56. Craven and Cate, *Torch to Pointblank*, 41–106; Orange, 1–44; Yergin, 339–343.
57. Alexander Orlov, *Handbook of Intelligence and Guerrilla Warfare* (Ann Arbor, MI: University of Michigan, 1963), 19.
58. Williamson Murray, *Strategy for Defeat* (Maxwell AFB, AL: Air University Press, 1983), 209–255.

59. Yergin, 346–348.

60. *United States Strategic Bombing Survey, Summary Report, European War*, hereinafter USSBS (Maxwell AFB, AL: Air University Press, 1987), 23; Yergin, 343–348.

61. USSBS, 30–31.

62. USSBS, 37.

63. Buell, *Master of Seapower*, 486. Admiral King himself was one.

64. Wesley Frank Craven and James Lea Cate, *The Army Air Forces in World War II, Vol. 3, Europe: Argument to VE Day* (Washington, DC: Office of Air Force History, 1983), 72–83; W. W. Rostow, *Pre-Invasion Strategy: General Eisenhower's Decision of March 25, 1944* (Austin, TX: University of Texas, 1981).

65. Omar Bradley and Clay Blair, *A General's Life: An Autobiography of General of the Army Omar Bradley* (New York: Simon & Schuster, 1983), 276–282.

66. Bradley and Blair, 353–360; Murray and Millett, 463–471.

67. Yergin, 348–349.

68. Paul Kennedy, *Rise and Fall of the Great Powers* (New York: Random House, 1987), 273.

69. Walt Boyne, "Missiles against the Roma," *Flying Review* (February 1968): 102–107; Albert N. Garland et al., *United States Army in World War II: The Mediterranean Theater of Operations, Sicily and the Surrender of Italy* (Washington, DC: Chief of Military History, 1965), 532–533; Charles H. Bogart, "German Remotely Piloted Bombs," *US Naval Institute Proceedings*, Vol. 102 (November 1976), 62–68; Alfred Price, *Luftwaffe* (New York: Ballantine, 1969, 1970), 106–107; Michael Russell Rip and James M. Hasik, *The Precision Revolution: GPS and the Future of Aerial Warfare* (Annapolis, MD: Naval Institute, 2002), 202–204.

70. Craven and Cate, *Matterhorn to Nagasaki*, 195; US Army Air Forces (AAF), AAF Board, Orlando, FL, "Controlled Missiles," Project No. GP 5, 29, copy in Technical Library, Air Armament Center, Eglin AFB, FL.

71. James Phinney Baxter III, *Scientists Against Time* (Boston: Little, Brown, 1946), 198–199; Wesley Frank Craven and James Lea Cate, *The Army Air Forces in World War II, Vol. 6, Men and Planes* (Washington, DC: Office of Air Force History, 1983), 258–259.

72. Clark G. Reynolds, *Admiral John H. Towers: The Struggle for Naval Air Supremacy* (Annapolis, MD: US Naval Institute, 1991), 360, in the Navy. Also, Admiral Towers at the head of the Bureau of Aeronautics approved the making over of 100 old torpedo bombers into attack drones before Pearl Harbor.

73. Craven and Cate, *Argument to VE Day*, 531.

74. Baxter, 198–199; Albert B. Christman and J. D. Gerrard-Gough, *History of the Naval Weapons Center, Vol. 2, The Grand Experiment at Inyokern* (Washington, DC: Naval History Division, 1978), 277–279. There is a splendid sample of the "BAT" in the museum at the Naval Air Warfare Center at China Lake, California.

75. Craven and Cate, *Men and Planes*, 234; J. Douglas Beason and Mark Lewis, "The War Fighter's Need for Science and Technology," *Air and Space Power Journal* (Winter 2005): 71–81.

76. Gorn, *Universal Man*, 108–109.

CHAPTER 6

1. Bernard Brodie, *Strategy in the Missile Age*, (Princeton, NJ: Princeton University, 1959, 1965), 73.

2. Gian P. Gentile, "Planning for Preventive War, 1945–1950," *Joint Forces Quarterly*, No. 24, (Spring 2000): 69.

3. MGEN Charles J. Dunlap, USAF, believes that soldiers even in 2007 feel that Air Force people are still obsessed with strategic bombing notwithstanding mountains of evidence to the contrary, "Understanding Airmen: A Primer for Soldiers," *Military Review* (September-October 2007): 130.

4. Robert F. Futrell, *Ideas, Concepts and Doctrine: Basic Thinking in the United States Air Force, Vol. I, 1907–1960* (Maxwell AFB, AL: Air University, 1987), 213.

5. US Air Force, Aircraft and Weapons Board, "Summary Minutes, First Meeting of the U.S. Air Force Aircraft and Weapons Board, 19–22 August 1947", in Box 181, RG 341, National Archives, College Park, MD, gives a rather good summary of the attitudes of the Air Force establishment at the birth of the USAF—still the ideal being a "balanced air force" with the emphasis on the strategic air attack mission; Report, US Air Force, DCS Development, First Aircraft and Weapons Board, (nd-August 1947), Box 182, RG 341, National Archives, College Park, MD.

6. The maximum strength of the AAF during World War II had been in August 1945 when there were 2,300,000 persons aboard. By March 1946, the total was down to 328,079, Herman S. Wolk, *Planning and Organizing the Postwar Air Force, 1943–47* (Washington, DC: Office of Air Force History, 1984), 135.

7. James R. Locher III, "Has it Worked? The Goldwater-Nichols Act," *Naval War College Review*, LIV (Autumn 2001): 96.

8. Wolk, 45–79, 149–178, is the authority on the subject. For an expert discussion of the period from a naval historian, see Jeffrey G. Barlow, *The Revolt of the Admirals: The Fight for Naval Aviation, 1945–1950* (Washington, DC: Naval Historical Center, 1994).

9. Michael H. Gorn, *The Universal Man: Theodore von Karman's Life in Aeronautics* (Washington, DC: Smithsonian, 1992), 116.

10. Capt. Ernest J. King, USN, "The Influence of National Policy on the Strategy of War," unpublished thesis, Naval War College, Newport, RI, 1932, copy in Library of Congress, Manuscripts Division, King Papers, Box 23, 8, wherein King argued that geography itself could dictate that seapower be the first line of defense but allowed that in the case of an island nation like Great Britain, airpower could run a close second. He concluded his 1932 argument with the notion that in the U.S. case the Navy remained the first line of defense; Steven L. Rearden, *History of the Office of the Secretary of Defense, Vol. 1: The Formative Years, 1947–1950* (Washington, DC: Office of the Secretary of Defense, 1984), 389, asserts that the Air Force heavyweights thought they now had the title and were not about to give it up.

11. Letters, Henry H. Arnold to Carl A. Spaatz, January 17, 1947, and Spaatz to Arnold, February 5, 1947, in Spaatz Collection, Manuscripts Division, Library of Congress, Box 256, in which Arnold laments that the Air Force did most of the compromising that enabled the Sherman-Norstad agreement that cleared the way for the unification act of that year. Spaatz replied that it was probably the only

compromise that could have a hope of passage because he was getting criticisms in equal volume and passion from all sides.

12. Carl H. Builder, *The Masks of War: American Military Styles in Strategy and Analysis* (Baltimore, MD: Johns Hopkins, 1989), 76.

13. Roger G. Miller, *To Save a City: The Berlin Airlift, 1948–1949* (Washington, DC: Air Force History & Museums Program, 1998), 24–25. Miller's fine monograph is current based on the latest sources, some of them coming from former Communist countries, and well written.

14. Conrad C. Crane, *American Airpower Strategy in Korea, 1950–1953* (Lawrence, KS: University Press of Kansas, 2000), 171–184, being the latest and most authoritative work on the subject.

15. Walton S. Moody, *Building a Strategic Air Force* (Washington, DC: Air Force History & Museums Program, 1996), 396.

16. William W. Momyer, *Air Power in Three Wars: World War II, Korea, Vietnam* (Washington, DC: USAF, 1978), 39–62. The entire theme of his book is the long struggle for the unified control of airpower at the theater level; the passage cited here relates to the Korean War and its background.

17. Stephen E. Ambrose, *Eisenhower, Vol II: The President* (New York: Simon & Schuster, 1984), 34–35, 106; Mark Clodfelter, *The Limits of Air Power* (New York: Free Press, 1989), 205.

18. Steven L. Rearden, "U.S. Strategic Bombardment Doctrine Since 1945," in R. Cargill Hall (ed.), *Case Studies in Strategic Bombardment* (Washington, DC: Air Force History & Museums Program, 1998), 450.

19. Harry R. Borowski, *A Hollow Threat: Strategic Air Power and Containment before Korea* (Westport, CT: Greenwood, 1982).

20. Vannevar Bush, *Modern Arms and Free Men* (Westport, CT: Greenwood, 1949, 1985), 81, 85, 121, though he also thought that the future of the manned bomber may be in doubt because short-range guided missiles might make them obsolete—that the balance would swing toward the defense.

21. Marshall L. Michel III, *Clashes: Air Combat over North Vietnam* (Annapolis, MD: Naval Institute, 1997), 1–4, 277–285; Ronald L. Banks, "Prejudicial Counsel: A Multi-Dimensional Study of Tactical Airpower between the Korean and Vietnam Wars," unpublished masters thesis, School of Advanced Air & Space Studies, 2001.

22. Rearden, "Strategic Bombardment Since 1945," 451; Maxwell D. Taylor, *The Uncertain Trumpet* (New York: Harper, 1960).

23. Lee Kennett, "Strategic Bombardment: A Retrospective," in R. Cargill Hall (ed.), *Case Studies in Strategic Bombardment* (Washington, DC: Air Force History and Museums Program, 1998), 630.

24. E. B. Potter, Nimitz (Annapolis, MD: US Naval Institute, 1970), 426; David A. Rosenberg, "American Postwar Air Doctrine and Organization: The Navy Experience," Alfred F. Hurley and Robert C. Ehrhart (eds.), *Air Power and Warfare: Proceedings of the Eighth Military History Symposium, United States Air Force Academy, 18–20 October, 1978* (Washington, DC: Office of Air Force History, 1979), 245.

25. Barlow, 40.

26. James R. Locher III, "Has it Worked? The Goldwater-Nichols Act," *Naval War College Review*, LIV, (Autumn 2001): 95.

27. Rearden, *History of the Office of the Secretary of Defense*, 390; Rosenberg, 253.

28. Barlow, 130.

29. Barlow, 191.

30. Rearden, *History of the Office of the Secretary of Defense*, 400–421. Among the foremost authorities on the subject is Barlow, *Revolt of the Admirals*; Admiral of the Fleet Ernest R. King had wings but he did not get them until he was a captain, and never had served as an aviator at the squadron level.

31. Philip A. Crowl, "Alfred Thayer Mahan: The Naval Historian," in Peter Paret (ed.), *Makers of Modern Strategy* (Princeton, NJ: Princeton University Press, 1986), 475–476, on naval recognition after 1945 of the newly increased importance of land attack; Frank Uhlig Jr., *How Navies Fight: The U.S. Navy and Its Allies* (Annapolis, MD: US Naval Institute, 1994), 410, on the great utility of the Navy even in the absence of enemy navies.

32. Nicholas E. Sarantakes, "The Short but Brilliant Life of the British Pacific Fleet," *Joint Forces Quarterly* (Issue 40, First Quarter 2006): 85–91.

33. Roger W. Barnett, "Naval Power for a New American Century," *Naval War College Review*, LV (Winter 2002): 46.

34. Delbert Corum et al., *A Tale of Two Bridges, Vol. 1: USAF Southeast Asia Monograph Series* (Washington, DC: Government Printing Office, 1976), 34–35; Lon O. Nordeen, *Air Warfare in the Missile Age*, 2nd ed. (Washington, DC: Smithsonian, 2002), 31.

35. In a semi-active scheme, the radar transmitter is aboard the attacking aircraft and the radar receiver is aboard the missile; in an active radar concept, both the transmitter and receiver are on the missile. The advantage of the latter is that the attacker does not have to remain pointed at the target after launch; the disadvantage is that the missile is more expensive and a transmitter is consumed with every shot.

36. Bill Gunston, *The Illustrated Encyclopedia of Aircraft Armament* (New York: Orion, 1988), 55; Frederick I. Ordway and Ronald C. Wakeford, *International Missile and Spacecraft Guide* (New York: McGraw-Hill, 1960), 34–35.

37. Stephen Budiansky, *Air Power* (New York: Viking, 2004), 351, where Radford is foursquare against strategic bombing.

38. Admiral Arthur Radford, "Modern Evolution of Armed Forces," Lecture, Naval War College, May 25, 1954, Naval Historical Collection, Naval War College, Newport, RI, RG 15.4.

39. The *Forrestal* was decommissioned in 1993.

40. It was still in service in 2006.

41. Theodore Roscoe, *On the Seas and in the Skies* (New York: Hawthorne, 1970), 622–626.

42. Adm. Robert B. Carney, "Role of the Navy in a Future War," Lecture, February 16, 1954, Naval War College, Newport, RI, Naval Historical Collection, RG 15, 7–8; Rosenberg, 268.

43. Rosenberg, 262; Barlow, 20–21, 115.

44. Edwin B. Hooper, *United States Naval Power in a Changing World* (Westport, CT: Praeger, 1988), 216–217.

45. Jacob Neufeld, *The Development of Ballistic Missiles in the US Air Force, 1945–1960* (Washington, DC: Office of Air Force History, 1990), 18–19.

46. Neufeld, 150, 173.

47. Scott R. Gourley, "From Atlas to Peacekeeper," *Air Force Space Command: 50 Years of Space & Missiles* (Tampa, FL: Faircount, n.d.), 16–21.

48. Newt Gingrich with Ronald E. Weisbrook, "Adapt or Die: The US Military's Responsibility to Protect America by Leading the Transformations in Science and Technology," *Strategic Studies Quarterly*, (Winter 2007): 29.

49. "Russia Remembers Space Hero," BBC News Online, April 12, 2001, accessed March 7, 2006, website: http://news.bbc.co.uk.

50. Bernard Nalty (ed.), *Winged Shield, Winged Sword: A History of the USAF, Vol. II* (Washington, DC: Office of Air Force History, 1997), 158.

51. Julius Pratt et al., *A History of United States Foreign Policy*, 4th ed. (Englewood Cliffs, NJ: Prentice-Hall, 1980), 414.

52. Eric Tegler, "Signs from Above," *Air Force Space Command: 50 Years of Space & Missiles* (Tampa, FL: Faircount, n.d.), 22–23.

CHAPTER 7

1. Herman S. Wolk, *Fulcrum of Power: Essays on the United States Air Force and National Security* (Washington, DC: Air Force History & Museums Program, 2003), 252–253, 259.

2. Donald J. Mrozek, *Air Power and the Ground War in Vietnam* (Maxwell AFB, AL: Air University Press, 1988), 31–32; Christopher C. S. Cheng, *Air Mobility: The Development of a Doctrine* (Westport, CT: Praeger, 1994), shows that the Army was trying hard to develop the air mobility concept in the 1950s, but its effort got a real boost when McNamara came to office in 1961 armed with ideas for flexible response and counterinsurgency warfare.

3. Cheng, entire volume; John A. Bonin, "Combat Copter Cavalry: A Study in Conceptual Confusion and Inter-service Misunderstanding in the Exploitation of Armed Helicopters as Cavalry in the U.S. Army, 1950–1965," unpublished masters thesis, Duke University, 1982; Major John A. Bonin, USA, "Toward the Third Dimension in Combined Arms: The Evolution of Armed Helicopters into Air Maneuver Units in Vietnam, 1965–1973," unpublished Command and General Staff College thesis, Fort Leavenworth, KS, April 22, 1986.

4. Mrozek, 55–56, shows that the Army was the leader in this, and to some extent the USAF was reactive to the political leaders and to the fear that the Army was building yet another air force; Robert F. Futrell, *The United States Air Force in Southeast Asia: The Advisory Years, To 1965* (Washington, DC: Office of Air Force History, 1981), 240.

5. Donald I. Blackwelder, "The Long Road to Desert Storm and Beyond: The Development of Precision Guided Bombs" unpublished masters thesis, School of Advanced Airpower Studies, Maxwell AFB, AL, 1992, on the origins of the LGB; Futrell, 241–242 on gunships; and Jack S. Ballard, *The Development and Employment of Fixed-Wing Gunships, 1962–1972* (Washington, DC: Office of Air Force History, 1982).

6. Bernard Nalty (ed.), *Winged Shield, Winged Sword: A History of the USAF*, Vol. II (Washington, DC: Office of Air Force History, 1997), 142–143.

7. On the whole, the Army users were quite satisfied about the level and timeliness of the support they received. In fact, there was some worry that the use of CAS

had been excessive, John J. Sbrega, "Southeast Asia," in Benjamin Franklin Cooling (ed.), *Close Air Support* (Washington, DC: Office of Air Force History, 1990), 472–473.

8. Sbrega, 413–414.

9. John Schlight, *Help from Above: Air Force Close Air Support of the Army* (Washington, DC: Air Force History & Museums Program, 2003), 316, 332; Sbrega, 444–445; Raymond Bowers, *Tactical Airlift* (Washington, DC: Office of Air Force History, 1983), 388–389; Ballard, entire work.

10. During World War II, General Henry Arnold convened a group of scientists under the leadership of Dr. Theodore von Karman. It produced a multi-volume work known as *Toward New Horizons*, which has gained fame as the USAF roadmap into the space age. Early in the 1950s, the USAF asked von Karman to write another edition of his report but he declined, saying that it was now beyond the capability of one person or his group. The USAF turned to an older group, the National Academy of Sciences, for guidance. The result was the Woods Hole Summer Study Group that met in 1957 and 1958 on the "Old Whitney estate." The scientists brought their families and it was a low-pressure setting, and there were many recreational activities; this was thought to be conducive to innovation. *Toward New Horizons* was reviewed at the outset. There was some feeling that it was remarkable for its conservatism. The original report included a recommendation for the launching of a space satellite. However, according to von Karman the USAF discouraged that during the intervening years because of the congressional feeling that it was pie-in-the-sky thinking and a waste of money. Then, in the fall of 1957 the USSR launched such a satellite. This so disturbed the United States and her scientists that it stimulated the next summer's meeting to some radical thinking on the possible scientific advances—one of the thoughts (arising within the Limited War Panel) being that laser light, just becoming known, might be used in weapon guidance, Michael H. Gorn, *The Universal Man: Theodore von Karman's Life in Aeronautics* (Washington, DC: Smithsonian, 1992), 113–122, 138–143.

11. Marshall L. Michel III, *Clashes: Air Combat over North Vietnam* (Annapolis, MD: Naval Institute, 1997), 7–20.

12. Forward of the target airplane, that is.

13. Michel, 7–20.

14. Alexander Berger, "Beyond Blue Four: The Past and Future Transformation of Red Flag," *Air and Space Power Journal* (Summer 2005): 43–56; Michel, 277–278.

15. Colonel John A. Doglione et al., *Airpower and the 1972 Spring Invasion*, Vol. II, in *USAF Southeast Asia Monograph Series* (Washington, DC: USAF, 1976, 1985), an anecdotal account of the last phases of the air war in Vietnam; Stephen P. Randolph, *Powerful and Brutal Weapons: Nixon, Kissinger, and the Easter Offensive* (Cambridge, MA: Harvard, 2007), 61, this work being the best available on this part of the war, perhaps the best of the entire air war in Vietnam.

16. Colonel Delbert Corum et al., *The Tale of Two Bridges*, Vol. I, *USAF Southeast Asia Monograph Series* (Washington, DC: USAF, 1976). It should be noted that the bridge was hit many times before, but in earlier attacks all the warheads were 750 pounds or less and the only precision-guided munitions used were the Bullpups.

17. The author was a pilot in the AC-130 squadron in Southeast Asia in 1974–1975.

18. Marshall L. Michel III, *The 11 Days of Christmas* (San Francisco: Encounter, 2002), 234.

19. Michel, *11 Days of Christmas*, 234.

20. Thomas G. Tobin et al., *Last Flight From Saigon* (Washington, DC: Government Printing Office, nd).

21. John F. Guilmartin, *A Very Short War: The Mayaguez and the Battle of Koh Tang* (College Station, TX: Texas A&M, 1995).

22. Stephen Peter Rosen, *Winning the Next War: Innovation and the Modern Military* (Ithaca, NY: Cornell, 1991), 58–59.

23. Xiaoming Zhang, *Red Wings over the Yalu: China, the Soviet Union, and the Air War in Korea* (College Station, TX: Texas A&M, 2002), shows that there is a wide variation in the kill ratios reported, and that the air superiority experience was much more complex than usually pictured.

24. Lon O. Nordeen, Jr., *Air Warfare in the Missile Age* (Washington, DC: Smithsonian, 1985), 207–209; David C. Isby, *Fighter Combat in the Jet Age* (London: HarperCollins, 1997), 84–93.

25. Michel, *Clashes*, 277–285; Isby, 84–93; Benjamin S. Lambeth, *The Transformation of American Airpower* (Ithaca, NY: Cornell, 2000), 41–42.

26. William W. Momyer, *Air Power in Three Wars: World War II, Korea, Vietnam* (Washington, DC: USAF, 1978), 65–107.

27. Lambeth, 48–51.

28. Lambeth, 86; George Lee Butler, "Disestablishing SAC," *Air Power History*, Vol. 40 (Fall 1993): 4–11.

29. John Schlight, *The United States Air Force: The War in Vietnam* (Washington, DC: Office of Air Force History, 1988), 215–221; Lambeth, 23.

30. Schlight, *War in Vietnam*, 214–215.

31. Mark Clodfelter, *The Limits of Air Power* (New York: Free Press, 1989), 30.

32. On interdiction in Vietnam, see Herman L. Gilster, *The Air War in Southeast Asia: Case Studies of Selected Campaigns* (Maxwell AFB, AL: Air University Press, 1993).

33. On Khe Sanh, see Bernard C. Nalty, *Airpower and the Fight for Khe Sanh* (Washington, DC: Office of Air Force History, 1986).

34. Charles G. Miller, *Airlift Doctrine* (Maxwell AFB, AL: Air University Press, 1988), 299–304.

35. For an articulate discussion of these issues, see Richard Devereaux, "Theater Airlift Management and Control: Should We Turn Back the Clock to be Ready for Tomorrow?" unpublished masters thesis, School of Advanced Airpower Studies, Maxwell AFB, AL, 1993.

36. Thomas A. Julian, "The Origins of Air Refueling in the United States Air Force," in Jacob Neufeld et al., *Technology and the Air Force* (Washington, DC: Air Force History and Museums Program, 1997), 75–99; Richard K. Smith, "Invisible Men, Invisible Planes: In-Flight Air Refueling," in *Air Mobility Symposium: 1947 to the Twenty-First Century* (Washington, DC: Government Printing Office, 1998), 59–63, the literature on air refueling being rather sparse, incidentally.

CHAPTER 8

1. Benjamin S. Lambeth, *The Transformation of American Airpower* (Ithaca, NY: Cornell, 2000), 156. For a credible and readable first-person account of the tribulations of the F-105 pilot in Vietnam, see Ed Rasimus, *When Thunder Rolled* (Washington, DC: Smithsonian, 2003); on the development of the F-117, see Ben R. Rich and Leo Janos, Skunk Works (Boston: Little, Brown, 1994).

2. Peter DeLeon, Report No. R-1312-1-PR, "The Laser-Guided Bomb: Case History of a Development" (Santa Monica, CA: RAND, 1974).

3. "Eglin's AMRAAMs Join War," *Northwest Florida Daily News* (February 22, 1991): 3, and Jeffrey Lenorovitz, "Allied Air Supremacy Keeps Air-to-Air Engagements Limited," *Aviation Week & Space Technology* (February 18, 1991): 45–46, and on the first kill of the new missile, "Hughes AMRAAM Intercepts Mig-25 in Iraq 'No-Fly' Zone," News Release, Hughes Aircraft Company, Canoga Park, CA, January 1992; Bill Sweetman, "Russia Sets the Pace in the race for Air-to-Air Missiles," *Jane's International Defense Review*, Vol. 30 (November 1997): 70–79.

4. Mark Hewish, Anthony Robinson, and Gerard Turbe, "Air-to-Air Missiles," *International Defense Review* (August 1990): 871–877; James W. Rawles, "AMRAAM: Better Late than Never," *Defense Electronics* (November 1988): 42–49; Doug Richardson, "Future Air-to-Air Missiles," *Military Technology* (July 1988): 92–96.

5. Thomas A. Keaney and Eliot A. Cohen, *Revolution in Warfare? Air Power in the Persian Gulf* (Annapolis, MD: Naval Institute, 1995), 191, 195.

6. Keaney and Cohen, 189–191; Lambeth, 155, 160–162.

7. Kenneth Werrell, *The Evolution of the Cruise Missile* (Maxwell AFB, AL: Air University, 1985), 142–144.

8. Wayne Thompson, *To Hanoi and Back: The U.S. Air Force and North Vietnam, 1963–1973* (Washington, DC: Smithsonian, 2000), 240; Alexander Berger, "Beyond Blue Four: The Past and Future Transformation of Red Flag," *Air and Space Power Journal* (Summer 2005): 43–56.

CHAPTER 9

1. The geographic commanders are those in charge of the joint forces in various parts of the world, like the Pacific (PACOM) and Europe (EUCOM).

2. Michael R. Gordon and Bernard E. Trainor, *The Generals' War: The Inside Story of the Conflict in the Gulf* (Boston: Little, Brown, 1995), 471; Peter L. Hays et al., *American Defense Policy*, 7th ed. (Baltimore, MD: Johns Hopkins, 1997), 122–129; Eliot A. Cohen, "Defending America in the Twenty-first Century," *Foreign Affairs*, Vol. 79 (November/December, 2000): 50; Lieutenant General David A. Deptula, USAF, "Toward Restructuring National Security," *Strategic Studies Quarterly* (Winter 2007): 5.

3. James R. Locher III, "Has it Worked? The Goldwater-Nichols Act," *Naval War College Review*, LIV (Autumn 2001): 95–115.

4. George Lee Butler, "Disestablishing SAC," *Air Power History*, Vol. 40 (Fall 1993): 4–11.

5. Edward C. Mann III, *Thunder and Lightning: Desert Storm and the Airpower Debates* (Maxwell AFB, AL: Air University, 1995), 175–179; see also Harold

Winton, "An Ambivalent Partnership: US Army and Air Force Perspectives on Air-to-Ground Operations, 1973–90," in Phillip S. Meilinger (ed.), *The Paths of Heaven: The Evolution of Airpower Theory* (Maxwell AFB, AL: Air University Press, 1997), 399–441.

6. Mann, 175–179; Winton, 399–441.

7. Thomas G. Tobin et al., *Last Flight From Saigon* (Washington, DC: Government Printing Office, 1978), 12–13, and the entire monograph for the confusion at Saigon during the last act.

8. Thomas A. Keaney and Eliot A. Cohen, *Revolution in Warfare? Air Power in the Persian Gulf* (Annapolis, MD: Naval Institute, 1995), 273.

9. Air Marshal Sir John Walker, RAF, "Did Air Power Work in the Balkans? — Of course it did!" *Journal of the Royal United Services Institute*, Vol. 145 (October 2000): 63–65, and James A. Winnefeld and Dana J. Johnson, *Joint Air Operations: Pursuit of Unity in Command and Control, 1942–1991* (Annapolis, MD: Naval Institute, 1993), 171.

10. Benjamin S. Lambeth, *The Transformation of American Airpower* (Ithaca, NY: Cornell, 2000), 271–273; Robert A. Pape, *Bombing to Win: Air Power and Coercion in War* (Ithaca, NY: Cornell, 1996), 240–241.

11. Keaney and Cohen, 80–87, shows that the interdiction results were mixed. The supply route from Baghdad to the theater would not have been able to deliver enough to support sustained operations; the Iraqi supply system in the theater collapsed, causing some units to have inadequate food and water; Lambeth, 129, on the losses.

12. Flavio Bessi and Francesco Zacca, "Introduction to 'stealth,'" *Military Technology* (May 1989), 68–78.

13. Walter Maine, Munitions Directorate, AFRL, Interview with David R. Mets, Eglin AFB, FL, April 13, 2000.

14. "AC-130 Gunship" (n.d.), available at http://www.specwarnet.com/vehicles/spectre.htm, accessed January 22, 2006; "AC-130U Spooky" (n.d.), available at http://www.globalsecurity.org/military/systems/ac-130.htm, accessed January 22, 2006. Until a new squadron was founded for the AC-130U, the call sign used by all AC-130s had been "Spectre," but the new unit chose to use the call sign formerly used by the AC-47, "Spooky."

15. Keaney and Cohen, 17. The 14 people on board were all killed, and that personnel loss amounted to almost ten percent of the total for the Coalition.

16. Stephen Budiansky, *Air Power* (New York: Viking, 2004), 405.

17. "Uninhabited Aerial Vehicles; Operations Desert Shield/Desert Storm" (n.d.), available at http://www.edwards.af.mil/articles98/cocs_html/splash/may98/cover/desert.htm, accessed January 22, 2006; US Department of Defense, "Unmanned Aerial Vehicles Roadmap, 2000–2005," April 2001, 4–5, available at http://www.globalsecurity.org/intell/library/reports/2001/uavr0401.htm, accessed January 22, 2006.

18. Keaney and Cohen, 180–181.

19. Tom Clancy and General Chuck Horner, *Every Man a Tiger* (New York: Putnam's, 1999), 244–247; Keaney and Cohen, 94–104.

20. Keaney and Cohen, 272; Williamson Murray, *Operations, Vol. II: Gulf War Airpower Survey* (Washington, DC: Government Printing Office, 1993), 15.

21. Keaney and Cohen, 155–160.

22. James K. Matthews and Cora J. Holt, *So Many, So Much, So Far, So Fast* (Washington, DC: Government Printing Office, 1996), 26–28.

23. Rick Atkinson, *Crusade: The Untold Story of the Persian Gulf War* (Boston: Houghton, Mifflin, 1993), 152.

24. James A. Winnefeld, *A League of Airmen: U.S. Air Power in the Gulf War* (Santa Monica, CA: RAND, 1994): 135; Gregory M. Swider, *The Navy's Experience with Joint Air Operations: Lessons Learned from Operations Desert Shield and Desert Storm* (Alexandria, VA: Center for Naval Analysis, 1993), 36–37.

25. Winnefeld and Johnson, 146–147; Clancy and Horner, 475; Keaney and Cohen, 136–137.

26. Atkinson, 219.

27. Benjamin S. Lambeth, "Air Force-Navy Integration in Strike Warfare," *Naval War College Review*, Vol. 61 (Winter 2008): 28–49.

28. Correlli Barnett, "The Fallibility of Air Power," *Journal of the Royal United Services Institute*, Vol. 145, (October 2000): 59.

29. Jacob Neufeld, *The Development of Ballistic Missiles in the US Air Force, 1945–1960* (Washington, DC: Office of Air Force History, 1990), 163, 230; Edwin B. Hooper, *United States Naval Power in a Changing World* (Westport, CT: Praeger, 1988), 216. The first Polaris submarine, the *USS George Washington*, went to sea in 1959.

30. Roger W. Barnett, "Naval Power for a New American Century," *Naval War College Review*, LV (Winter 2002): 59.

31. Rowan Scarborough, *Rumsfeld's War: The Untold Story of America's Anti-Terrorist Commander* (Washington, DC: Regnery, 2004), 32.

32. Carl H. Builder, *The Masks of War: American Military Styles in Strategy and Analysis* (Baltimore, MD: Johns Hopkins, 1989), 25, on the traditional pecking orders in the Navy; on the changed situation for submarine and anti-submarine forces, John Morgan, "Anti-Submarine Warfare: A Phoenix for the Future," available at http://www.fas.org/man/dod-101/sys/ship/docs/anti-sub.htm, accessed January 29, 2006.

33. Keaney and Cohen, 133, 144, 193. Inertial navigation systems (INS) are dependent upon inertial measurement units (IMU) made up of very precise measurement devices. Often, one will measure changes in forward and aft movements and left and right displacements. Another measures changes in rotary movement by means of a gyroscope—lately, a laser gyroscope. Once those measurements are generated, they are then converted into commands for steering systems. Long in use for submarine navigation underwater where neither celestial nor LORAN measurements were possible, in small packages INS mechanisms tend to precess over time and must be corrected. That was long a formidable problem, but the Global Positioning System came on line in the 1990s, easing the difficulty. A constellation of satellites is in position and emits signals that permit the GPS receiver to determine its location with great precision in three dimensions: longitude, latitude, and altitude. That can be used to nearly instantaneously update the accuracy of an IMU even during the short time-of-flight of a gravity bomb. The downside is that in theory, GPS signals can be jammed, but in short-range weapons the INS by itself can deliver fairly accurate results.

34. Eric H. Biass, "The Guided Dispenser: The Ultimate Attack Weapon?" *Armada International*, Vol. 15 (Aug/Sep 1991): 6–15.

35. Rebecca Grant, *The B-2 Goes to War* (Arlington, VA: Iris Press, 2001), 73–74; Edward J. Walsh, "Air Force, Navy Precision Weapons Pack Power in Economical Packages," *National Defense*, LXXXI (May/June 1997): 34–35; US Air Force, Headquarters Air Combat Command/DRPW, "Final Joint CAF and USN Operational Requirements Document for Joint Direct Attack Munitions," August 23, 1995.

36. Stanley B. Alterman, "GPS Dependence: A Fragile Vision for US Battlefield Dominance," *Journal of Electronic Defense* (September 1995): 52–55; "US Reviews GPS Policy," *Military Technology* (May 1996): 8–9; Stephan M. Hardy, "Will the GPS Lose Its Way?" *Journal of Electronic Defense* (September 1995): 56–61; Interview, Col. Harry V. Dutchyshyn, Jr., Munitions Directorate, Air Force Research Laboratory, with David R. Mets, Eglin AFB, FL, April 11, 2000.

37. In the initial stages of development, it was known as the Small Smart Bomb, in the 250-pound range with GPS/INS guidance and about 50 pounds of explosive in its warhead.

38. Ryan Hansen, "SDB: Doing More with Less for the Warfighter," *Eglin Eagle* (March 17, 2006): 20–21.

39. Ryan Hanson, "JDAM: Not your Father's Version, but Still the Warfighters Weapon of Choice," *Eglin Eagle* (March 10, 2006): 18–19.

40. Roy Braybrook and Eric Biass, "Not-Too-Close Encounters of the Air-to-Ground Kind," *Armada International* 20 (February/March 1996): 36; James W. Canan, "Smart and Smarter, JSOW and JDAM: The 'Most Significant' New Weapons," *Seapower* (March 1995): 93–96; Interview, Mario J. Caluda, AAC Executive Director with David R Mets, April 12, 2000, Eglin AFB.

41. Even the ones that hit the Chinese Embassy were a technical success in that they hit the target at which they were launched—the problem there was inaccurate intelligence, not inaccurate delivery. Programs have been undertaken to add GPS kits to USAF LGBs, GBU-15s (guided bombs using either television or infrared seekers), and AGM-130s (GBU-15s modified by adding a rocket motor to give them additional standoff).

42. Ryan Hansen, "JASSM: The Air Force's Next Generation Cruise Missile," *Eglin Eagle* (March 3, 2006): 20–21.

43. Rebecca Grant, "The Echoes of Anaconda," *Air Force* (April 2005), available at http://www.afa.org/magazine/april2005/0405anaconda.asp, accessed March 25, 2006.

44. "Global Hawk High Altitude, Long Endurance Unmanned Reconnaissance Aircraft, USA," available at http://www.airforce-technology.com/projects/global, accessed April 4, 2004; "U.S. Drones Crowd Iraq's Skies to Fight Insurgents," *New York Times* (April 5, 2005); General Atomics, news release, "Predator Finds Home at U.S. Air Force Museum," May 15, 2001, available at http://www.ga.com/news.php?subaction=showfull&id=989913600&archive=&start_from=&ucat=1&, accessed April 4, 2004.

45. Scarborough, 32.

46. "Predator RQ-1/MQ-1 Unmanned Aerial Vehicle," available at http://www.airforce-technology.com/projects/predator, accessed March 31, 2005.

47. Brooke Davis, "First Ever Coordinated UAV Flight Makes History," available at http://www.edwards.af.mil/archive/2004/2004-archive-2, accessed April 4,

2005; Mark Cantrell, "The Pilot Who Wasn't There," *Military Officer* (January 2005): 46–53.

48. Kevin Whitelaw, "No Rest For a Cold Warrior," *U.S. News & World Report* (October 1, 2007), available at http://ebird.afis.mil/ebfiles/e200770924547188.html, accessed September 24, 2007.

49. Donald L. Kunz, "Modeling of Automated Aerial Refueling," Blue Dart Submission, March 15, 2007, available at http://www.afit.edu/pa, accessed August 10, 2007; Michael Sirak, "Air Force Says Reaper Armed Unmanned Aircraft Now Operating in Afghanistan," *Defense Daily* (October 12, 2007), available at http://ebird.afis.mil/ebfiles/e20071012552300.html, accessed October 12, 2007.

50. "Global Hawk High Altitude, Long Endurance Unmanned Reconnaissance Aircraft," available at http://airforce-technology.com/projects/global, accessed April 4, 2005; Air Force Link, "Global Hawk," available at http://www.af.mil/factsheets/factsheet.asp?fsID=175, accessed March 31, 2005.

51. John A. Tirpak, "The Struggle over UAVs," *Air Force Magazine* (November 2007), available at http://www.afa.org/magazine/nov2007/1107UAV.asp, accessed November 9, 2007.

52. Demetri Sevastopulo, "US Military in Dogfight Over Drones," *Financial Times* (August 20, 2007), available at http://ebird.afis.mil/ebfiles/e20070820537336.html, accessed August 20, 2007; John A. Tirpak, "UAV Executive Agency—Denied," *Air Force Magazine* (November 2007), available at http://www.afa.org/magazine/nov2007/1107watch.asp, accessed November 9, 2007; Deptula, 12–13.

53. Ryan Henry, "Defense Transformation and the 2005 Quadrennial Defense Review," *Parameters* (Winter 2005–2006): 5–15. As of 2005, the Office of the Secretary of Defense held that the uncertainties required that the Department be prepared to (a) "Defend the Homeland," (b) "Operate effectively in four strategic areas: Europe, Northeast Asia, the East Asian Littoral, and the Middle-East and Southwest Asia," (c) "Fight two major combat operations nearly simultaneously," and (d) "Win decisively in one of the two major operations . . . including, if necessary, regime change." Steven Lambakis, "Reconsidering Asymmetric Warfare," *Joint Forces Quarterly*, No. 36 (n.d.): 106.

54. Arthur K. Cebrowski, Testimony, House Armed Services Committee, in *Transformation Trends* (March 2, 2004): 1.

55. John H. Dalton, Admiral Jeremy M. Boorda, USN, and General Carl E Mundy, Jr., USMC, "Forward . . . From the Sea," in Peter L. Hays et al. (ed.), *American Defense Policy*, 7th ed. (Baltimore, MD: Johns Hopkins, 1997), 366–369.

56. Scott F. Smith, "Boots in the Air," unpublished masters thesis, School of Advanced Airpower Studies, 2000; John Gordon IV and Jerry Sollinger, "The Army's Dilemma," *Parameters*, 34 (Summer 2004): 41, argue that the Army's emphasis on making the whole force rapidly deployable is misguided because the decision makers will almost always go for an option involving precision fires at minimum risk as first choice—precision and standoff by Navy and Air Force airpower.

57. Michael R. Worden, *The Rise of the Fighter Pilot Generals: The Problem of Air Force Leadership, 1945–1982* (Maxwell AFB, AL: Air University Press, 1988); Builder, 17–43.

58. Richard K. Smith, "Invisible Men, Invisible Planes: In-Flight Air Refueling," in *Air Mobility Symposium: 1947 to the Twenty-First Century* (Washington, DC:

Government Printing Office, 1998), 59–63; LGEN William J. Begert, USAF, "Kosovo and Theater Air Mobility," *Aerospace Power Journal*, XIII (Winter 1999): 16–18; LTCOL Richard Simpson, "Command of Theater Air Mobility Forces During the Air War Over Serbia: A New Standard or a New Data Point," *Airlift/Tanker Quarterly*, Vol. 8 (Summer 2000): 11; Thomas A. Julian, "The Origins of Air Refueling in the United States Air Force," in Jacob Neufeld et al., *Technology and the Air Force* (Washington, DC: Air Force History and Museums Program, 1997), 75–94; John A. Tirpak, "Is the USAF Going Out of Business," *Air Force Magazine* (November 2007), reporting on a speech by Secretary of the Air Force Michael W. Wynne, who warned that the USAF modernization program is not being sufficiently supported to maintain its capability as a first-rate force, not only in tankers but also in fighters and space systems as well, available at http://www.afa.org/magazine/nov2007/1107watch.asp; Eric Rosenberg, "Boeing Predicted to get Tanker Deal," *Seattle Post-Intelligencer* (December 17, 2007), available at http://ebird.afis.mil/ebfiles/e200712175568315.html, accessed December 17, 2007.

59. I realize this is an oversimplification. The KC-135 fleet received a major upgrade that had the effect of multiplying its numbers when it was re-engined. But then, the C-141 fleet was similarly upgraded when it was given a fuselage extension and air refueling plumbing, also effectively multiplying its numbers.

60. Keaney and Cohen, 154–155.

61. John A. Tirpak, "Crunch Time for Air Mobility," *Air Force Magazine* (December 2007), available at http://www.afa.org/magazine/dec2007/1207mobility.asp, accessed December 3, 2007.

62. Grant, B-2 Goes to War, i–iii.

63. Rebecca Grant, "When Bombers Will Be Decisive," *Air Force Magazine* (November 2007), available at http://www.afa.org/magazine/nov2007/1107bombers.asp, accessed November 9, 2007.

64. US Air Force, Air Force Basic Doctrine, AFDD-1, September 1997, with an updated edition published in 2003.

65. Actually the two functions, Research and Development and Procurement, were in a unified Air Materiel Command in the late 1940s, but were separated into Air Research and Development Command (later Air Force Systems Command) and Air Materiel Command (later Air Force Logistics Command) in 1950 on the theory that procurement involved so much more money that it would overwhelm the development mission were they in the same command; Stephen B. Johnson, in *The United States Air Force and the Culture of Innovation* (Washington, DC: Air Force History & Museums Program, 2002), 223.

66. "AEF: Dawn of a New Era," *Airlift/Tanker Quarterly*, Vol. 8 (Winter 2000): 12–20; John A. Tirpak, "The Long Reach of On-Call Airpower," *Air Force*, Vol. 81 (December 1998), for a summary of the AEF, available at http://www.afa.org/magazine/1298airpower.html; Richard G. Davis, *Anatomy of a Reform* (Washington, DC: AF History & Museums Program, 2003).

CHAPTER 10

1. YuLin G. Whitehead, "Information as a Weapon: Reality versus Promises," unpublished masters thesis, School of Advanced Airpower Studies, Maxwell AFB,

AL, 1997, 1–3; Lieutenant General David A. Deptula, USAF, "Toward Restructuring National Security," *Strategic Studies Quarterly* (Winter 2007): 10.

2. P. C. Emmett, "Airpower in the Information Age," in Stuart Peach (ed.), *Perspectives on Air Power* (London: The Stationery Office, 1998), 167–171.

3. "Barksdale Gets Cyber Command—At Least for a While," *Air Force Magazine* (November 2007), available at http://www.afa.org/magazine/nov2007/1107world.asp, accessed November 9, 2007.

4. Steven Lambakis, "Reconsidering Asymmetric Warfare," *Joint Forces Quarterly*, No. 36 (n.d.): 106; David T. Fahrenkrug, "The Age of Cyber Warfare," *The Wright Stuff* (December 2007), available at http://www.maxwell.af.mil/au/aunews/archive/0222/articles/theageofcyberwarfre.html, accessed December 3, 2007.

5. David G. Chandler, *The Campaigns of Napoleon* (New York: Macmillan, 1966), 678.

6. Theodore Ropp, *War in the Modern World* (London: Collier, 1962), 368.

7. Joseph F. Kreis (ed.), *Piercing the Fog: Intelligence and Army Air Force Operations in World War II* (Washington, DC: Air Force History & Museums Program, 1996), 1–4.

8. Alexander Orlov, *Handbook of Intelligence* (Ann Arbor, MI: University of Michigan, 1963), 2–3, on Generals Dwight Eisenhower and Omar Bradley testifying of the sorry state of U.S. intelligence and on the British lead in the discipline; Kreis, on the reluctance of air commanders to accept the recommendations of intelligence officers.

9. Thomas B. Buell, *The Quiet Warrior: A Biography of Admiral Raymond A. Spruance* (Annapolis, MD: Naval Institute Press, 1987), 160; Ensign George Gay, Interview, October 12, 1943, available at http://www.ibiblio.org/hyperwar/USN/ships/logs/CV/cv-8-EnsGay.html, accessed December 9, 2005.

10. Orlov, 5; see Williamson Murray, "Retrospect," in John F. Kreis (ed.), *Piercing the Fog: Intelligence and Army Air Force Operations in World War II* (Washington, DC: Air Force History & Museums Program, 1996), 420–421, on the attitudes of senior flying officers of the Army Air Forces toward their intelligence people.

11. Kreis, 3; Murray, 396.

12. Murray, 184–185.

13. Donald MacKenzie, "Technology and the Arms Race," *International Security*, Vol. 14 (Summer 1989): 161–176, explains in a review of Matthew Evangelista's *Innovation and the Arms Race* how thinking differs in a pluralistic society, where ideas often go from the bottom up, as opposed to an authoritarian one where they usually travel from the top down.

14. Williamson Murray laments that the cultural conceit of Americans was a factor in the technological surprise in Japanese airpower at the outset of World War II, "Retrospect," 397, 400, 413.

15. William H. McNeill, *A World History* (London: Oxford, 1967), 315–321, 367–368, 373–378.

16. Forrest E. Morgan, *Compellence and the Strategic Culture of Imperial Japan* (Westport, CT: Praeger, 2003), 66; Paul Kennedy, *The Rise and Fall of the Great Powers* (New York: Random House, 1987), 4–9.

17. Kennedy, 9–13.

18. Orlov, 12, 17.

19. Interview, Ira Eaker with David R. Mets, Washington, DC, April 26, 1982.

20. Arthur S. Link, *Woodrow Wilson and the Progressive Era* (New York: Harper & Row, 1954), 164–167, 271–273; Julius Pratt et al., *A History of United States Foreign Policy*, 4th ed. (Englewood Cliffs, NJ: Prentice-Hall, 1980), 243–239; Kennedy, 271.

21. Peter Calvocoressi, *Top Secret Ultra* (New York: Ballentine, 1980), 106–107; Anthony Cave Brown, *Bodyguard of Lies* (London: W. H. Allen, 1977), 57; Orlov, 9; Daniel Yergin, *The Prize: The Epic Quest for Oil, Money, and Power* (New York: Free Press, 1991), 335.

22. Among the best is Barbara Wohlstetter, *Pearl Harbor: Warning and Decision* (Stanford, CA: Stanford University, 1962).

23. Yergin, 305.

24. Calvocoressi, 48–51; Williamson Murray and Allan R. Millett, *A War to be Won: Fighting the Second World War* (Cambridge, MA: Belknap, 2000), 464–465.

25. Kreis, 2, on the differing needs of strategic air intelligence; and Murray, in Kreis, 401, on the intelligence complications in the campaign against German industry.

CHAPTER 11

1. Ronald Scott Mangum, "NATO's Attack on Serbia: Anomaly or Emerging Doctrine," *Parameters*, XXIX (Winter 2000–2001): 40–52.

2. Robert C. Owen, *Deliberate Force: A Case Study in Effective Air Campaigning* (Maxwell AFB, AL: Air University, 2000), 455–515, for an analysis of the Bosnian Campaign.

3. Dana Priest, *The Mission: Waging War and Keeping Peace with America's Military* (New York: Norton, 2003), 53; Benjamin S. Lambeth, *NATO's Air War for Kosovo* (Santa Monica, CA: RAND, 2001), xiii.

4. Among the criticisms are: John Barry and Evan Thomas, "The Kosovo Cover-Up," *Newsweek*, Vol. 135, (May 15, 2000): 22, available at http://ehostgw4.epnet.com, whose complaints were that damage of fielded forces from altitude was proven ineffective, and the bombing of the targets in Serbia proper was against civilians and therefore of questionable morality; Lt. Colonel Robert S. Bridgford, USA, et al., "Lessons Learned from Operation Allied Force in Kosovo," *Field Artillery* (January-February 2000), 10–13, in an article little related to the bombing campaign concludes with no reservations that Kosovo proves that airpower cannot do it alone; and Jonathan Eyal, in "Kosovo: Killing the Myths after the Killing has Subsided," *Royal United Services Institute Journal*, Vol. 145 (February 2000): 20–27, concludes that airpower did not win but rather the victory was limited and was achieved by a combination of NATO unity, the threat of a ground war, and Russian diplomacy; and finally, Norman Friedman, "Was Kosovo the Future?" *U.S. Naval Institute Proceedings*, Vol. 126 (January 2000): 6, 8, asserts that it really was not much of a victory, and that the "strategic bombing" was wasted whereas such effects that airpower had arose from the damage done to tactical forces in Kosovo, the latter being facilitated by the operations of the KLA ground forces; as the Navy supplies airpower and is increasingly committed to power projection ashore, it makes it difficult for some of its advocates to criticize, but Scott C. Truver in "The U.S. Navy

in Review," *U.S. Naval Institute Proceedings*, Vol. 126 (May 2000): 78, available at http://ehostgw2.epnet.com, wherein he emphasizes the importance of the ground threat and Russian diplomacy in the outcome—and asserts that Milosevic remains in power (at that time) as a partial failure of the campaign—as do many other analysts.

5. General Clark defended his targeting in (among other places), Vince Crawley, "Clark Explains Choices Made in Air War," *Air Force Times* (June 26, 2000): 25, available at http://ehostvgw2.epnet, and General Wesley Clark, "Airpower in NATO's Future," *NATO's Nations and Partners for Peace* (February 1999): 10–12.

6. Barry Posen, "The Air War for Kosovo," *International Security*, Vol. 24 (Spring 2000): 58; Major General Robert H. Scales, Jr., "Adaptive Enemies: Achieving Victory by Avoiding Defeat," *Joint Force Quarterly* (Autumn/Winter 2000): 12.

7. Jonathan Eyal, "Kosovo: Killing the Myths after the Killing has Subsided," *Journal of the Royal United Services Institute*, Vol. 145 (February 2000): 26; Elaine M. Grossman, "U.S. Military Debates Link Between Kosovo Air War, Stated Objectives," *Inside the Pentagon* (April 20, 2000): 3, available at http://ebird.dtic.mil/apr2000; Lt. Col. Timothy C. Hanifen, "The Themes of Airpower Theory, Joint Vision 2020, and Some Comparative Implications for Marine Aviation," *Marine Corps Gazette*, Vol. 84 (May 2000): 89; Gene Myers, "Public Perceptions of the Air War Over Serbia," *Aerospace Power Journal*, Vol. 14 (Spring 2000): 85–89, available at http://ebhostvgw2.epnet.com.

8. Karl Mueller, "Coercive Air Power in Bosnia and Kosovo," unpublished paper, School of Advanced Air Power Studies, Maxwell AFB, AL, November 7, 1999, 9; Myers cites the Chief of Staff of the Air Force, General Michael Ryan, on the point; Andrew J. Bacevich, *American Empire: The Realities & Consequences* (Cambridge, MA: Harvard, 2002), 185.

9. General Wesley Clark, interview with Lt. Col. Mason Carpenter, USAF, and Lt. Col. Jeff Paulk, Washington, DC, November 6, 2000, wherein Gen. Clark claims to know Milosevic better than the reverse as Clark had spent much time studying the Serbian president; Daniel A. Byman and Matthew C. Waxman, "Kosovo and the Great Airpower Debate," *International Security*, Vol. 24 (Spring 2000): 8, pointing out that it is impossible to know what went on in Milosevic's mind; Bacevich, 189.

10. Which is the conclusion of Byman and Waxman, 19.

11. Lambeth, xiv–xv; 230–250.

12. Bacevich, 234; Sean M. Maloney, "Afghanistan: From Here to Eternity?" *Parameters* (Spring 2004): 4–15, available at http://carlisle-www.army.mil/usawc/parameters/04spring/maloney.htm, accessed March 26, 2006.

13. Rebecca Grant, "The Echoes of Anaconda," *Air Force* (April 2005), available at http://www.afa.org/magazine/april2005/0405anaconda.asp, accessed March 25, 2006.

14. Richard W. Stewart, review of *Not a Good Day to Die: The Untold Story of Operation Anaconda*, by Sean Naylor, in *Army History* (Winter 2006): 53–56; Stephen Budiansky, *Air Power* (New York: Viking, 2004), 435–436; Elaine Grossman, "Was Operation Anaconda Ill-Fated from the Start," *Inside the Pentagon*, July 29, 2004, available at http://www.d-n-i.net/grossman/army_analyst_blames.htm,

accessed March 24, 2006; Benjamin S. Lambeth, *Air Power Against Terror* (Santa Monica, CA: RAND, 2005), 163–221.

15. Maloney, 5–14, asserts that after Anaconda, the campaign continued to progress to the point where the adversary could no longer mount operations like that but was limited to ambushes and the like in no more than platoon-sized operations.

16. Williamson Murray and Robert H. Scales, Jr., *The Iraq War: A Military History* (Cambridge, MA: Harvard, 2003), 32–44.

17. To be "painted" is to have one's airplane illuminated by the radars on the ground.

18. John Gordon IV and Jerry Sollinger, "The Army's Dilemma," *Parameters* (Summer 2004): 33–45, available at http://carlisle-www.army.mil/usawc/parameters/04summer/gor&soll.htm, both the authors being retired Army officers and employed by RAND Corporation.

19. Shane Story, "Transformation or Troop Strength," *Army History* (Winter 2006): 25; Rowan Scarborough, *Rumsfeld's War: The Untold Story of America's Anti-Terrorist Commander* (Washington, DC: Regnery, 2004), 29–30.

20. Bob Woodward, *Plan of Attack* (New York: Simon & Schuster, 2004), 402.

21. Murray and Scales, 180; Lieutenant-General David A. Deptula and Major-General Charles D. Link, USAF (Ret.), "Modern Warfare: Desert Storm, Operation Iraqi Freedom and Operation Enduring Freedom," *Air Power History* (Winter 2007): 41.

22. Murray and Scales, 174, 176.

23. JSTARS = Joint Surveillance and Target Attack Radar System, an airplane developed on a Boeing 707 airframe that can track moving vehicular traffic over a wide area through any kind of visibility obscuration. It is a high-value target, so it cannot be used in non-permissive environments without heavy protection.

24. Murray and Scales, 164–165; Gordon and Sollinger, 33–45.

25. JSOW = Joint Standoff Weapon, a unpowered glide bomb carried on fighter aircraft. It has guidance similar to the JDAMS but is equipped with folding wings that give it extended range with the same accuracy as JDAMS.

26. Adam Hebert, "New Horizons for Combat UAVs," *Air Force* (December 2003), available at http://www.afa.org/magazne/dec2003/1203uav.asp, accessed November 27, 2004.

27. Michael Russell Rip and James M. Hasik, *The Precision Revolution: GPS and the Future of Aerial Warfare* (Annapolis, MD: Naval Institute, 2002), 167.

28. G. W. Rinehart, "Toward Space War," *High Frontier* (Winter 2005): 47.

29. Budiansky, 436–440; on asymmetry, see Colin S. Gray, "Thinking Asymmetrically in Times of Terror," *Parameters* (Spring 2002): 5–14, available at http://carlisle.www.army/usawc/Parameters/02spring/gray.htm, accessed June 12, 2002, in which he warns that sometimes the reaction to the terrorist attack can turn out more damaging to us than the attack itself.

30. AWACS = Airborne Early Warning and Control System. Built on a four-engine jet airframe, this aircraft contains the radar, the communications, and the many crew members needed to control an air-to-air battle.

31. "Europe: The Danube's Bonny, Bloody Banks," *Economist*, November 6, 1999, available at http://newfirstsearch.oclc.org.

32. For an articulate discussion of the subject, see Lt. Col. Kent Laughbaum, *Synchronizing Airpower and Firepower in the Deep Battle* (Maxwell AFB, AL: Air University Press, 1999).

33. Robert Coram, "The Hog that Saves the Grunts," *New York Times* (May 27, 2003), available at http://www.robert.coram.com/op_ed.html.

34. James Kitfield, "The Permanent Frontier," *National Journal* (March 17, 2001): 1–13, available at http://ebird.dtic.mil/mar2001; see also Peter L. Hays et al. (eds.), *Spacepower for a New Millennium: Space and U.S. National Security* (New York: McGraw-Hill, 2000), and Major-General William E. Jones, USAF (Ret.), "Air Power in the Space Age," in Stuart Peach (ed.), *Perspectives on Air Power: Air Power in its Wider Context* (London: The Stationery Office, 1998): 196–218.

35. Jones, 197.

36. Kitfield, 1–13; Mike Moore, "Space: Non-Aggressive Weapons," *Bulletin of the Atomic Scientists* (March/April 2001): 17–23, available at http://ebird.dtic.mil/mar2001; Hays et al., 4.

37. Stew Magnuson, "Darkened Skies: Murky Picture of What's Happening in Space Worries Air Force Officials," *National Defense* (December 2007): 28.

38. Moore, 17–23.

39. David A. Umphress, draft article, "Flying and Fighting in Cyberspace" (2006), author being an AFRES lieutenant-colonel with a doctorate from Texas A&M, and holds an associate professorship in Computer Science at Auburn University.

40. The Naval Air Transport Service of World War II was merged with the Air Transport Command to form MATS in the late 1940s. Naval transport crews had an important role in the Berlin Airlift, and continued to fly in MATS until the 1960s. In those days, an admiral was the vice commander of MATS.

41. Allen G. Peck, "Airpower's Crucial Role in Irregular Warfare," *The Wright Stuff* (September 2007), available at http://www.maxwell.af.mil/au/aunews/articles/AirpowersCrucialRoleinIrregularWarfare.html, accessed September 3, 2007.

42. Robert C. Owen and Carl P. Mueller, *Airlift Capabilities for Future Counterinsurgency Operations* (Santa Monica, CA: RAND, 2007), 33–61.

43. Owen and Mueller, 33–61; Max Boot, *The Savage Wars of Peace* (New York: Basic Books, 2002), 330–332; Peck.

44. Admiral William A. Owens, "Emerging System of Systems," *U.S. Naval Institute Proceedings*, Vol. 121 (May 1995): 35–39.

45. Eric Tegler, "Signs From Above," *Air Force Space Command: 50 Years of Space & Missiles* (Tampa, FL: Faircount, n.d.), 29.

46. J. R. Wilson, "AFSPC History," *Air Force Space Command: 50 Years of Space & Missiles* (Tampa, FL: Faircount, n.d.), 48.

47. Moore, 17–23; Stew Magnuson, "Strategic Command Selling Itself to Field Commanders," *National Defense* (December 2007), 30.

CHAPTER 12

1. Kevin C. Holzimmer, "Joint Operations in the Southwest Pacific, 1943–1945," *Joint Forces Quarterly*, No. 38, (n.d.), 105–108.

2. James Winnefeld and Dana Johnson, *Joint Air Operations* (Annapolis, MD: Naval Institute, 1993), 171.

3. E. B. Potter, *Nimitz* (Annapolis, MD: Naval Institute, 1976), 221n, 242; Herman S. Wolk, "George C. Kenney, "MacArthur's Premier Airman," in William M. Leary (ed.), *We Shall Return! MacArthur's Commanders and the Defeat of Japan* (Lexington, KY: University Press of Kentucky, 1988), 96.

4. Walter W. Rostow, *Pre-Invasion Strategy: General Eisenhower's Decision of March 25, 1944* (Austin, TX: University of Texas, 1981), on command and control.

5. Herman S. Wolk, *Planning and Organizing the Postwar Air Force* (Washington, DC: Office of Air Force History, 1984), 171–178; Edwin B. Hooper, *United States Naval Power in a Changing World* (Westport, CT: Praeger, 1988), 191.

6. Robert F. Futrell, *The United States Air Force in Korea* (Washington, DC: Office of Air Force History, 1983), 47; Walton S. Moody, *Building a Strategic Air Force* (Washington, DC: Air Force History & Museums Program, 1996), 352, 396–397; William W. Momyer, *Air Power in Three Wars: World War II, Korea, Vietnam* (Washington, DC: USAF, 1978), on command and control citation.

7. Momyer, on command and control in Vietnam.

8. Winnefeld and Johnson, 146–147; Tom Clancy and General Chuck Horner, *Every Man a Tiger* (New York: Putnam's, 1999), 475.

9. Dana Priest, *The Mission* (New York: Norton, 2003); Clark A. Murdock and Richard W. Weitz, "New Proposals for Defense Reform," *Joint Forces Quarterly*, No. 38, (n.d.), 34–41; Tucker R. Mansager, "Interagency Lessons Learned in Afghanistan," *Joint Forces Quarterly*, Issue 40 (First Quarter 2006): 80–84; Bob Woodward, *Plan of Attack* (New York: Simon & Schuster, 2004), 414.

10. Richard Szafranski, "The First Rule of Modern Warfare: Never Bring a Knife to a Gunfight," *Air and Space Power Journal* (Winter 2005): 18–26, Szafranski himself being a retired Air Force pilot, albeit a bomber man; Michael Rosenwald, "Pentagon May Support Air Force Bid for More F-22 Fighters," *Washington Post* (December 4, 2007), available at http://ebird.afis.mil/ebfiles/e20071204565ll.html, accessed December 4, 2007.

11. John T. Bennett, "Mullen: 4% of GDP Needed for Military," *Defense News* (December 3, 2007), available at http://ebird.afis.mil/ebfiles/e20071203565020.html, accessed December 3, 2007.

12. During the Vietnam War, surface-to-air missilery was in its infancy, and the nomenclature of those produced by the Soviets had but one digit, as in SA-2, SA-3, SA-6, and SA-7. Since then, the newer ones have gotten into the double digits, and the term is an euphemism for "latest" or "modern."

13. Szafranksi, 18–26.

14. Rep. Terry Everett (R-AL), "Arguing for a Comprehensive Space Protection Strategy," *Strategic Studies Quarterly* (Fall 2007): 21–23; Donald Alston, "Perpetuating an Integrated Space Force," *The Wright Stuff* (September 2007), available at http://www.maxwell.af.mil/au/aunews/Articles/PerpetuatinganIntegratedSpaceForce.html,accessed September 3, 2007.

15. Everett, 24.

16. J. Christopher Moss, "Bridging the Gap: Five Observations on Air and Space Integration," in Kendall K. Brown (ed.), *Space Power Integration: Perspectives*

from Space Weapons Officers (Maxwell AFB, AL: Air University Press, 2006), 171–187; B. Singaraju et al., "Space Superiority—Enabled by High Risk, High Payoff Technologies," *High Frontier* (May 2007): 17–21.

17. Singaraju et al., 17–21; Moss, 177–181.

18. An argument has long raged to the effect that the atomic bombs at Hiroshima and Nagasaki actually saved many more lives, including Japanese lives, than were lost.

19. George D. Kramlinger, "Narrowing the Global-Strike Gap with an Airborne Aircraft Carrier," *Air and Space Power Journal* (Summer 2005): 85–98; Rebecca Grant, "When Bombers Will Be Decisive," *Air Force Magazine* (November 2007), available at http://www.afa.org/magazine/nov2007/1107bombers.asp, accessed November 9, 2007.

20. Kramlinger, 85–98.

21. Jack Sine, "Defining the 'Precision Weapon' in Effects-Based Terms," *Air and Space Power Journal* (Spring 2006), 81–88.

22. Kramlinger, 85–98. Incidentally, no B-52s were ever lost to enemy aircraft, yet their sole gun installation, that in the tail, did kill two MiGs in Linebacker II.

23. Kramlinger, 85–98.

24. John A. Tirpak, "Next, The Unmanned Bomber?" *Air Force* (March 2006), available at http://www.afa.org/magazine/March2006/0306watch.asp, accessed March 25, 2006.

25. Lt. Col. Jay Stout, USMC (Ret.), "Close Air Support Using Armed UAVs?" *Naval Institute Proceedings* (July 2005): 1–4, available at http://www.military.com/NewContent/0,13190,NI_705_air—P1,00.html, accessed December 12, 2005.

26. Roger W. Barnett, "Naval Power for a New American Century," *Naval War College Review*, LV (Winter 2002): 51.

27. Barnett, 53.

28. The last time large American carriers were lost was in 1942, although the *USS Franklin* came close to destruction in 1945.

29. US Department of Defense, Defense Science Board, "Future of the Aircraft Carrier," October 2002.

30. John F. Guilmartin, *A Very Short War: The Mayaguez and the Battle of Koh Tang* (College Station, TX: Texas A&M, 1995), 39.

31. Barnett, 56.

32. Alan Lee Boyer, "Naval Response to a Changed Security Environment," *Naval War College Review* (Summer 2007): 73–100.

33. Ann Scott Tyson, "U.S. Steps Up Anti-Piracy Actions," *Washington Post* (December 16, 2007), available at http://ebird.afis.mil/ebfiles/e20071216567915.html, accessed December 16, 2007; Richard Halloran, "The New Line in the Pacific," *Air Force Magazine* (December 2007), available at http://www.afa.org/magazine/dec2007/1207pacific.asp.

34. Christopher J. Lamb, "Information Operations as a Core Competency," *Joint Forces Quarterly*, No. 36, (n.d.), 94; Thomas G. Mahnken, "War in the Information Age," *Joint Forces Quarterly* (Winter 1995–1996): 39–43.

35. Guilmartin, entire work.

36. Thomas G. Tobin et al., *Last Flight From Saigon* (Washington, DC: Government Printing Office, 1978).

37. F. J. Bing West, "Maneuver Warfare: It Worked in Iraq," *Naval Institute Proceedings* (February 2004), available at http://www.military.com/NewContent/0,13190,NI_WAR_0104,00.html, accessed December 14, 2005.

38. Gordon R. Sullivan and James M. Dubik, "War in the Information Age," unpublished paper, Strategic Studies Institute, US Army War College, 1994.

39. Thomas A. Keaney and Eliot A. Cohen, *Revolution in Warfare? Air Power in the Persian Gulf* (Annapolis, MD: Naval Institute, 1995), 210–211; Lieutenant-General David A. Deptula and Major-General Charles D. Link, USAF (Ret.), "Modern Warfare: Desert Storm, Operation Iraqi Freedom and Operation Enduring Freedom," *Air Power History* (Winter 2007): 40, 42.

40. Lamb, 88–96.

41. Peter W. Wielhouwer, "Toward Information Superiority," *Air and Space Power Journal* (Fall 2005): 85–96; Mahnken, 41.

42. Sullivan and Dubik; Thomas Hone, "Why Transform?" *Transformation Trends* (July 2, 2004): 1, in which the author shows that though there was some awareness at the division and brigade levels during the penetration of Baghdad in 2003, at the lowest levels there still were large gaps in the situational awareness among the troops in contact; David J. DiCenso, "IW Cyberlaw," *Airpower Journal* (Summer 1999): 86–102, warns that the huge information advantage the United States enjoys gives it more to lose than others, and thus forethought must be given to the subject of IW in both legal and policy terms.

43. Roger W. Barnett, *Technology and Naval Blockade: Past Impact and Future Prospects* (Newport, RI: Naval War College Press, 2002).

44. Barnett, *Technology and Naval Blockade.*

45. Barnett, *Technology and Naval Blockade.*

46. Ed Tomme and Sigfred Dahl, "Balloons in Today's Military? An Introduction to the Near Space Concept," *Air and Space Power Journal* (Winter 2005): 39–49.

47. Bernard Schriever, "Foreword," in Peter L. Hays et al. (eds.), *Spacepower for a New Millennium: Space and U.S. National Security* (New York: McGraw-Hill, 2000), vii–ix, in which General Schriever, the recognized father of American missile and space programs, uses the airpower analogy to lament the limitations of space force application capabilities and the total absence of space control technologies—in direct contradiction of space sanctuary advocates.

48. Bruce M. DeBlois, "Ascendant Realms: Characteristics of Airpower and Space Power," in Phillip Meilinger (ed.), *Paths of Heaven: The Evolution of Airpower Theory* (Maxwell AFB, AL: Air University Press, 1997), 570. Strangely, the Moffett example of successfully integrating aviation in the sea service is seldom, if ever, cited in the space literature.

49. DeBlois, 564.

50. DeBlois, 529–571.

51. Brian Sullivan, "Spacepower and America's Future," in Peter L. Hays et al., *Spacepower for a New Millennium: Space and U.S. National Security* (New York: McGraw-Hill, 2000), 269; Everett C. Dolman, *Astropolitik: Classical Geopolitics in the Space Age* (London: Cass, 2002), 88, 100, 119, 137–141, albeit that Dolman is not a fan of the Treaty nor of the internationalization of space, as suggested by his title.

52. Ryan Hansen, "A Weapon of Miraculous Capabilities," *Eglin Eagle* (March 24, 2006): 22–23.

53. Matthew Dalton, "Big Coal Tries to Recruit Military to Kindle a Market," *Wall Street Journal* (September 11, 2007), available at http://ebird.afis.mil/ebfiles/e20070911543277.html, accessed September 11, 2007.

54. A point made by John Gordon IV and Jerry Sollinger, "The Army's Dilemma," *Parameters*, 34 (Summer 2004): 41, as well as by Winnefeld and Johnson.

Index

About the Author

DAVID R. METS is Professor Emeritus, School of Advanced Air and Space Studies at the USAF Air University. He is a retired air force navigator, pilot, commander, and academy professor. He has authored four books and previously served as editor of *The Air University Review.*